T0329051

DREAMS OF A NATION

DREAMS OF A NATION

VERSO

London • New York

First published by Verso 2006
© in the collection, Verso 2006
© in the contributions, the individual contributors 2006
All rights reserved
The moral rights of the authors and editor have been asserted
1 3 5 7 9 10 8 6 4 2

Verso
UK: 6 Meard Street, London W1F 0EG
USA: 388 Atlantic Ave, Brooklyn, NY 11217
www.versobooks.com

Verso is the imprint of New Left Books

ISBN-13: 978-1-84467-088-8
ISBN-10: 1-84467-088-0

British Library Cataloguing in Publication Data
A catalogue record for this book is available from the British Library

Library of Congress Cataloging-in-Publication Data
A catalog record for this book is available from the Library of Congress

Typeset in Garamond by Hewer Text UK Ltd, Edinburgh
Printed in the United States

For The Warrior:
Abu Said

CONTENTS

LIST OF ILLUSTRATIONS

PREFACE

Edward W. Said

The following is the text of the keynote speech that Edward Said delivered at the opening night of our Dreams of a Nation: A Palestinian Film Festival, on 24 January 2003 at the Roone Arledge Cinema, Lerner Hall, Columbia University, New York.

I'd like to make a brief series of reflections on what the significance of Palestinian films might be, and then try to relate it to the more general problem – political, aesthetic, historical – of the visible, to the dialectic of the visible and the invisible, so far as Palestinians are concerned. I will explain by way of an anecdote, from a book I wrote many years ago called *After the Last Sky.*[1]

In 1983, I was a consultant to a United Nations International Conference on the Question of Palestine called UNICQP, which was held in Geneva; over a hundred countries were involved. From the moment that we started to work on this conference, it was clear that the United States and Israel would not approve nor participate. But the one difficulty I didn't at all anticipate is connected to the subject of this festival, namely the problem of visual material and Palestinians.

Some of the problems were predictable. For example, one of my tasks was to commission papers for the conference (the UN loves to produce papers). Every delegate who came to the conference was supposed to get ten or so papers commissioned on, for example, the history of Palestine, the problem of colonialism, the history of Zionism, the history of Israel, etc. We gathered fifteen or twenty papers from experts from all over the world. But at a UN conference, any country can veto a paper without giving a reason. So in the end only three were allowed. (In the case of the Turkish delegation, for example, they vetoed the paper on the history of the region by one of the foremost experts in the world, a French professor called Maxime Rodinson, because it mentions the Armenians.)

We had commissioned a very well-known Swiss photographer called Jean Mohr, whom I had met through John Berger.[2] Mohr had spent years in the late 1940s working for the Red Cross. Later he went around Gaza, Jordan, Lebanon, Egypt, the West Bank, and inside Israel, taking pictures of Palestinians. He had amassed an archive of six or seven thousand photographs. Since he lived in Geneva, it seemed to me a logical and interesting idea to have his pictures at the entrance hall of the conference center, at the Palais des Nations, where the old UN, League of Nations, headquarters was. And so they were thus exhibited.

Then something unexpected happened: the photographs were shown in the hall, but only very limited captions were permitted. So there was a picture, for example, of a family, but instead of there being a label describing the family, what year the picture was taken, or what the family was doing there, the only identification allowed was "Gaza."

It became obvious to me that the relationship of Palestinians to the visible and the visual was deeply problematic. In fact, the whole history of the Palestinian struggle has to do with the desire to be visible. Remember the early mobilizing phrase of Zionism: "We are a people without a land going to a land without a people?" It pronounced the emptiness of the land and the non-existence of a people.

This brings to mind an article I read in *Haaretz* on 22 January 2003 by the wonderful Israeli reporter Amira Haas. The title of the piece is "You can drive along and never see an Arab." It is a description of the road system on the West Bank and Gaza built by the Israelis since the occupation, more particularly in the last few years, tying together all the settlements – around 150 or 160 settlements. These are roads on which Arabs and Palestinians cannot travel; if you are an Israeli citizen and settler, you can drive on them and not see any Arabs.

> A person could travel the length and breadth of the West Bank without ever knowing not only the names of the villages and cities whose lands were confiscated in order to build the Jewish settlements and neighborhoods, but even the fact that they exist. Most of their names cannot be found on the road signs. And from a distance, the calls of the muezzins

and the streets empty of people (after all, there is nothing to go out for) seem like an aesthetic decoration. A Jew traveling on the almost empty roads of the West Bank would think that there no longer are any Arabs: they do not travel on the wide roads used by the Jews.[3]

The people who planned the settlements, large and small, twenty years ago or more also knew that they must prevent the "natives" from harming the settlements or their residents – in other words, that they must build roads that would isolate every Palestinian city and village, that would divide them from each other and from the main roads, to such an extent that now all it takes is an earthen barrier to block a village's access to the road or to its olive groves, or a city's access to its industrial zone.[4]

Palestinian cinema must be understood in this context. That is to say, on the one hand, Palestinians stand against invisibility, which is the fate they have resisted since the beginning; and on the other hand, they stand against the stereotype in the media: the masked Arab, the *kufiyya*, the stone-throwing Palestinian – a visual identity associated with terrorism and violence.

Palestinian cinema provides a visual alternative, a visual articulation, a visible incarnation of Palestinian existence in the years since 1948, the year of the destruction of Palestine, and the dispersal and dispossession of the Palestinians; and a way of resisting an imposed identity on Palestinians as terrorists, as violent people, by trying to articulate a counter-narrative and a counter-identity. These films represent a collective identity.

The Palestinians are a dispersed people. Their films come from different places: the West Bank, Gaza, Israel, Europe, the United States. One of the efforts of these films is to recollect and gather together what has been lost since 1948, often in the most simple terms of everyday life. In the film I made in 1998, called *In Search of Palestine*, I filmed a family in the Deheshye Camp, outside Bethlehem, who insisted on bringing to me the key of their family house, which had been visible from near the camp inside Israel proper. The house had been destroyed, but they still had the key.

Things like keys, title deeds (useless now), family photographs, newspaper clippings, school certificates, marriage licenses – these are the bedrock of Palestinian memory.

In Michel Khleifi's *Fertile Memory*, there is a superb scene in which an elderly woman is taken to see the piece of land that she owns. She has been dispossessed of

A scene from Michel Khleifi's *Fertile Memory* (1980).
(Picture courtesy of Omar al-Qattan, Sindibad Films).

the land, which is now occupied by the Israelis, inside Israel. She is taken to see it because her son tells her that some people want to buy the land, and they want to acquire it legally from its owner. There is a scene in which this woman – elderly, large, not well-educated, who works as a seamstress in an Israeli swimsuit factory – visits her land for the first time. She is radiant as she stands there and for the first time feels the ground beneath her. This point of contact between her and the land from which she's been alienated – and which she no longer owns, and which the present inhabitants want to buy from her – illuminates the screen like an epiphany. The affirmation of her identity is conveyed in a totally unsentimental way. I think this is one of the keystones of Palestinian cinema.

In its attempt to articulate a national narrative, Palestinian cinema discovers a world that has been frequently hidden, and the making visible, sometimes in very subtle and eloquent ways, as in the cinema of Elia Suleiman, or in folkloric ways in the later films of Michel Khleifi, is very exciting indeed.

INTRODUCTION

Hamid Dabashi

Here, on the slopes before sunset and
At the gun-mouth of time
Near orchards deprived
Of their shadows
We do what prisoners do:
We nurture hope.

Mahmoud Darwish

PALESTINE: THE PRESENCE OF THE ABSENCE

Making a case for the cause and consequences of Palestinian cinema as one of the most promising national cinemas cannot stop at the doorsteps of simply proposing that its local perils and possibilities are now transformed into a global event. The proposition itself is paradoxical and it is through this paradox that it needs to be articulated and theorized. How exactly is it that a stateless nation generates a national cinema – and once it does, what kind of national cinema is it? The very proposition of a Palestinian cinema points to the traumatic disposition of its origin and originality. The world of cinema does not know quite how to deal with Palestinian cinema precisely because it is emerging as a stateless cinema of the most serious national consequences. I have edited this volume in part to address the particulars of this paradox – at once enabling and complicating the notion of a "national cinema."

The most notorious recent case that has dramatized this paradox is the refusal of the Academy of Motion Picture Arts and Sciences to consider Elia Suleiman's *Divine Intervention* (2002) for the Oscars, objecting that he is a stateless person. This happened in a year that the Cannes Film Festival had accepted three Palestinian films in its various venues. As for Elia Suleiman's nationality, well, he is officially an Israeli citizen – and the fact is that he would be accepted into the Academy if he were to submit his film as an Israeli, except that he was born into a Christian Palestinian family and does not have equal citizenship rights in the Jewish state. "The Academy does not accept films from countries that are not recognized by the United Nations," an official of the Academy told reporters. The same UN resolution that recognized the formation of the state of Israel, however, partitioned the historical Palestine into two states, and the other one is Palestine. So if Palestine is not a state, the same is true about Israel. The Academy further stated that to be eligible for the Best Foreign Film category, a film must first be released in the country of its origin. But how would that be possible in the case of Palestine? With East Jerusalem, the West Bank, and Gaza Strip – as indeed the rest of Palestine – under full Israeli military occupation, and most of the population under curfew, there are almost no functioning cinemas left and few Palestinians have the financial means to attend them. With the systematic destruction of Palestinian civil society and cultural institutions, and decades of Israeli military censorship, how could such a demand be met?

In February 2004, when I helped organize a Palestinian film festival in Jerusalem, the Palestinian cultural organization that hosted us (Yabous) had to transform the lobby of a YMCA into a makeshift movie theater – with foldable chairs, a rented projector, and a pull-out screen. Our audience had to negotiate their way through a labyrinth of Israeli military checkpoints to get to the festival. During the following summer, I traveled through a series of Palestinian refugee camps in Lebanon and Syria, with a backpack full of Palestinian films, showing them to Palestinian refugees on the rooftops of dilapidated buildings – projected on walls from a mismatched constellation of equipment running on stolen electricity. Which of these "movie theaters" did the Academy have in mind in order for *Divine Intervention* to be seen by Palestinians in "their country?"

Today we are witnessing the spectacular rise of a national cinema – predicated on a long history of documentary filmmaking in pre-1948 Palestine and a subsequent dispersion of Palestinian filmmakers throughout the Arab world – precisely at a moment when the nation that is producing it is itself negated and denied, its ancestral land stolen from under its feet and militarily occupied by successive bands of white European and American colonial settlers. That paradox does not only preface the case of Palestinian cinema, it occasions it and gives it a unique and exceptionally unsettling disposition. What precisely that disposition is will have to be articulated through a close reading of its films – a principal reason behind the compilation of this volume. Palestinian filmmakers dream their cinema – the visual evidence of their being-in-the-world – in a forbidden land that is theirs but is not theirs. These dreams, as a result, always border with nightmares – hopes transgressing into fears, and at the borderlines of that im/possibility of dreaming and naming, the Palestinian cinema is made im/possible.

It is crucial to keep in mind that the origin of Palestinian cinema pre-dates the dispossession of their historical homeland. The first Palestinian film to have ever been made was a short documentary by Ibrahim Hasan Serhan, which recorded the visit of King Abd al-Aziz bin Abd al-Rahman bin Faysal al-Saud (1888–1953; reigned 1932–53) to Palestine, and his subsequent travels between Jerusalem and Jaffa. In the history of Palestinian cinema there dwells a sense of continuity that outlives the current political predicament of Palestinians and the disrupted course of their nationhood.

At the end of the nineteenth century, groups of white European settlers – escaping persecution from acts of religious, racial, and ethnic violence endemic to Europe, or else colonial opportunists taking advantage of that fact – began to move into Palestine and gradually took it over, forcing its native inhabitants to live in exile or be crammed into refugee camps, or else subjugated into second-rate citizenship in their own homeland. Mobilized by the memories of their pogroms and then a genocidal Holocaust, perpetrated against millions of European Jews, white Europeans sought to assuage their guilty conscience by granting the descendants of those they had sought to exterminate a state that was built on the broken back of another nation, which had absolutely nothing to do with the criminal atrocities committed by one group of Europeans against another. Thus the Palestinians were robbed of their ancestral homeland and the State of Israel – the first religious (Jewish) state in the region (preceding an Islamic Republic by more than a quarter of a century) – was born in 1948. Palestinians call this event

Nakba or "Catastrophe," and to this day it remains the central traumatic moment of their collective identity.

At the beginning of the twenty-first century, Israel has mutated into a military machine no longer even true to the original design of pioneering Zionists in the nineteenth century, who dreamt of an exclusively Jewish state. Today, Israel is a military camp completely given over to the imperial designs of the United States. Most cases of colonialism have ended in indignity: the French packed up and left Algeria, the Italians Libya, the British India, so did the Portuguese, the Spaniards, the Belgians, and the Dutch. Those such as the Afrikaners who did not leave and stayed put with a shameless insistence on apartheid were finally swept away by the force of history, and had to abandon their racist practices and concede to the will of the nation they had subjugated. But the Zionists remain. The fact that Jewish communities have lived in Palestine since time immemorial is as much an excuse for the formation of a Jewish State in Palestine as the equally historical presence of Muslim or Christian Palestinians is an excuse for the creation of an Islamic or Christian republic. Palestine belongs to Palestinians – whether Jews, Christians, or Muslims.

At the core of the Palestinian historical presence is thus a geographical absence. The overriding presence of an absence is at the creative core of Palestinian cinema, what has made it thematically in/coherent and aesthetically im/possible.

Abdel Salam Shehada's gut-wrenching film *Debris* (2002) is an example *par excellence* of the active mutation of body and soil in Palestinian cinema. "Every time I saw a tree being uprooted," says the young Palestinian boy to the camera as he remembers the scene of Israeli bulldozers razing his parents" olive grove, "I felt a part of my body was being ripped out." The elders claim the land with their memory, as their children and their olive trees grow on it. Populating the land with Palestinians becomes the key element in preventing the question of Palestine to remain a question, or to become only a metaphor. "Palestine is an issue," interjects Mahmoud Darwish at one point in the course of a conversation with Edward Said in Charles Bruce's *In Search of Palestine* (1998), "not an essence."

In most world cinema, the active formation of such globally celebrated traditions as Soviet Formalism, Italian Neorealism, French New Wave, or German New Cinema have been formed in the aftermath of a major political upheaval and national trauma. The Russians discovered and articulated their cinema in the aftermath of the Russian Revolution of 1917; Italians did the same in the immediate decades after the

Mussolini era and in the throes of massive poverty caused by the war; the French followed suit in the aftermath of their colonial catastrophes in Africa; while the Germans did the same in the aftermath of the Holocaust. Hiroshima was as definitive to Akira Kurosawa's cinema as the Chinese, Cuban, and Iranian revolutions were to the Chinese, Cuban, and Iranian national cinema. The central trauma of Palestine, the *Nakba*, is the defining moment of Palestinian cinema – and it is around that remembrance of the lost homeland that Palestinian filmmakers have articulated their aesthetic cosmovision.

TRAUMATIC REALISM

In what particular way can a Palestinian cinema have a claim to an aesthetic that corresponds to or transcends the fact of its politics? The paramount feature in Palestinian cinema is a subdued anger, a perturbed pride, a sublated violence. What ultimately defines what we may call a *Palestinian cinema* is the mutation of that repressed anger into an aestheticized violence – the aesthetic presence of a political absence. The Palestinians' is an aesthetic under duress – and this book is a preliminary attempt at navigating its principal contours.

What happens when reality becomes too fictive to be fictionalized, too unreal to accommodate any metaphor? Palestinian filmmakers have taken this mimetic crisis, and turned it into one of the most extraordinary adventures in cinematic history.

The Palestinian cinematic will to resist power, ranging from Michel Khleifi, Rashid Masharawi, and Mai Masri at one end to Elia Suleiman, Hany Abu Assad, and Annemarie Jacir at the other, is the crowning achievement of its traumatic realism. That traumatic realism is integral to its cinematic mannerism – whether factual or fictive. What we witness in Palestinian documentaries, for example, is not a plain act of certificating a past history. A certain fear of loss, a worrisome look at the historical evidence, and keeping a sustained record of an endangered memory inform much of what we see in Palestinian documentaries. Documentaries, as a result, are also a form of visual "J'accuse" – animated by a tireless frenzy to create an alternative record of a silenced crime, to be lodged in a place that escapes the reach of the colonizer as occupier. There is an obvious anxiety about the narrative pace of these documentaries, a *traumatic documentation* of events beyond the pale of memory. Consider, for example, Kais al-Zubaidi's *Palestine: A People's Record* (1984) and its compulsive meticulousness in safeguarding and narrating the archival footages of the earliest history of Palestine in moving pictures. To over-compensate for that *traumatic anxiety*, notice the polished accent of the voice that narrates the documentary – a feature of Palestinian documentaries now completely taken over by the accented voice of the filmmakers themselves narrating their own stories. The formality of this official voice – about Palestine but not of a Palestinian – is matched by the formal dressing of the interviewees – invariably wearing ties and suits – adding authority and authenticity.

Orality is a strong element in the making of this documentation because it gives it immediacy and urgency. We see old people reminiscing, "I can remember . . ." The underlying meaning is, "Let me tell what the books won't tell you," or "I hold the truth, I was there." The people delivering their *shahada*, or testimonial reports, convey what took place when the world had its back turned. Their account serves to redress the record in the hope of redressing the injustice. The absence of a Palestinian state does not imply amnesia. In fact, the documentary film becomes itself that ledger, the document of these crimes.

Most Palestinians who are interviewed in these documentaries are old people, evidence of memory on the edge of disappearance. What factually emerges from the documentary – that Zionism was integral to European colonialism as it is now to the US imperialism, and that the Ottoman, Syrian, and Lebanese absentee landlords sold their lands to Zionist settlers entirely unbeknownst to their Palestinian tenants – is almost secondary to the urgent necessity of preserving the fading memory of a people and their material culture.

The mutation of the politically repressed into the aesthetically representational becomes a defining moment of Palestinian cinema. This representational im/possibility is deeply rooted in Palestinian realism and constitutional to its crisis of mimesis. Integral to Palestinian realism is its particular fascination with turning rural landscape into urban legends. Films such as Michel Khleifi's *Fertile Memory* and Abdel Salam Shehada's *Debris* have an obsession with Palestinian rural life – with open air, fertile land, and olive trees at their centers. But in films such as Elia Suleiman's *Chronicle of a Disappearance* (1996), Alia Arasoughly's *This is not Living* (2001), Hazim Bitar's *Jerusalem's High Cost of Living* (2001), Akram Safadi's *Songs on a Narrow Path: Stories from Jerusalem* (2001), Muhammad al-Sawalmeh's *Night of Soldiers* (2002), Hany Abu Assad's *Ford Transit* (2002), and *Jerusalem on Another Day: Rana's Wedding* (2002)

A scene from Mohammad Bakri's *Jenin, Jenin* (2002).

Mohammad Bakri (as Haifa) in Rashid Masharawi's *Haifa* (1995).

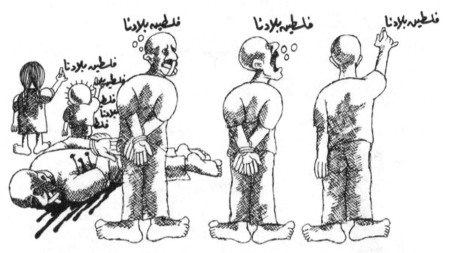

A cartoon by Naji al-Ali, the Palestinian cartoonist. By the time he was murdered on July 22 1987, Naji al-Ali had crafted an extraordinary body of work about the brutal predicament of Palestinians. The writing on the wall reads: "Palestine is our Homeland." Naji al-Ali is known and loved for his principal creation, the character of Hanzalah, who always appears in his cartoons, with his back turned to the audience and his face towards the event – a witness to history. In this cartoon, Hanzalah is standing next to the murdered Palestinian and by the young Palestinian girl, both of them writing on the wall "Palestine is our Homeland!."

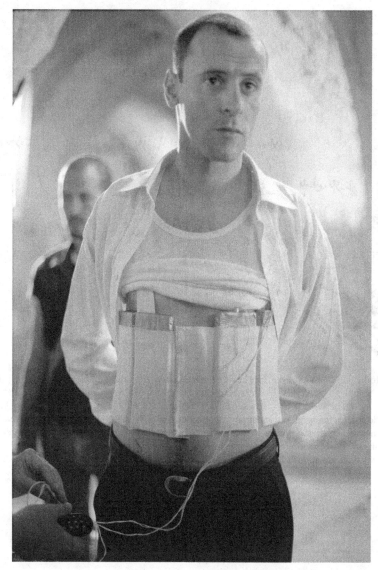

Ali Suleiman (as Khaled) in Hany Abu Assad's *Paradise Now* (2005)
(Picture courtesy of Augustus Film.)

we also see a common concern with Palestinian urbanity. To see the rhyme and reason behind this sustained gaze at Palestinian cities, we need first to visit a Palestinian refugee camp.

In Mohammad Bakri's *Jenin, Jenin* (2002), the camera follows the director from behind as he walks over the ruins of this camp. The camera does not come anywhere near his face. This device is reminiscent of Hanzalah, the central character in Naji al-Ali's cartoons. Before he was murdered on July 22 1987, Naji al-Ali had crafted an extraordinary body of work about the brutal predicament of Palestinians. In all of these cartoons, Hanzalah is defiant, angry, and bitter (and thus his name "Hanzalah"), with his back turned to the people watching Naji al-Ali's cartoons. This gesture has two important functions: (1) he turns his back in anger on a world that refuses to watch, wonder, and respond; and (2) he acts as the unflinching conscience of his people, as an eyewitness to a systematically denied and denigrated history. Mohammad Bakri pays homage to Naji al-Ali, mutates into Hanzalah, and thus partakes in the iconography of his people.

Throughout Sabra and Shatila Palestinian refugee camps, when I visited them in July 2004, there were myriad murals ranging in subject matter from defiant cries for a return to Palestine to asking the inhabitants of the camp to keep it clean, and they were all written and articulated from the position of Hanzalah, with his tiny little figure at a corner of the mural encouraging his fellow Palestinians to do one thing or another. One may also read in a similar way the silent and observant figure of ES, the screen version of Elia Suleiman himself in his cinema.

Leading Mohammad Bakri into the Jenin refugee camp is a deaf and dumb man who has witnessed the massacre and yet has no language to speak out about it. The man motions, pleads, leads, moves, gestures, and gesticulates to express the dread he has witnessed. In a sense, that deaf and dumb man is Palestine: having witnessed but not able to bear witness to the crime he has seen. He has to invent, *to will*, a language, to speak out against a massive propaganda machinery that denies its very existence. "I am a dumb man who has seen a nightmare," goes a proverbial poem in Persian. "Facing a crowd both blind and deaf / I cannot tell the terror I have seen / And the crowd incapable of comprehension."

The Jenin refugee camp was established to house the residents of Lydda, once a thriving port-city with a long and thriving history of urbanization. The inhabitants of Lydda were expelled by the Zionists and shipped to a concentration camp for a few years then settled in Jenin, while the old city itself is today hailed as a gem of architectural preservation and restoration, marketed to Yuppie Zionists. What is a refugee camp other than the negation of one's claim to urbanity? Mohammad Bakri's *Jenin, Jenin* encapsulates the trauma of Palestine's arrested urbanity in the ruins of a refuge camp – the brutal irony of being robbed of one's urbanity, condemned to a refugee camp, and yet subjected to even more destructive terror in the middle of that deprived urbanity.

The Palestinian claim to a stolen *civitas* in the broad daylight of history creates a traumatic amnesia, a phantom pain. Sawalmeh Mohammed's *Night of Soldiers* (2002) is a deeply moving reflection, this time on Ramallah. Sawalmeh Mohammed's camera stays behind closed doors and nervously looks through windows, creating a mood of claustrophobia and fear. *Night of Soldiers* is a mournful elegy, adopting the gaze of a lonely young woman sitting and remembering.

The traumatic realism at the heart of Palestinian cinema weaves its agitated rural and denied urban imagination together, at once suggestive and arrested. Consider Rashid Masharawi's *Haifa* (1995), a successful experimentation with the trope of madness – narrated around a village idiot – by way of defying the limits of representation in a deliberately rambunctious way. Haifa, the lead character, is the schizophrenic displacement of Haifa, the city. In Haifa's madness dwells the insanity of dispossession, and in his representation of Haifa as occupied territory the ravages of colonialism. Everything in *Haifa* is misplaced – Haifa lives in Gaza; Gaza dreams of Haifa; Haifa is a madman; Haifa is an occupied urbanity depleted and deprived of its rightful inhabitants. In the ravaged mind, depleted body, and emptied gaze of Haifa, Rashid Masharawi maps out the history and geography of the dispossessed Palestinians – of Palestine.

The traumatic realism at the heart of Palestinian cinema breaks through the history that has been mandated. History cannot be reversed, but it can be re-imagined.

TOWARDS AN AESTHETICS OF THE INVISIBLE

This volume begins with a short reflection by the late Edward Said on the problem of visibility for Palestinians. His preface is the text of the keynote speech that he delivered at the opening night of our Dreams of a Nation: A Palestinian Film Festival, on Friday 24 January 2003 at Roone Arledge Cinema of Lerner Hall, Columbia University.

Next is a short chapter by Annemarie Jacir, who curated the film festival. Very few people, in my judgement, know Palestinian cinema better than Annemarie Jacir, herself an accomplished filmmaker. In this chapter she reflects on the trials and tribulations of putting a project of this sort together, as well as making and archiving films.

Joseph Massad's scholarship, over the last decade, has facilitated a critical conversation about the vagaries of politics and the transformative power of culture, towards which he sustains an unflinchingly critical perspective. His wide range of writings on the modern Arab artistic and intellectual disposition uniquely qualifies him to place Palestinian cinema in the context of the Palestinian national liberation movement. In his chapter, Massad makes a persuasive argument about the integral function of Palestinian art in general and cinema in particular in the historic struggle of the Palestinian people to liberate their country from colonial occupation.

Michel Khleifi is widely considered the founder of contemporary Palestinian cinema. Born in Nazareth in 1950, two years after the *Nakba*, Khleifi entered the world a disinherited Palestinian. In 1970 he left his occupied homeland for Europe and settled in Belgium, where he turned to theater and cinema as the principal mode of his creative reflection on the predicament of his people. Beginning in 1978 he made a succession of documentaries in and on Palestine. But it was his first feature film, *Wedding in Galilee* (1987), that garnered him and Palestinian cinema global recognition. In his chapter, published in its Spanish translation for the first time in February 1997 in *El Pais* and now translated from original Arabic into English for this volume by Omar al-Qattan, Khleifi gives his own reflection on the causes and consequences of the aesthetics and politics of a Palestinian cinema.

Khleifi's documentaries and feature films have crafted a microcosmic universe in which the Palestinian national liberation movement finds its universal texture and dexterity, to reveal and to intervene in the historic fate of his people. Particularly important in Abu-Manneh's chapter is the link that he establishes between Khleifi's cinema and the rise of Intifada – the popular uprising of Palestinians against the colonial occupation of their homeland.

One of the principal concerns I had in editing this volume on Palestinian cinema was not to isolate it within its immediate cultural confinements and to link both its liberating forces and particular predicament to a larger – more emancipatory – frame of reference. I asked Ella Shohat, a feminist critic of nationalism, to contribute a chapter. She offers a critique of a nationalized cinema that is quite relevant to Palestinian filmmaking.

Years ago I had read Hamid Naficy's pioneering essay on Palestinian cinema as a form of epistolary narrative. When I was putting this volume together, I asked Naficy to update and expand it as a chapter to be included here. Particularly important is his placing of Palestinian cinema in the context of what he calls "accented cinema," namely a cinema produced by artists accompanying massive labor migrations around the world, particularly from the former European colonies such as Algeria into France. As Naficy notes, the case of Palestinian cinema is a unique historical example in which the condition of exile is "structural" to its narrative and is not caused by forces of global labor migration.

Nizar Hassan is a distinguished Palestinian documentary filmmaker, born in Nazareth, Palestine, in 1960. His short chapter, written originally in Arabic and published in *Al-Ayyam al-"Iliktruniyya* on July 20 2004, and now translated into English for the first time by Taoufiq bin Amor, speaks directly to the predicament of Palestinian filmmakers and national identity. Nizar Hassan's hilarious yet resolute take on a certain incident shows his determination to be identified as a Palestinian filmmaker and the wider range of implications for the fate of this national cinema.

First-person narratives by Palestinian filmmakers are rare. I was very happy that Omar al-Qattan agreed to join us in this volume not only by translating Michel Khleifi's account of his career as a filmmaker but also by writing his own. These two statements, plus those of Annemarie Jacir and Nizar Hassan, provide an exceptionally important account of the extraordinary challenges and opportunities faced by Palestinian filmmakers and producers.

In the final chapter of this book, I discuss what I believe to be the quintessential force of Elia Suleiman's cinema – his uncanny visual command of cinematic frivolity, exceptionally rare in world cinema. I believe Elia Suleiman is the most creative Palestinian filmmaker of his generation and one of the most brilliant filmmakers anywhere in the world. Aspects of his cinema can be (and have been) traced to the French filmmaker Jacques Tati or even to the American comedian Buster Keaton. But such similarities, I believe, are superficial. There is something unique about Elia Suleiman's cinema and the visual vocabulary he is creating. I believe what James Joyce said about his *Ulysses* (1922) – that he "put in so many enigmas and puzzles that it will keep the professors busy for centuries arguing over what I meant, and that's the only way of ensuring immortality" – is also true about Elia Suleiman's cinema. My purpose in this Introduction is to offer a manner of reading Elia Suleiman's visual vocabulary, and thus his cinema, that is rooted in the crisis of mimesis in Palestinian cinema – how is a Palestinian filmmaker to attend to the impossibility of representing his or her national trauma? What I have termed "traumatic realism" as the defining moment of Palestinian cinema assumes a particularly creative effervescence when we come to Elia Suleiman's cinema, and the manner in which he has sought to tell the trauma at the fractured center of his nation.

In the summer of 2004, I met a young Palestinian cultural historian in Damascus. His name is Bashar Ibrahim and he has written an excellent book on the history of Palestinian cinema, *al-Sinama al-Filastiniyyah fi al-Qarn al-"Ishriyn* ("Palestinian Cinema in the Twentieth Century," Damascus: National Organization for Cinema, Syrian Ministry of Culture, 2001). He lives in a Palestinian refugee camp on the outskirts of Damascus and devotes his life to collecting and archiving Palestinian film. It was after getting to know about Bashar Ibrahim's archive that I realized that putting together a comprehensive filmography of Palestinian cinema is a daunting task. While the occupiers of Palestine have enjoyed mega-million-dollar endowments to establish various forms of cultural institutions in "Israel," thus seeking to fabricate a non-existent legitimacy for their colonial settlement, including a major Cinematheque and a corresponding archive and a very lucrative annual film festival, every conceivable dimension of Palestinian cultural life is in a state of shambles, the bits and pieces of their national heritage scattered all over the map and at times heroically salvaged by devoted Palestinians such as Bashar Ibrahim. The task of archiving Palestinian films has technical problems as well. As Kamran Rastegar, who prepared and annotated the selected filmography at the end of this book, explains, one has to address the issue of what exactly accounts for the inclusion of a film in this category. Certainly filmmakers who are Palestinian by birth and breeding, national origin, and parental descent are included in this filmography. However, there are also films made by other Arab filmmakers for Palestinian cultural institutions which equally belong to this category. In his prefatory remarks to this volume, the late Edward Said addresses the larger issue of placing Palestinian cinema in the context of Arab cinema. By no means is the filmography that Kamran Rastegar has prepared exhaustive: it is a task much in need of further careful archival research and systematic documentation. For now, Kamran Rastegar's filmography, combining his own original research with information in existing Arabic filmographies, will be a reliable guide for further research.

Kamran Rastegar has also prepared a suggested bibliography that can facilitate further reading and research into aspects of Palestinian cinema. The bibliography is largely limited to English and French sources, with a number of important sources in Arabic as a few prominent exceptions. There is an increasing body of writing on Palestinian cinema on the Internet. The site we have created, www.dreamsofan.org, provides such a database on Palestinian cinema, with links to many related sites.

This volume is a labor of love by a group of scholars and activists, a token of our collective admiration for one of the greatest cinematic traditions around, and a preliminary step towards a much wider appreciation of Palestinian cinema. But above all I offer it as a sign of hope, a modest gift, and an olive branch to all the rightful inhabitants of the historical Palestine – Jews, Christians, Muslims, agnostics, or otherwise – in the hope that they will all one day live in peace, prosperity, and an all-encompassing forgiveness of a brutish history, in anticipation of a brighter future, when justice underlies peace, and when equality sustains freedom, and when "Arabs" and "Israelis" come out of their compromising quotation marks and embrace their common and liberating humanity.

Hamid Dabashi
New York
April 2006

ONE

"FOR CULTURAL PURPOSES ONLY": CURATING A PALESTINIAN FILM FESTIVAL

Annemarie Jacir

I remember when we were in Bethlehem in the 1970s and 1980s and it was illegal to show red, white, black, and green together because they represented the Palestinian flag. Israeli soldiers were ordered to shoot at, if not to kill, those who exhibited these colors.[1] We were also forbidden to gather in groups, and when we were on the streets, we would always separate from each other so as not to attract the unwarranted attention of the Army.

As Palestinians, our memories were affected by these policies and we thus learned the power of representations and images. We also learned that many of our daily activities were considered a threat by our occupiers and thus criminalized, and that our personal expression was not to be taken for granted. Through our daily lives, we found out that colors, symbols, and images were invested with dangerous or emancipatory powers. But we also found how sensitive our adversaries were to these symbols – wherever we were in the world, we felt limitations, sometimes even internalized ones, on the quality, quantity, and variety of representations available to us – and rarely, if ever, did we see representations of Palestinians *by Palestinians*.

In New York, as I began curating the Dreams of a Nation film festival in 2002, these memories returned to me. This project, of which the festival was a part, of presenting, archiving and studying Palestinian cinema, is an effective manner to support the continuing struggle of Palestinians to use colors, symbols, and images to represent ourselves in the peril of the destruction of our culture. The Palestinian

The prominent Palestinian–Chilean filmmaker Miguel Littin, by the wall that Israelis have erected around Palestine (February 2004). Miguel Littin had come to Palestine from Chile to participate in the Dreams of a Nation Film Festival organized in collaboration with the Palestinian cultural institution Yabous. (Photo by Annemarie Jacir.)

colors and flag were targets, but this only is the surface of a military campaign to prevent the emergence of Palestinian cultural and civil institutions. Over the course of the recent Intifada, Israeli forces have continued to systematically destroy and dismantle the cultural infrastructure of Palestinian civil society. In organizing Dreams of a Nation we wanted to highlight and discuss the impressive feat that Palestinian filmmakers were attempting – to develop an aesthetically and socially relevant body of filmmaking just when decades of cultural development in the West Bank, Gaza, and elsewhere, were being newly threatened, and we wanted to intervene and contribute to the present rather disappointing cultural discourse on Palestine in the US by introducing the nuanced and compelling work we were seeing from Palestinian filmmakers around the world.

THE THREAT TO PALESTINIAN CULTURAL LIFE

Last year, all across Palestine, cultural organizations, media outlets, and educational and research facilities have been targeted in raids and incursions by the Israeli Army. Files and computers from the ministries of education, agriculture, industry, civil affairs, and finance have been seized. The Land Registry Office, Central Bureau of Statistics, Palestinian Legislative Council, various human rights organizations, numerous medical institutions, as well as private radio and television stations, have been searched and ransacked – the greatest damage occurring in the full-scale reoccupation of all major Palestinian cities during April and May 2002.

This matter has historical roots. In 1948 and the years that followed, 418 Palestinian towns and villages were depopulated, destroyed and occupied and 780,000 Palestinians became refugees.[2] Some of those villages were later populated by new Israeli immigrants, others remain empty to this day. In a few villages, not all buildings were razed or destroyed, as in the case of Qisariya (Caesarea), where the old village mosque remains, but has been converted into a bar and restaurant. For those Palestinians who remained in the new state of Israel, nearly twenty years of internal military rule (from 1948 to 1966) would ensure cultural stagnation and retreat. For those outside, it would also take years of work and development for active cultural institutions to emerge.

During the 1970s and onwards, Israel has engaged in a mass campaign to eliminate Palestine's greatest artists, intellectuals, and leaders. This operation included the assassinations of novelist Ghassan Kanafani in Beirut (and his 16-year-old niece, who was in the car with him), writer Wael Zuaiter in Rome, intellectual Mahmoud Al-Hemshari in Paris, poet Kamal Nasser, Kamal Idwan, Ali Salameh, and Mohammad Yousef Al-Najjar (and his wife) in Beirut, Hussein Abu al-Khair in Cyprus, feminist leader Nada Yashruti in Beirut, Majed Abu Sharar in Rome, Khalil Al-Wazir in Tunis, and Atef Bseisso in Paris, to name only a few.

Unfortunately, this is not only a historical reality but also reflects a continuing system of destruction that in many ways serves as the backdrop to the difficulties we faced organizing our Palestinian film festival in New York. The threat of ridding Palestine not only of its native inhabitants but also of destroying and erasing all remnants of Palestinian cultural and civil life is still very real.[3]

The Khalil Sakakini Cultural Center is a non-profit and non-political community organization in Ramallah, where it serves as a frequent location for art exhibits, concerts, literary events, film screenings, lectures, and children's activities. In the April 2002 invasion of Ramallah, the center was targeted by the Israeli army as it swept through the city. The Sakakini Center, whose building is a masterpiece of Palestinian architecture, had four offices broken into – including that of the acclaimed poet Mahmoud Darwish. Irreparable damage was caused to artwork in the building and to the antique original iron door. In addition to ransacking the offices and destroying equipment, the hard drive of the main computer was stolen and the telephone switchboard and alarm system destroyed.[4]

Similar destruction befell the Kasaba Theater and Cinematheque, also in Ramallah, which had, one week earlier, hosted an event of poetry, music and dance with Mahmoud Darwish. This same institution, only a few weeks before, had hosted Nobel Literature Prize laureates Wole Soyinka and José Saramago, who had been visiting Palestine on a solidarity mission. Again, the offices of the theater were ransacked, and files and computers destroyed.

This is the context in which our Palestinian film festival, Dreams of a Nation, took place in New York in January 2003. There was a communal urgency in curating the Dreams of a Nation festival for precisely these reasons – it was part of widespread and determined activities carried out by Palestinians worldwide, to resist the systematic destruction of the cultural infrastructure of Palestinian civil life and the further fragmentation of our society.

IMPLICATIONS FOR FILMMAKING

Just as the military authority issued orders prohibiting our adoption of our national colors, so too did they attempt to impose the occupation through systems of colors and signs.

Colors are also used to differentiate license plates for cars belonging to Palestinians in different areas and identity cards issued to Palestinians and which must be carried at all times: these identity cards and permits come in a palate ranging from orange to blue, depending on whether one is a Palestinian from Gaza, the West Bank, or from inside Israel.[5]

The tactic of separation as a method of Israeli control is also evident in the numerous military checkpoints that surround every Palestinian town and village, preventing Palestinians from any real kind of freedom of movement or contiguity.[6] In such circumstances, social cohesion erodes, institutions weaken, and connections unravel. This was an inescapable fact during the planning stages of our festival. Curating the film festival from New York hinged on having someone in Palestine who could physically gather the tapes – since Palestinians in various parts of the West Bank and Gaza are under different levels of military curfew and are often not allowed to leave their homes, let alone to venture to a post office to mail videotapes. This made even the mundane details of receiving copies of films for the festival a major difficulty, often requiring sophisticated planning and execution by parties both inside and outside of Palestine.

In one case, we solicited a film titled *Local*, made by three Ramallah-based filmmakers, a film which had never been seen outside of Ramallah. My sister Emily in the West Bank, who has the advantage of having a US passport, helped to facilitate the sending of the tape to us in New York. She was usually able to travel across checkpoints while the filmmakers were not. When the tape was initially requested, a full curfew prevented any effort to obtain it. When the curfew was lifted, Emily went to the home of the filmmakers, picked up the tape, crossed the checkpoints to Jerusalem, and mailed the tape to us via Federal Express. After two weeks, the tape had not yet shown up. Emily once again traversed the checkpoints from Ramallah and returned to the Federal Express office in Jerusalem, where she was informed that the tape had not been sent and was being held for "security reasons." After much consternation, we were finally able to get another copy of the tape out of

Palestine and to New York through an acquaintance who was willing to carry it out through the airport and mail it from Europe.

Eventually, each with its own story, the tapes began to arrive in our office at Columbia University, all duly marked on the package with the conventional phrase, "For cultural use only, no commercial value" – this is the way films are sent through international customs as submissions to film festivals. In our case, however, I felt that the "cultural use" disclaimer could be seen as an impediment rather than facilitating the process of crossing borders. The films and videotapes arrived from all corners of the globe, however, in every format and system imaginable, and we proceeded to prepare for their screening.

In addition to the difficulty of getting tapes from within Palestine, it was also a challenge to locate some of the Palestinian films and filmmakers we hoped to feature from the rest of the world. There is no central archive or central location in which information on these films exists. (It should be noted that in Lebanon an effort was made to create such an archive. The archive there contained footage from the 1940s to the late 1970s. After the Israeli invasion of Beirut in 1982, the Palestinian film archives there "disappeared" and, to my knowledge, have never resurfaced in their entirety.)

The act of filmmaking in Palestine is also subject to interference and barriers due to the nature of the occupation and its policies on the ground. Last year, when I finished shooting a short fiction film, as I tried to leave Ben Gurion Airport, Israeli airport security confiscated the unprocessed film I was taking out of the country to be developed. As part of a long interrogation, as well as three body-searches, it was clear that "security concerns" were not the only reasons for their actions. Among other things, the security officers demanded that I give them a script of what had been shot, as well as the names and whereabouts of the cast and crew who had worked with me. After several hours (I had long since missed my flight), they decided to let me go, but kept the film with them for another day until they had determined that it was not a "security threat." What is clear to me is the fact that for airport security, the initial concern was not for the security of the airplane, but rather reflected a deep unease about the fact that a Palestinian had simply made a film. In that sense, not much has changed since the days of the first Intifada, when the colors of the Palestinian flag were banned – in the present context, colors, symbols, and images are still subject to criminalization.

As the checkpoints multiply and the destruction of Palestinian cultural activities and institutions occurs, young filmmakers across the West Bank and Gaza are picking up their cameras and creating works that both record and resist these destructive policies. In addition to the several, mostly foreign-financed or produced fiction films shown in the Dreams of a Nation festival, it was crucial to include the daring new works of those documentary filmmakers in Palestine who continue to work alone in such adverse conditions.

This is precisely why our primary criterion for the films in the festival was for its director to be Palestinian. I often heard "there are also many non-Palestinian filmmakers working in solidarity with Palestinians. Why can't they be included?" There is no doubt that I find the work of those filmmakers important, but we did not consider this a festival about political solidarity. We conceived this as a chance for Palestinians to have a forum to tell their own stories. This was an occasion to celebrate our own cinema and in fact celebrate our own different voices, politics, stories and ways of seeing. For me, this is a matter of our survival, of resisting our culture's disappearance.

Like many colonized peoples, Palestinians have been the subjects of other people's films and research, and have often been perceived as exotic others, as victims, or as terrorists. We have been subject to other groups' gazes, and yet, ironically, whether we live in Palestine or in the Diaspora, we have come to understand how we have been made invisible through the complete absence of our own voices and images. Instead, we have seen our experiences and lives represented and mediated through the work – sometimes good, sometimes bad, sometimes well intentioned, sometimes not – of others

PRESENTING PALESTINIAN FILM IN NEW YORK

Another imperative of the festival was to introduce Palestinian cinema to the US, and more specifically to film audiences in New York City. In addition to bringing these new films to New York audiences, the importance of the festival lay in the fact that most Americans have never had the opportunity to view Palestinian films before and that these images and stories are rarely, if ever, seen in the US. Historically, Palestinian voices in the US have been systematically silenced.

This is why the range of films we chose was meant to include both fiction, documentary, and experimental work, and to give a forum to well-known filmmakers such as Elia Suleiman, Rashid Masharawi, Michel Khleifi and Mai Masri, as well as new voices and visions. We also wanted to bring together Palestinian filmmakers in the Diaspora with those in Palestine. The agenda was ambitious. We were able to program over thirty-four films, of which three were world premieres, twelve US premieres, and five New York premieres. I wondered what the audience in New York would think of the festival.

Sadly, there were difficulties in organizing the festival beyond simply logistical issues. As we began the preparations for the film festival, suddenly certain websites appeared attacking our festival. We also began to receive a barrage of hate mail, personal attacks, and death threats. The day before the festival was to begin, campus security and the New York police department became involved, upon receiving word that anti-Palestinian extremists were threatening to violently obstruct the festival. Our computers were hacked, our emails spammed, our voicemails flooded with racist, obscene, and threatening messages. The festival's academic sponsor, Hamid Dabashi, came under pressure as head of the department hosting the event, and was made to explain numerous times to various university and other authorities the nature of the festival, so as to prevent the event from being cancelled.

"Americans for a Safe Israel" was one among many groups who incited a campaign not only to call the president of Columbia University and threaten that "donations will be withheld and that concerned citizens will use whatever influence they have" to prevent the festival from occurring but were also urged to call President Bush at the White House and remind him "of the need to honor God's Covenant with Israel."[7] Other websites published a statement claiming that the films in the festival "oppose Israel's existence and call for Arab migration to 'Zionist controlled territory.'"[8] Due to this coordinated campaign, the university was finally forced to release a public statement defending the rights of academic and artistic freedoms where the film festival was concerned.

These responses seemed excessive and absurd. Who opposes *film festivals?* What is so threatening about such an event? Is it the filmmakers, the issues they deal with, or something much more fundamental: the symbols, images and representations they bring forth? Or is it simply the fact that for the first time Palestinians had represented their own experiences themselves without mediation and commentary?

Many of these organizations seemed most disturbed by the festival poster—a map of historic Palestine with doves flying from it overlaid on a strip of film. In a basic way, the poster was clearly representing the land from which these filmmakers originate. No one can dispute the fact that one million Palestinians inside the State of Israel are part of the larger community of Palestinians, which also include millions in the Diaspora who originate from within these borders – and yet indicating their inclusion through the use of a map of *where we come from* was deemed an act of symbolic violence. On the website of a self-proclaimed believer "in human rights for the Palestinians," the festival was attacked for "obliterating my country!"[9] For those who fear the very existence of Palestinians and deny our right to personal expression, the use of imagery indicating our symbolic unity, even on a poster, is clearly still a threat.

Despite all of this, the festival was a huge success. For the four-day event, thousands of people turned up. I was surprised to find that people drove from as far as Iowa and Texas to attend the festival. Some came in solidarity, others for curiosity, and many for their love of cinema. This is a testament, no doubt, not only to the persistence of Palestinian culture but also to the fact that many people in the U.S. and in other parts of the world *want* to see these films to increase their understanding of the Palestinian culture, or simply to enjoy them as works of art.

The attempts at suppressing Palestinian cultural identity have only led to more resistance, and the evolution of cultural production by Palestinians continues, despite the loss of lives, the loss of land and property, despite dispossession and exile. With cameras, we tell our own stories, represent our experiences, and resist being made invisible. This book is a celebration of Palestinian persistence.[10]

TWO

THE WEAPON OF CULTURE: CINEMA IN THE PALESTINIAN LIBERATION STRUGGLE[1]

Joseph Massad

It is said that when Göbbels heard the word culture, he reached for his pistol. Göbbels clearly understood the effective force of cultural life in inflicting foreign domination as well as in mobilizing resistance to it. Such an understanding was also shared by resistors to colonial oppression. Amilcar Cabral was clear from his own African experience that for a colonial power "to take up arms to dominate a people is, above all, to take up arms to destroy, or at least to neutralize and to paralyze, their cultural life. For as long as part of that people can have a cultural life, foreign domination cannot be sure of its perpetuation."[2] Indeed, Cabral could have added that people survive as people only if their culture survives, for what would the notion of peoplehood signify outside the notion of culture?

The place of culture in national liberation has always been a contested terrain. This is more so at the time the struggle for liberation is being waged, as the demands of contingency limit the space of debate. While revolutionaries have mobilized culture as a weapon of resistance, they have had to confront colonial powers who also mobilized culture as a weapon of domination. Negotiating the terms of cultural battles then becomes crucial for strategies of liberation. It is in this context that the aesthetic may be sacrificed for the sake of political instrumentalism and instrumentalism itself is transformed into an aesthetic. This was evident in a number of post-revolutionary contexts, beginning with Soviet socialist realism, and extending to China, Cuba, and Iran, and in pre-liberation contexts such as South Africa and Rhodesia. In this chapter, I will provide a brief history of Palestinian cinema, and reflect on the role of the aesthetic in it and on the nature of the audiences it sought and seeks to reach.

The 2003 Columbia University Palestinian Film Festival took place on the thirtieth anniversary of the first Palestinian Film Festival, which convened in Baghdad in March 1973. Like Hegel's *Geist*, Palestinian film festivals seem to move from East to West, following money, resources, and the solidarity movement. From its early beginnings (as the expression of Palestinian revolutionaries' intent on defeating Zionist colonialism) to its most recent blossoming since the Oslo Accords (in the context of official Palestinian capitulation), Palestinian cinema, along with other Palestinian cultural expressions more generally, has been integral to Palestinian resistance.

The Palestinian experience with Zionist colonialism is hardly unique in this regard. If Golda Meir had declared once that "the Palestinian people does not exist,"[3] Portugal's Antonio Salazar had declared before her that "Africa does not exist."[4] If Göbbels wanted to shoot culture, more recently Ariel Sharon followed that strategy by ransacking and pillaging Palestinian institutions of culture, prominent among them, the Sakakini Cultural Center in Ramallah, which was vandalized by Israeli occupation soldiers in April 2002.[5] Yet Palestinians have continued to resist in the last half-century Israel's oppression in all its extensions – whether racist laws applied against its Palestinian citizens and those Palestinians it exiled and refuses to allow back, or its racist military occupation of the West Bank and Gaza for the last thirty-seven years. Culture has been one of the more important venues for such resistance. In song, music, dance, painting, theater, poetry, novels, and cinema, Palestinians have mounted a cultural resistance that refuses to sever the connection they have to their lands and homes, despite Israel's continuing conquests and ravages of their lives.[6] As Cabral put it, "if imperialist domination has the vital need to practice cultural oppression, national liberation is necessarily an *act of culture*."[7]

CINEMA AND STRUGGLE

While Arab commercial cinema to date is yet to produce a single feature film about the Palestinian tragedy, many films were made from the late 1940s on depicting aspects of that tragedy. Egyptian commercial films were more interested in Egyptian soldiers' own psychic and family dramas than in the tragic fate of the Palestinians.

This is apparent in Mahmud Dhulfuqar's *Fatat min Filastin* (*A Young Woman from Palestine,* 1948 – featuring Su'ad Muhammad and Mahmud Dhulfuqar) as well as in Kamal al-Shaykh's *Ard al-Salam* (*The Land of Peace,* 1957 – featuring Omar Sharif and Fatin Hamamah). These films depict Egyptian soldiers falling in love with Palestinian women who end up leaving Palestine to marry them and live in Egypt. Aside from the relatively poor quality of these films, in aesthetic and production terms, their message was hardly a hopeful one, much less possible, for the majority of Palestinians.

Syrian and Lebanese films released in the late 1960s and early 1970s sensationalized the Palestinian guerrillas in B-rated adventure films inspired by Hollywood Westerns. Such films included *'Amaliyyat al-Sa'ah al-Sadisah* (*The 6 O'Clock Operation,* 1969) directed by Sayf al-Din Shawkat and *Thalathat 'Amaliyyat fi Filastin* (*Three Operations in Palestine,* 1969) directed by Muhammad Salih al-Khayyali. Others included Gary Garbidian's *Kulluna Fida'iyyun* (*We Are All Guerrillas,* 1969). There are of course important exceptions to these trends. Two films stand out in this regard: *The Duped* (*al-Makhdu'un,* 1971) directed by the Egyptian Tawfiq Salih and produced in Syria, is based on Ghassan Kanafani's novella *Men in the Sun,* and *Kafr Qasim* (1974), directed by the Lebanese Burhan 'Alwiyyah, depicts the 1956 massacre of Palestinian Israelis by the Israeli army on the eve of Israel's invasion of Egypt. Although neither of these films depicted the *Nakba,* or the 1948 Palestinian catastrophe, they were attempts to portray some of the tragic events and experiences of Palestinians *after* the *Nakba.* The absence of any thorough cinematic treatment of *al-Nakba,* the foundational trauma of the Palestinian struggle, seems related to its unrepresentability. To represent the Palestinian tragedy and trauma is to relive it and to give credence to its permanence, which most directors avoided. Egyptian director Yousry Nasrallah has just attempted such a feat. He adapted to cinema Lebanese novelist Elias Khouri's novel *The Gate of the Sun.* His film premiered at the 55th Cannes Film Festival in May 2004.

Due to the absence of any Palestinian institutions of culture that survived the catastrophe, the emergence of a Palestinian cinema had to wait until such a rubric emerged. The Arab governments' establishment of the Palestine Liberation Organization in 1964 was to provide an institutional setting for a number of cultural projects, which, however, remained mostly undeveloped until after the 1967 war and the Palestinian guerrillas' take-over of the PLO in 1969. This was the heyday of what was then called the Palestinian revolution, which sought to revolutionize every aspect of Palestinian life.

The Palestinian revolution paid attention to cinema since its early years. The Palestine Film Unit (Wihdat Aflam Filastin) was founded in 1968 under the auspices of Fatah and undertook its revolutionary mission of recording and documenting the Palestinian revolution for the future. Other Palestinian groups founded their own units in the early 1970s and produced their own films. These include the Democratic Front's "Artistic Committee" (founded in 1973) and the Popular Front's "Committee for Central Information" (founded in 1971) in addition to the PLO's "Division of Artistic Education" (founded in 1973).[8]

The founders of these units were keen on recording revolutionary events, as they did not want to replicate the experience of previous revolutions that failed to record their pre-victory period on film, leaving such tasks to outsiders. Although the foundational mission of the Palestine Film Unit was documentary and pedagogical, the aesthetic dimension of films formed much of the debate about the first film that the Unit produced, namely, "With our souls and our blood," a title borrowed from the political chant "With our souls and our blood, we sacrifice ourselves for you Oh Palestine." The film, which documented the Black September massacres in Jordan in 1970, was a collective effort by camerawoman Sulafah Jadallah (who was shot during the 1970 onslaught causing her partial paralysis), and camera man and director Hani Jawhariyyah (murdered in 1976 with camera in hand during the Lebanese Civil War) and director Mustafa Abu 'Ali. Jawhariyyah and Abu 'Ali had met in Britain during their schooldays in the mid-1960s, and had been collaborating since 1968 on different cinematic projects.[9] Jawhariyyah's camera had also recorded much of the available footage of Palestinians being expelled over the bridges of the River Jordan during the 1967 War.

Although it was ultimately Abu 'Ali who finished the film with the help of a large team of technicians and artistic advisors, he did so after arduous debates about the form and style the film should have. While the debate centered on what would be the best pedagogical form, namely whether the film should be a documentary or a "revolutionary struggle" film, the question of representation came to the fore. The team decided to subject the film to a revolutionary political analysis that would substitute for a traditional script, and that the mission of the technical team was to interpret it cinematically. A number of experimental montage effects were undertaken, especially with regard to the rhythmic pace of the film (fast or slow concatenation of images were tried, for example), as well as use of cartoons "to clarify" for the Palestinian audience the content of the film. When portions of the experimental montage were shown to a refugee audience at the Wihdat refugee camp outside Amman, it was decided to drop the fast rhythm of cartoon images and replace them with child actors in a scene that was viewed as "more realistic" than cartoons and "closer to the comprehension of our masses." Having undertaken this popular referendum, the team decided to drop symbolism altogether from the film.[10]

The question of canvassing the Palestinian audience for what they would find most effective in film was taken up seriously by the Unit. Field studies were undertaken involving questionnaires that would be distributed before screening films produced by the Unit, and collected afterwards. One of the findings based on the questionnaire was that audiences preferred the "realist" style to other "artistic" and experimental styles.[11] It was in this context that instrumentalism, wherein film is seen as a pedagogical tool to incite people to politics, became prominent, as did audience tastes and desires. In this sense, what Palestinian filmmakers were negotiating was something akin to the debate between avant-gardist and populist schools of aesthetics, current in revolutionary thought since World War I.[12]

Palestinian films began to be produced at a relatively prolific rate throughout the 1970s, the highest number being twelve in 1973, slowing down by the end of the decade and reaching a trickle after the Israeli invasion of Lebanon in 1982. Most copies of the films were lost or stolen in the mayhem of the invasion while the remaining copies were scattered around the world, where they remain to this day. Baghdad hosted the next two Palestinian film festivals (in 1976 and 1980) before that venue was closed after the start of the Iran–Iraq war.

Funding for film had come from the PLO and its constituent guerrilla groups and thus was limited in scope. Palestinians, however, were not the only ones making films about Palestine. This had been a productive period also for international filmmakers who made films about Palestine, from across the Arab World, Western and Eastern Europe, and the Third World (Leipzig in East Germany had important film festivals which showed films about the Palestinians directed by Palestinians and non-Palestinians alike). International filmmakers who ventured into Palestinian cinematic territory included Jean-Luc Godard *Ici et ailleurs* (*Here and Elsewhere*, 1974), and Manfred Vosz *Palästina* (*Palestine*, 1971), and *Für Er Ist Palästinenser*

(*Because He is Palestinian*, 1972). Production of films about Palestine and the Palestinians was such that at the 1973 Baghdad festival, 150 films were shown, fifty of which were made outside the Arab World. That number was to change drastically by the 1980 third film festival in Baghdad where a hundred films were shown, of which only five were made by Arab directors.

The films of the 1970s were characterized by their purpose of inciting politics and critiquing it simultaneously, which is the reason why all of them – with one exception – were documentary films (*Returning to Haifa*, 1982, by Iraqi director Qasim Hawal, with PFLP funding).[13] In addition to the higher costs needed for feature films, the cultural outlook of the Palestinian revolution at the time necessitated the documentation of Palestinian lives in the face of the continuing erasure of Palestinian history by the State of Israel. These documentaries attempted to provide a narrative of the history, present, and future of Palestine and the Palestinians. As they were banned in many Arab countries, few of these films had any popular audiences outside Lebanon and the Palestinian refugee camps, where most of them were produced under PLO auspices (although in addition to Iraq, many films would be shown in Syria, Algeria, Libya, South Yemen, and Egypt).

This would change after the expulsion of the PLO from Lebanon in 1982 and the crisis faced by the revolutionary generation in the face of Egyptian–Israeli peace and Israeli defeat of the PLO. The 1980s were to witness the first attempts by Palestinians outside the sphere of the PLO or its constituent parts to make films. Michel Khleifi's beautiful 1980 film *Fertile Memory* was to be followed by the first ever Palestinian feature film directed by a Palestinian, namely Khleifi's *Wedding in Galilee*, released in 1988. With European funding, the talented and innovative Khleifi was able to cover the costs of his film, which differed markedly, not only in style, but also in purpose, from the films of the 1970s. A Palestinian Israeli based in Belgium, Khleifi dramatized Palestinian life through a story that mixed the social and the political, the sexual and the aesthetic in a new mélange contextualized by Israel's usurpation of Palestinian lands and control of Palestinian lives. It would be another decade before other directors would join Khleifi in making feature films. While PLO funding for such artistic production dried up by the late 1980s, European funding was substituted in the individual case of Khleifi.

The 1990s ushered in a new age of Oslo and PLO capitulation, which brought its own financial rewards. The flooding of the West Bank and Gaza with internationally funded NGOs and the availability of new US and European money, as well as funding from the Palestinian business community, for different types of cultural projects, including films, changed the filmic terrain drastically. As evidenced by the films shown in the 2003 Columbia University Dreams of a Nation film festival, the majority of the films were produced in the previous five years. Encompassing shorts and long feature films as well as documentaries, the aesthetic and political composition of these films differ markedly from those of the 1970s. While many of the recent films are still involved in documenting Palestinian lives, their role is less pedagogical and aims less at an incitement to politics than at a commentary on it. One could posit that Palestinian cultural production, including films, in recent years, is constitutive of the simultaneous despair and hope that Palestinians are experiencing. The innovative experimental styles used by the different directors reflect the experimental nature of the new modality of the Israeli occupation under PA rule. Palestinian artists, like the rest of the Palestinian people, are committed to resist the occupation, exile, and racism, but are not decided as to what ways would lead to victory.

The 1970s were characterized by diaspora filmmakers, but today, Palestinians from Israel, the West Bank, and Gaza, as well as the diaspora, are engaging in this cultural form of expression. Their new films are deployed in an important battle of images with the Zionist-friendly international media covering the Israeli occupation. The 1970s films were mostly made for a Palestinian and other Arab audiences whose tastes the directors wanted to address and cater to; the new films, however, clearly have a local and international audience as a target and are more mindful of international tastes (indeed, many films display credits only in English while others have bilingual credits. Few, if any, have them in Arabic only.) This is a reflection not only of the new international funding generated by the Oslo capitulation but also by the continued onslaught of Zionist images in the international sphere which have a monopoly on the representations of Palestinians. Palestinian films shown in Leipzig in the 1970s addressed a sympathetic audience, in New York in 2003, they addressed, at best, a mixed one.

Clearly, being mindful of international tastes and interests engages a different politics of reception than those envisaged by the Palestinian directors of the early 1970s. Indeed, when Palestinian director Mustafa Abu 'Ali and Palestinian film critic Hassan Abu Ghanimah discussed in 1973 Tawfiq Salih's important film *al-Makhdu'un* (*The Duped*) and how it would be received by a European or American audience, they both saw the need for the film to be preceded by a "written introduction . . . that explains to the audience the real history to the events of the film and the actual situation within which our people were living in the period [that the film depicts] . . . We are aware that events today have bypassed what the film engages and therefore we acknowledge that *The Duped* could lead the foreign spectator to a relatively wrong understanding."[14] Such problems have been clearly bypassed by contemporary Palestinian directors, as the politics of reception of foreign, read Western, audiences are always already internalized by the filmmakers of today, making any *ex post facto* contextualization for their benefit gratuitous.

If political instrumentalism defined the aesthetics of the films of the 1970s, the new crop of films engage both European avant-garde as well as Palestinian folk aesthetics. These two types of aesthetics are deployed in images of resistance and oppression, images of frustrated and impossible love stories of the romantic variety, as well as the Palestinians' emotional and physical attachment to their lands and their love of it. The test for the new generation of Palestinian filmmakers, however, remains aesthetic and political. Which audiences are these films targeting, and what aesthetic forms and political messages do they want to communicate? The nature of international funding and the nature of political power in the West Bank and Gaza will have strong roles to play in both.

Perhaps *Four Songs for Palestine* stands out in this regard, as being one of the more beautiful and effective of such recent films. The film, directed by Palestinian Israeli director Nada El-Yassir (who lives in Canada) in 2001, is a short that depicts a woman at home, with the television blaring in the background. Her daily life seems to enact every aspect of the Palestinian experience, symbolized by the colors of the Palestinian flag. If capitalism, as Marx has taught us, transforms "all that is solid into air," Israeli military occupation transforms all that is solid in the Palestinian experience into *liquid*. This liquefaction is registered by the film in the daily activities of this generic Palestinian woman. We are treated to her lining her eyes with kohl, drops of which transform into a shimmering black color against a white background that overtakes the screen in a highly aestheticized form. The blackness also registers the dark days of mourning that so many Palestinians have endured for a hundred years. Indeed, in the opening scene, as this Palestinian woman looks into the mirror before washing her face, all she can see in the mirror reflection is the occupation forces shooting Palestinians. As she prepares breakfast and accidentally cuts her finger while slicing tomatoes, the bright redness of her blood overwhelms the screen against a black background, reminding us of the thousands of gallons of spilled Palestinian blood at the hands of the Israeli occupation and the concomitant mourning of Palestinians over their dead loved ones. Later as she prepares Palestinian tea with fresh mint, the greenness that the mint gives to the tea registers that other color of the Palestinian flag, reminding us of the product of the land that Palestinian peasants work so hard to till. The greenness is quite strong and challenges the black background that threatens to overtake it. Finally, we are made aware of a small baby in a crib. The mother approaches, embraces it and begins to nurse it. The whiteness of the mother's milk against the black background completes the circle of the four Palestinian flag colors, insisting on the centrality of motherhood and maternal nurturing to the Palestinian struggle and Palestinian resistance. It is after all the cycle of Palestinian life that the Israeli occupation seeks to interrupt, however unsuccessfully. As the mother nurses her baby, we see young Palestinians demonstrating on television against the occupation and we are informed by the newscaster that twenty young Palestinians have been shot by the Israeli occupation forces. The aestheticized rendering of the four colors as emerging from the daily chores of a Palestinian woman, confined as she was to her dilapidated house as a result of the Israeli-imposed curfew, emblematizes without the slightest didacticism the sense of oppression that all Palestinians undergo on a daily basis. No words are necessary to explain anything in the film, the blaring television and radio notwithstanding. El-Yassir clearly wanted to communicate in images – the cinematic language by definition – what words are inadequate to explain. Her meticulous rendering of the Palestinian experience, especially that of Palestinian women, makes her film one of the best of the new crop.

In this sense, El-Yassir follows in the footsteps of Palestinian film director Elia Suleiman, whose films, like those of Khleifi, have increasingly acquired international interest and audiences. Suleiman's films, whether *Homage to Assassination* (video), or his two features *Chronicle of a Disappearance* and *Divine Intervention*, insist on the visual register as the primary mechanism for expression, relegating verbal discourse to secondary status. Indeed, while Suleiman, as actor, has the starring role in all three films, we never hear his voice. On one occasion, when he was invited to speak in Nazareth at a community event in *Chronicle of a Disappearance* (1996), external factors (the microphone malfunctions, people's cell-phones ring incessantly) conspire to silence him completely. But while he is unable to utter words with a silenced voice, his imagination manifesting in the films that he makes is free to wander. In his latest film, *Divine Intervention* (2002), he turns to fantasy as the realm of wish fulfillment in resisting occupation. It is this visual imagery that Suleiman insists is the only language of his cinema. The influence of avant-garde European filmmakers on his novel aesthetic is clear throughout. The originality and beauty of his films led to international acclaim and a number of prizes that Suleiman received at international film festivals, including at Cannes.

Another masterful production is the most recent three-part documentary *Route 181*, directed by Michel Khleifi and Israeli director Eyal Sivan. *Route 181* is perhaps the best exposition of the Zionist movement and of Israeli society that the Palestinians have been confronting for a century. The understated style of the film, which asks simple questions of ordinary Israelis and Palestinians across all walks of life along the demarcation lines set by the United Nations Partition Plan, otherwise known as UN Resolution 181, from which the film gets its title, is matched by the exhilarated and liberated tone of Israeli Jews who speak of massacres of Palestinians, of expulsions, destruction of homes, confiscation of lands, "sweeping" Palestinians off the land to "cleanse" it, and much more in the most ordinary fashion. Israeli soldiers interviewed in the film assert that they are simply doing their jobs by manning the checkpoints. An educated Israeli soldier, who flexes his intellectual muscles by telling Sivan about the philosophers he reads, is inquisitive about Hannah Arendt's book on Eichmann – wanting to learn what "the banality of evil" really means. He gets it in theory but sees no connection to what he is engaged in. The banality of Zionist evil is indeed everywhere in evidence in this amazingly subtle yet revealing film, which mesmerizes audiences for the four-and-a-half-hours duration. An Israeli contractor who supplies the Israeli army with barbed wire to cordon off Palestinian land is just doing his job, oblivious to his part in the evil, as are those who live on confiscated Palestinian land – although one of the latter cries about the oppression of his European Jewish mother (who later became a refugee in Palestine) by an anti-Semitic soldier, while at the same time insisting that he goes to sleep without any "guilt" about Palestinian refugees. *Route 181* provides a portrait of Israeli Jews and their Palestinian victims as they are, engaged in their daily living of oppressing and resisting respectively, representations that send shivers up the spines of all feeling audiences without resorting to didacticism. Khleifi's masterful versatility as a director of documentaries

A scene from Michel Khleifi and Eyal Sivan's *Route 181: Fragments of a Journey to Palestine-Israel* (2004).

and feature films makes him unique among Palestinian directors. His international acclaim has meant that his films are not only *objets d'art* but also central parts of a growing Palestinian cinematic arsenal.

Such beautiful and intelligent films aside, the Palestinian narrative of exile and dispossession is yet to be told in film, whether to a Palestinian or an international audience. Palestinian directors, as is the case with other Arab directors, have not attempted to represent the foundational trauma of the *Nakba*, except with documentary footage. The unrepresentability of the *Nakba* in this aesthetic realm haunts Palestinian and Arab cinema like no other dimension of the Palestinian story. If the film *Exodus* dramatized the Zionists' original sin of colonial conquest as a story of liberation, it remains to be seen how Palestinian filmmakers can resist this foundational lie in their own films. Read another way, if the *Nakba* as trauma, as the Palestinian traumatic event *par excellence*, lies by definition outside the circuit of representation, and therefore cannot be represented aesthetically, then it cannot be missing or lacking after all. In this sense, it would seem that the very unrepresentability of the *Nakba* is what has structured Palestinian cinema all along, which is why this cinema fails to say what it must but cannot say.

Egyptian director Yousry Nasrallah adapted to the screen Elias Khouri's novel *The Gate of the Sun*.[15] His film, shown at international festivals around the world to wide acclaim, was released in the spring of 2004. In it Nasrallah reproduces moving scenes of the Palestinian exodus and of Israeli massacres without the slightest sensationalism. While the film is about a love story between two Palestinians, whose arranged marriage begins in Palestinian landed time and whose love and lives end in Israeli and diasporic landless time bifurcates the two parts of this almost five-hour film. In contrast with nationalist romantic accounts of exile and the land, the film, like the novel, which does not ignore the monumental loss of land and home, seeks to represent the affective loss instantiated by the 1948 catastrophe among fellow Palestinians, separated by exile and colonialism. That the metaphor of longing is registered through a reproductive heterosexual love story is significant and hardly incidental to the political (national and colonial) ideology of reproduction and demographics. Perhaps inspired by Edward Said's famous demand that the Palestinians be granted "permission to narrate,"[16] the film and the novel are narrations by third parties (Dr. Khalil, Umm Hasan) about the lives of the two major protagonists, whether Nahila, now dead, or her husband, Yunis al-Asadi, comatose and dying in a

Palestinian refugee hospital in Beirut. The narration begins again to tell the story of the Palestinian exodus as one that does not *end* Palestinian existence but rather *begins it anew*, through a narrative that can be picked up by one Palestinian and then another without interruption, as Umm Hasan picked it up from Dr. Khalil. Indeed, the famed phrase of the comatose Yunis, repeated many times in the film and the novel, is to start over again "from the beginning." *The Gate of the Sun* thus renarrates the Palestinian story in a cinematic language that straddles the individual and the universal without subsuming them into one another. With his latest film, Nasrallah has produced the Palestinian *Exodus* precisely by reproducing and insisting that the real Palestinian exodus formed but a new beginning for Palestinian lives, and *not* an end.

What Palestinian filmmakers have succeeded in doing in the last thirty years is to tell many important Palestinian stories that the world had never heard before. In this vein, the talented Elia Suleiman has shown more interest in a satirical imaging of Israeli militarism, which if it did not have such violent consequences would be laughable for its buffoonery. However, Zionism's use of the cultural weapon remains its most effective anti-Palestinian weapon in the international arena, where its misrepresentations of the Palestinian people and of its colonial project, in film or in the news media, remain supreme. What Palestinian filmmakers have succeeded in doing so far is to deploy and instrumentalize their films as weapons of resistance in the international arena and to infiltrate this bastion of Zionist power slowly.[17] Herein lies their contribution and promise. The hope, however, is that Palestinian cinema will not only remain a *weapon of resistance* but that it will also become a *weapon and an act of culture*. As the late French philosopher Gilles Deleuze put it, the cry of the Zionists to justify their racist violence has always been "we are not a people like any other," while the Palestinian cry of resistance has always been "we are a people like all others."[18] It is this message that is being communicated most effectively by Palestinian cinema.

THREE

FROM REALITY TO FICTION –
FROM POVERTY TO EXPRESSION

Michel Khleifi

In 1948 two major events took place in the Middle East: the creation of the State of Israel and the onset of the Palestinian tragedy. Two different realities have since evolved: the State of Israel became strengthened into a regional power with a formidable military, economic and technological arsenal; while the Palestinian cause has continued to marginalize itself within the Arab World – itself plagued by civil wars and military or monarchic regimes that are still denying their people basic democratic rights. The intensity of the bitter struggles in the Middle East, however, have contributed to the radical change that slowly and gradually took hold after the October 1973 War, first with the visit of President Anwar al-Sadat to Jerusalem in 1977 and then, in the mid-1990s, the signing of a peace treaty between some Arab countries and the State of Israel. This development was considered by some as a capitulation and by others as a strategic choice designed to remedy and re-stabilize the Middle East.

After the Gulf War (1990), the Palestine Liberation Organization (PLO) and the State of Israel launched negotiations and treaties of mutual recognition. By some force of history, these two entities, once enemies, became alter egos and are now, perhaps, partners, for better or for worse.

Within this context of anger and revolt, I began my film career in the beginning of the 1980s. This was the result of my personal, political, and cultural experience, which was influenced by my childhood in the Nazareth of the 1950s and 1960s – a place that, for me, was a ghetto at the heart of the Galilee under Israeli rule. At that

Michel Khleifi (Courtesy of Omar al-Qattan, Sindibad Films.)

time we were cut off from the Arab world, every progressive opinion was suppressed by the military power, and our people were scattered among the Arab countries. The education curriculum was reviewed, reshaped and imposed on us by the new state. For us, this was a time of fear and isolation – indeed, of solitude.

My first cultural benchmark was when I discovered poetry, theatre, and literature in outstanding writers such as Pablo Neruda, Federico Garcia Lorca, Nazim Hikmet, Paul Eluard, Vladimir Mayakovsky, Emile Zola, Victor Hugo, O'Henry, Bertolt Brecht, August Strindberg, Henrik Ibsen, Anton Chekhov, and others – not to mention Arab poets and writers whose works reached us from time to time. All these writers and poets provided us with small windows to the world and the hope for freedom, which every person needs to humanize his or her daily life and to make it more bearable. At that time, in Nazareth's only movie theater, we used to share with the viewers of the rest of the world the pleasure of watching Hollywood films from the 1950s and 1960s, before the emergence of television, which was going to eventually close this wonderful window of dreams. In fact, even now, when I catch a glimpse of a film from that period, I feel I am a child again, and I realize the impact of these productions on what is made today.

Within that context, the 1967 Arab–Israeli War had negative consequences for Arab societies in general and particularly for Palestinian society, and, later, for Israeli society as well. It is only now that we have become aware of the negative consequences of that war, which saw Israel defeating all the Arab armies and occupying a huge territory, forcing it to rule a large civilian population. The 1967 War reunited the Palestinian territory and opened our society to the Arab world after twenty years of isolation. The situation became explosive and revolutionary. The PLO asserted itself on a political, military, and ideological level, and consequently its influence became great. Through the rallying of most Arab and Palestinian intellectuals, a PLO culture thus emerged. Literature, poetry, cinema, and folk expressions were part of the activities favored by the PLO in order to renew an Arab–Palestinian identity.

The 1967 War saw the end of innocence while the time of building political and national foundations was beginning. It was also a revolutionary time all over the world: the Vietnam War, the movements in favor of democratization in the Eastern bloc, the tide of protest in the US- and the post-1968 period, which paved the way for a real cultural revolution in Europe.

After 1967, I became aware that without a true cultural movement, which would advocate a genuine change in our thinking and which would recognize the individual as a citizen with his/her rights safeguarded within the structures of existing and future Arab states (the Palestinian state, for example), the hope to have a liberated society would remain a remote dream. I also became aware of the need to decolonize cultural action from the domination of political and ideological discourse. How can we create a culture that could retain within itself its own originality and specificity, while still being universal? How can we create a cinema, which could carry the Palestinian human experience, vertically (historically) and horizontally (on the basis of people's daily reality)? Is there really a culture of the poor, and if yes, how to protect it? These questions were on my mind before leaving for Belgium at the beginning of the 1970s.

During the 1970s, Palestinian cinema was the political expression of the PLO. These films directly focused on the events experienced by the Palestinian populations in Jordan until 1970 and in Lebanon thereafter. Towards the end of the Civil War in Lebanon, this cinema slowly died away without having ever shined, because its role was taken over by television cameras, which rushed out to film the Middle East. As far as I was concerned, the Palestinian cause was a just one, but the way it was being fought was wrong. We had to provide the world with another way of talking about us. At the time, we had the simplistic idea that the world was against us and that Zionists were everywhere. From the time of my childhood I had a specific viewpoint and I wanted it to be at the heart of my cinematic expression. The strength of Israel stems from our weakness, and our weakness does not stem from Israel's strength but rather derives from Arab society's archaic structures: tribalism, patriarchy, religion and community life, where there is no recognition of the person as an individual nor of men's, children's and, above all, women's rights.

These were the axes around which I wanted to organize my work. By protecting the individual from various oppressive regimes, the Arab World will achieve a new culture; by moving towards other individuals, with all our contradictions but no fear, we will recover our faith in the past, the present and the future of our common destiny. As to the confrontation with Israel, it is around the human rights principles that it must be settled. No one should compromise these legitimate rights or the principle of equality before the law. From now on, our daily life should be organized around civil law and not around the laws of religious and archaic mythologies.

So, as you can see, making a film about or for Palestine is not an easy task. One is faced with many internal and external elements of our multiple histories: a history defined differently by different people – Israelis or Palestinians, Jews or Arabs, Arab–Muslim and Western Judeo-Christianity. One is faced with commercial, technological, ideological, and historical war machines. We, cursed citizens of this under-developed world, this Third World of miseries, what can we do? We must keep on producing, creating, and fighting for life. We must be part of one of the most dynamic and progressive intellectual movements, whether cultural, aesthetic or philosophical. We must appropriate the world, take charge of it. Thought does not recognize borders, it is as free as the wind, ready to abandon any language or region if it is defeated by repression.

My films are part of a school of thought that always attempts to liberate languages from their ruling systems, whether ideological or commercial. My cinematographic roots stem from the history of direct cinema, which anchored itself in people's reality. As a filmmaker, I wanted to reach a universal cinematic language. A century after cinema was invented, we must go beyond differences, trends, and schools of filmmaking. We cannot separate the documentary from the fictional film. The question I ask myself is: How can I manage, with sound and picture, to make a film that will integrate drama, theatre, action, and reportage all into one work? Let's not forget that I come from a Third-World background of poverty, so the culture of the poor was always in the back of my mind, pushing me to find solutions in order to be creative. Perhaps one's viewpoint could combine all this because looking is also a way of thinking about cinema as a piece of writing. Literature can combine all these notions. In a novel, a documentary description can follow a fictional scene and then a poetic evocation of one detail: light, color, and movement, without creating a problem for the reader. I think that in our case, the only way to confront the power of commercial cinema is to use a camera as you would use a pen.

In order to develop this concept, I had to ask many questions:

1. What is "direct cinema?" Are the directors Robert J. Flaherty, Dziga Vertov, Joris Ivens, Henri Stork, Alain Resnais, Chris Marker, JeanRouche, Jean-Luc Godard all anchored in reality?
2. Does the obsession with objectivity presented by TV reporting really hold up to scrutiny?

3. What is *subjectivity* and how is it manifested? Is it in the collective vision of a team, from a philosophical, social, cultural point of view? Is it in the technical aspect of a medium, in the framing, the film stock, the sound track? Or is it with the journalist or the director who acts as the viewer's proxy, does he/she grasp the language of film?

4. What are the limits and strengths of militant cinema, and how are young filmmakers, with no financial means, managing to film reality as if it were fiction or fiction as if it were reality, as with neo-realism, new wave, nova Brazilian cinema, and independent American cinema?

5. How is poetry used by different cinematographic schools? (For Italian neo-realists Roberto Rossellini, Vittorio de Sica, and Cesare Zavattini, poetry serves the subject; in Pier Paolo Pasolini's films, the subject serves the director's poetry; in Andrej Tarkovski and the Taviani Brothers' films, poetry is like a subject serving the viewer; in the cinema born from the French *Nouveau Roman* – Marguerite Duras, Alain Robbe-Grillet, Claude Simon, Alain Resnais – poetry is perversion.)

All these questions led me to one conclusion: cinematic expression bears in itself a logic of narration. It must narrate a story, and every story is the result of a subjective discourse, which comes from (an) individual(s). I decided as a free individual to dedicate my work to showing the Palestinian experience *according to my perception of the world*, through film . . . because these questions taught me to watch a film in order to watch reality, to hear voices and resonances in order to listen to people's cries and joys. To look and to listen, as Godard said.

MY APPRENTICE YEARS

Between 1977 and 1980, I took part in the directing of several documentaries in Palestine/Israel for Belgian TV. At that time, the documentaries we made were essentially based around a journalist's voice-over, reading a commentary analyzing the subject and illustrating it with pictures. These sequences were punctuated with political interviews. From my first TV film, I had the voice-over reduced – I diminished the politicians' speeches and I concentrated on powerful situations that expressed the complexity of reality. I was giving voice to the people who were experiencing the event. After the first documentary, I had the feeling that the logic of television was limited to the event and was unable to get deeper into the subject to see and to hear the hidden reasons behind these events. The subject was always being "covered' instead of being *revealed* to show the roots of events. This was (and is) the huge contradiction of TV films.

On the other hand, the individual was always shown as an abstraction: the Palestinian, the Israeli, the army, the *fedayyeen* (freedom fighters). Who are they? How do they live, what do they think about, do they dream, hope or despair? Where do they come from and where are they heading? The idea of *Fertile Memory* (1980), my first film, stems from these questions. I thought that if I wanted to make a film about my society, I had to raise uncompromising questions: If Palestinians are the victims of the Israelis, then who are the Israelis? The victims of inhuman repression who then became the tormentors of the Palestinian people? But the Palestinians – are they only victims or are they also both victims and tormentors? They are tormentors, but towards women and children . . . Everything should be taken on its own level, and only to ascertain the damage done will not show who is the victim or the tormentor. We can only reach the truth by denouncing the logic and the systems that transform us into potential tormentors and victims.

This is how I decided to make a film for – and not about – the women of Palestine, and through them, a film for Palestine.

In *Fertile Memory*, Palestine – its history, its reality, its future, and its contradictions – appear through the portraits of two women, who are almost marginal in the eyes of society: a widow and a working woman. They become the archetype of their people's experiences. Here was how a subdued society oppresses half of its population. *Fertile Memory* was for me the vision of the present towards the past for a better future. I tried to push the real scenes from daily life towards fictionality, by exploring the two women's external and internal worlds. I had to suppress the boundaries between reality and fiction, document and narration. Is not Palestine the essence of the mythical country, in spite of its reality?

This film turned the PLO's militant cinema upside-down. It demonstrated that it is more important to show the thinking that leads to the political slogan rather than the expression of this slogan that is political discourse. For the first time, we could see Palestinian women in their private environment, all by themselves. Their memory was becoming subject, since they were themselves the subjects of their people's drama. Thus *Fertile Memory* is impregnated with Palestinian poetry "from within," as a number of commentators have observed – i.e. from the Palestinian society inside the Israeli state.

After I completed this film in 1981, events took a dramatic course in the Middle East: a direct war between Israel and the PLO in South Lebanon, President Sadat's assassination, inter-Palestinian civil wars in Lebanon in the presence of the Syrian and the Israeli armies in the South, which was going to result in the occupation of Beirut, which would in turn result in the PLO leaving Lebanon.

It was in this context of new defeats that I started to write *Wedding in Galilee* (1987). At that time, producers only wanted strong scenarios written on the American model, with a happy ending. Without success, I had been looking for a production team to work on a project called *A Season in Exile* that would have represented an aesthetic and dramatic continuity to *Fertile Memory*. It was the description of a young Palestinian woman who had fled her village to follow her lover to Europe.

For *Wedding in Galilee*, the idea came to me through the story of a quack doctor who was faced with a newly wed couple unable to make love on their wedding night, creating unbearable tension in a village. From this idea, I wrote a modern tragedy in which two "gods" confront each other, representing two systems, military and modern, one of the Israeli military governor and the other the patriarchal and archaic authority of the Palestinian *Mukhtar*, or mayor of the village. As each tries to pull destiny his way, it is the fate of the people of the village that is at stake. The question is: who will win?

In this film, for which I also wrote the script, I wanted to erase the boundaries between fiction and reality. The characters came from my imagination but they were played by non-professionals who had been chosen for their fictive resemblance to the scenario's characters. Here, I was interested in the theme of joyfulness and resilience under occupation. I tried to multiply the points of view from realism to formalism, theatrical documentary, etc. The overpowering immanence of Palestinian society and the way it is anchored in vertical reality, in the historical and cultural reality of this land – these had to be shown. I had also to concentrate on the visible elements of confrontation (Israeli/Palestinian, soldier/civilian, power/emotion, etc.) and other invisible elements (old/young, men/women, sexuality/tradition, symbols/needs). By limiting the drama within one space and one timespan, I wanted to have a go at the Manichean rigidity of the Arab and Palestinian way of thinking on the one hand, and at the Israelis and their supporters on the other hand. Sergei Eisenstein once said: "You can find the world's complexity in a dew-drop," so how can we describe such a formidable reality as that of the Middle East?

Anna Condo (as Bride) in Michel Khleifi's *Wedding in Galilee* (1987)
(Courtesy of Omar al-Qattan, Sindibad Films.)

This film was made during a very confused period, when the protagonists of the drama did not know where they were heading (between 1983 and 1987): all paths were open. There was a sort of quiet before the storm: the film was completed and screened in Cannes six months before the onset of the first Intifada, while three years later it was the turn of "Operation Desert Storm" to destroy the Middle East.

Wedding in Galilee had an incredible impact. Apart from the numerous international prizes it was awarded, it has been shown all over the world, sparking exciting debates and provoking viewers whenever it is shown. Some could perceive through this film the possibility of a co-existence in the Middle East, others saw it as a poetic and humanist work, others as a denunciation of the archaism of Arab-Palestinian society. I think that with this film I followed my path: to make films that raise questions rather than films that give answers. I genuinely think that questions generate life and answers death! I always believe in active viewers and never in passive ones. All readings are right but they are always incomplete, like life itself.

While Palestinian poets had influenced me through the making of *Fertile Memory*, I read almost every Palestinian short story and novel before writing *Wedding in Galilee*. The film refers to the works of Emile Habibi above all but also of Mohammed Naffa' and others. But the poet who influenced me most in the writing and the direction of this film was Yannis Ritsos, the great Greek poet who passed away a few years ago.[1]

At the end of the film, the Palestinian villagers take to the streets and rebel against the military occupation. Six months after the first world screening of this film at the Cannes Film Festival, where it was awarded the International Critics' Prize, the Palestinian people of Gaza, and later on, of the West Bank, rebelled and the First Intifada (1987–94) set the whole country ablaze. I think that many people saw in the film a glimpse of hope in the dark and violent reality of the first years of the Intifada. That was good. But I was already feeling the urgency to do something that would narrate the suffering of the people of the Intifada: families, women, men and above all, children who were dying from the army's bullets.

In 1989 I had just completed a screen adaptation of the first novel of a Belgian friend, *L'Ordre du Jour*, which was about bureaucracy, individualism and corruption in Belgium, an approach which you could call Kafkaesque. I was excited about the idea of making a film that would give a fictional, anthropological reflection on the life of this bureaucratic class, the largest class in today's developed countries. I thought I would film the existential exile of the European individual at the end of the twentieth century. However, urgency made me put this project aside and head for Jerusalem to shoot a new film called *Canticle of the Stones*.

The initial project was to make a poetic, impressionistic investigation based on the portraits of some of the children killed by Israeli repression. Again, I had to go beyond the reductive images conveyed by the numerous international television reports, especially by CNN. The Palestinians already had an automatic discourse, a sort of "ready-to-wear" language for journalists. There, I turned the problem around and I started filming the theme of sacrifice as a subject of the Intifada. This was a universal approach, since sacrifice is part of all human experience. "Everybody is always sacrificing something," says the male protagonist, whoever it is for – family, loved ones, children, work – everybody has to sacrifice a little bit of his/her dignity and freedom. So, instead of talking of the dead as martyrs, an idea verging on fascism, I wanted to emphasize their universal value, to understand their death as a form of sacrifice.

First, I wrote a poetical dialogue with two voices: she and he. While I was writing it, I realized that there was some similarity with *Hiroshima, mon amour*, by Marguerite Duras, adapted in Alain Resnais' outstanding film. I thought about this resemblance and I realized that the Middle East and Palestine, destroyed by war, looked like postwar Europe at the end of the 1940s. Towns and villages, land, houses, and, above all, souls were damaged. Fifty years on, it is more or less the equivalent of several atomic explosions. Why not have the literary and cinematographic references of *Hiroshima mon amour*? Besides, it was a way to draw attention to the fact that Marguerite Duras had always held a stubborn pro-Israeli position even during the invasion of Lebanon and the occupation of Beirut in 1982. To talk about Hiroshima is also to reject all situations of violence and repression everywhere in the world. It is to uphold all demands for dignity and freedom, which arise all over the world and to be in solidarity with these demands. You cannot be selective when it comes to the implications of these questions. The film was shown in Cannes and, as expected, sparked heated discussions and debates.

After the Gulf War, I directed my first Belgian film. The subject, location, and characters all came from the novel of my friend Jean-Luc Outers. As I explained, it was an almost anthropological look at the bureaucrats of the end of this century.[2] A critic wrote the following: "the film casts a critical and ironic eye on our changing

Western world . . . through a poetic-lyrical study of our bureaucratic societies where surrealistic absurdity often mixes with reality." I won't dwell on that film, which to this day remains a painful memory for me: through the irrational rejection of this film in Europe, I discovered that European society refuses, in an intolerant manner, any external viewpoint on its own reality. It seemed to me that the prevailing opinion ("what does an Arab filmmaker have to do with this?") was similar to the blunt refusal, which is also a form of censorship, of most of the Arab regimes of my films, and toward *Wedding in Galilee* in particular. The two sides are similar and disconcerting in their attitudes: This image does not resemble us! The Arabs don't acknowledge a woman's real problems, the problem of, for example, her virginity, or a man's real problems, in his sexuality. And the Europeans do not want their bureaucratic and state-run systems to be inspected, the very systems that provide tens of millions of men and women with work. Both were accusing me, each in their own way, of being hostile to them. Arabs thought I was too Westernized and Europeans thought that I, the "Oriental," was filming them with no love. In other words, the film was a blow to me; it was hard to live with, especially when there was such misunderstanding.

And then I wrote and directed *Tale of the Three Jewels* in Gaza, just before Arafat entered. It was like taking the road to Palestine once again by exploring a new aspect of the human adventure of my people: the theme of childhood in the midst of the pain endured under occupation and violence. And the need to rebuild the world of the children of Gaza and their right to dream and to be as free as any other citizen of the world who claims his or her right to life. A society cannot be built without its children's creativity. In the Middle East, it is necessary to get children, including Israeli children, to consider their region's history on the basis of a whole tradition: in other words, it is necessary to get them to understand that the history of their region belongs to them all. This way, I could build the scenario from the elements of the region's popular and religious cultural traditions: Tales, holy books, popular beliefs, Jins, etc. Historical space cannot be divided into communitarian and confessional parts – Jewish, Christian, Muslim; and I would add atheism as well, for I believe everyone has the right to inherit the cultural and historical legacy of the region, including the pre-monotheistic legacy of yesterday and the secularism of today.

I have always worked on the problem of narration because I think that an identity needs to be narrated. Look at the role of American cinema in the building of American national identity. Before creating *Tale of the Three Jewels*, I challenged myself to produce a modern tale using the traditional form of the oriental tale. World cinema, and particularly American cinema, has, from the beginning, based itself on biblical narrative (Old Testament) or on *The Arabian Nights*. Therefore, our task was to cross the resources of our imaginary, that vertical dimension of our culture, with the reality we are living nowadays. The result was a love story, with a fantastical dimension, between two 12-year-old children, against the background of the blunt reality of the cursed Gaza Strip.

As a conclusion, I would like to define the intricate relationship between my cinematographic language and the prevalent political language. The prevalent political language aims at determining a harmony of concrete interests. It is a uniform language that emphasizes the difference between what is similar and what is different within a very precise geographical and economical area. On the other hand, my cultural action, and not cultural language, aims at liberating spaces where everyone can be moved, can rediscover the real nature of things, marvel at the world, think about it and immerse oneself in the world of childhood. Finally, politics excludes the imaginary, unless it can be used for ideological or partisan ends. But my films' cultural world is made up of both reality and the imagination, both of which are vital to the creation of my films. It is like a child's quest for identity: he or she needs these two levels – reality and dream – to approach life in a balanced and non-schizophrenic way.

Translated by Omar al-Qattan

FOUR

TOWARDS LIBERATION: MICHEL KHLEIFI'S *MA'LOUL* AND *CANTICLE*

Bashir Abu-Manneh

> *The subject was always being "covered" instead of being revealed to show the roots of events.*
> Michel Khleifi

For the last twenty-five years, Michel Khleifi and Palestinian film have been nearly synonymous. From his earliest documentary *Fertile Memory* (1980) to his latest *Route 181: Fragments of a Journey in Palestine–Israel* (2004), co-directed with Israeli Eyal Sivan, Khleifi has been at the forefront of charting the human condition of Palestine–Israel.[1] Deeply preoccupied with ordinary life under conditions of dispossession, inequality, and occupation, he has uniquely captured the dialectic of Israeli creation and Palestinian destruction. His cinematic project is thus essentially dyadic: to *reveal* Palestine and to *intervene* in its transformation. Knowledge of roots and causes is coupled with a vision of national and social emancipation.

Khleifi's *oeuvre* is marked by a particular preoccupation with time. Its centrality in his cinema is best conveyed in two of his documentary films, *Ma'loul Celebrates Its Destruction* (1985) and *Canticle of the Stones* (1990). It is here, much more than in his other more famous films, *Fertile Memory* and *Wedding in Galilee* (1987), that the place of time in Palestinian actuality is powerfully re-created. The years 1948, 1967, 1982, and 1987 are all deeply ingrained in Palestinian consciousness, signifying social and political upheavals, traumas, defeats, and transformations: respectively, *Nakba* (The Catastrophe)/the establishment of Israel on most of Palestine; *Naksa* (The Setback)/Israel's occupation of the remainder of Palestine (West Bank and Gaza);

Israel's invasion of Lebanon and its expulsion of the PLO from Beirut; and, finally, the outbreak of the Intifada. For Khleifi, this temporality of Palestinian existence has entailed a specific reading of the present. Here, the repressed past and the immanent future are both evoked and existent, producing a dynamic picture of collision, struggle, and potential regeneration. Present and past become springboards for a desired future. Nostalgia for a pre-colonial past is as equally rejected as accommodation with the colonial present. This, I would like to suggest, is what makes Khleifi's cinema truly revolutionary: it challenges existing forms and relations of domination and anticipates a future of freedom and emancipation.

As Benita Parry has convincingly argued, such a practice of looking backwards only in order to look forwards (deployed in Alejo Carpentier's wonderful phrase "Memories of the Future") is at the heart of revolutionary forms of anti-colonial struggle. These, moreover, "register a rupture with dominant forms of Western thinking, and far from articulating nostalgia for the past, contemplate a condition transcending both the pre-colonial and the colonial."[2] This ruptural politics of national liberation, clearly expressed by Cabral and Fanon, involves eliminating colonial oppression in such a way so as to *enable* the cultural and political dominance of the masses and *prevent* that of the national bourgeois elite.[3] It thus seeks to construct an anti-imperialist nationalism deeply connected to social and political transformation. As Fanon has argued: "But if nationalism is not made explicit, if it is not enriched and deepened by a very rapid transformation into a consciousness of social and political needs, in other words, into humanism, it leads up a blind alley."[4]

Such is also the revolutionary ambition of what I see as Khleifi's radical anti-colonial humanism.[5] As he explains in his cinematic testimony, "From Reality to Fiction – From Poverty to Expression": "How can we create a fighting and competitive culture, which would bear within itself its own originality and specificity, while still being universal? How can we create a cinema, or films, which would carry the Palestinian human experience, vertically (historically) and horizontally (on the basis of people's daily reality)? Is there really a culture of the poor, and if yes, how to protect it?"[6] For Khleifi, as my reading of *Ma'loul* and *Canticle* below shows, culture becomes a tool to critique both national oppression and domination and a nationalism that advocates *partial* emancipation. Similar to Fanon, Khleifi believes that the collective struggle for self-determination necessarily has to empower individual self-liberation if it is to achieve the desired emancipation: "The liberation of the individual does not follow national liberation. An authentic national liberation exists only to the precise degree to which the individual has irreversibly begun his own liberation."[7] Fanon's conception of authenticity, or the liberation of the individual through the collective, thus becomes the end point of Khleifi's cinematic project – and it is that project that gives his films their real value, both as artistic productions and as forms of interventions in Palestinian culture and society.

I will begin with *Ma'loul* and the past, and then proceed to discuss *Canticle*, the meaning of liberation, and the future. Ma'loul is one of hundreds of villages occupied, depopulated, and destroyed by Jewish troops in 1948.[8] Most of its 690 residents (in 1944/45), who primarily worked in cultivating grain and olives, were expelled to Nazareth in July 1948. The village was subsequently leveled, though its mosque and two churches still stand and are sometimes used as cowsheds by residents of the neighboring kibbutz. According to the Israeli Absentees Property Law of 1950, Ma'loul land was designated as "absentee property" and its owners were denied their ownership rights. The state's cruel and unjust definition of an "absentee" was broad enough to include anyone who for whatever reason left his town or village after the 1947 Partition Plan. As a result of the Israeli expulsion of 1948, most Palestinian landowners fell under this category. For Ma'loul residents specifically, this law created the unique definition of "present absentee" landowners. Their fate was shared by thousands of other Palestinians who became citizens of the newly established Israeli state. As Sabri Jiryis explains in his groundbreaking *The Arabs in Israel*: "Thus property valued at millions of pounds has been confiscated from Arabs who are regarded as citizens of the country, voting in local and Knesset elections. This is how the Absentees Property Law came to be dubbed the 'law of the present absentee.' " He adds: "Thus the land belonging to 'absentees' living in Israel suffered the same fate as that of refugees outside Israel: in both cases it was given to Zionist foundations and Jewish settlements."[9]

Since Jews owned only 6 per cent of the land in Palestine in 1948, a massive expropriation and confiscation of Palestinian land was conducted mainly by force, and later legitimized by state law. Since 1948, the particular tragedy of "present absentees" like Ma'loul residents has been that they could still visit the site of their destroyed village but couldn't redeem their expropriated lands or settle there again. They thus became "internal refugees" in a state that regarded them as its citizens but granted exclusive use of their property to Jews. For the new Israeli colonists, Ma'loul land (and that of most of Palestine) was part of their wider project of "liberating," "emancipating," and "redeeming," the land.[10] For the Palestinians, places like Ma'loul came to epitomize their dispossession and disenfranchisement by Israel. They also revealed the particularist nature of the Jewish state that by law enforced discriminatory and repressive measures against its own non-Jewish citizens.[11] By choosing Ma'loul as a subject of his documentary Khleifi was thus tackling the fundamentals of Israeli state foundation and its discriminatory policy towards Palestinians in Israel.

The film starts with opening shots from the Israeli invasion of Lebanon in 1982 just two years earlier. Accompanied by a screeching emergency sound and that of warplanes in the background, images of destruction, death, fear, and injury flash by in fast forward. Lebanon is seen as it is suffering under the heel of Israeli brutality and screaming out in outrage.[12] War images continue, and lead back to shots from Mandate Palestine: British withdrawal, expulsions, demolitions, and, finally, refugees. For Khleifi, Lebanon leads back to Palestine: to understand Lebanon one has to understand 1948. The roots of Israeli aggression lie there. Images of an abandoned building in a forest then appear, followed by rubble. The footsteps of a visitor are heard and seen: with him the camera explores the width and breadth of the site. Though his identity is never disclosed, his presence allows Khleifi to chart the topography of a destroyed village. He also provides a connecting thread in the unfolding narrative. Over shots of the explorer's footsteps, sounds of children playing are heard. It slowly becomes clear that through a mixture of voice, sound, and image, Khleifi is attempting to reconstruct and bring to life a silenced and repressed history. As the mural painting of the village suggests, around which some elderly villagers sit and chat to the director, reconstructing the past is forging a link with it in the present: remembering is an act of actively constructing the present as an outcome of loss and dispossession. The past is also evoked directly: shots of imagined village life are dispersed throughout the film. Glossed over in a golden light and shot in slow motion, they convey the rootedness of villagers and the range of their productive preoccupations; while now all that remains is rubble and destruction.

The past is also directly narrated. Villagers' accounts are contrasted with a history lesson in an Arab school: the Zionist version of a "promised land," "redeemed" by victims of the Holocaust is compulsory education.[13] The clash between official and oral history is sharpened by the fact that the documentary is shot during Israel's 36th Independence Day celebrations. What for Israelis is "Independence" for Palestinians is "The Catastrophe," (*Nakba*). On this day, *Ma'loul Celebrates Its Destruction*, as the full title of the documentary clearly states. On Israel's Independence Day, Ma'loulees commemorate the *Nakba* by revisiting the site of their destroyed village. Khleifi joins them on their annual return.[14] An official national holiday is thus transformed, as Khleifi shows, into a day of defiant remembrance of ruined origins and forbidden times. As Jean Genet put it: "For the Palestinians of Maaloul [*sic*] the anniversary is a renaissance, a feast for the dead. For one day there's a village again – it may be only a lifeless facsimile but it's extremely vivid. Not just a thing of the past but also a reincarnation, as New York is of York."[15] The past is thus resurrected in the present for a day. The ritual of return, then, provides more than just an opportunity for nostalgic remembrance and reconstruction. It becomes an act of reaffirming violated rights and denied aspirations. As one Ma'loulee tells Khleifi: "rights don't disappear as long as someone claims them." What Khleifi clearly captures in *Ma'loul* is the extent to which Palestinians are resilient in their struggle for justice and self-determination. Challenging the official propagandist history recounted in the Arab classroom, the documentary shows that the route to justice has to go through a recognition of the historical truth of the *Nakba*. Any such recounting must emphasize the position and experience of the expropriated and oppressed. For Khleifi, to tell what really happened is to tell it from the position of the dispossessed. Truth and justice are thus inseparably connected. As Norman Geras has argued: "If there is no truth, there is no injustice. Stated less simplistically, if truth is wholly relativized or internalized to particular discourses or language games or social practices, there is no injustice. The victims and protestors of any *putative* injustice are deprived of their last and often best weapon, that of telling what really happened."[16] Zionism, therefore, cannot be understood if it excludes "the standpoint of its victims" – as Edward Said succinctly put it.[17] It is only on such a foundation that any notion of justice can rest.

The link between truth and justice is made strikingly clear in one of the most moving and powerful sequences in *Ma'loul*: an interview with one of the elderly villagers, Abu-Zaid. The camera follows him as he slowly tries to make sense of his surroundings and re-chart the borders and topography of his demolished home. This proves to be somewhat difficult since the Jewish National Fund has covered over the remains of Ma'loul with a pine forest (called Balfour Forest, ironically.)[18] Among the pine trees, Abu-Zaid recognizes his own trees: almond, blackberry, fig, olive, and cactus fruit. Memories come flooding back, and even more objects are identified. Remembering, however, also unleashes his deep sense of fear and insecurity. At some point after the camera departs the scene, he comes rushing back to speak to the director's team; he is visibly panicked. He's extremely worried, he tells the director, about what he's been recounting to them. The following exchange ensues. "This interview . . . must be illegal. What could you do for me . . . if they were to arrest me?" "They won't," a voice tries to reassure him. "They will! And they"ll squash my tongue as well!" "But what are you scared of?" the voice again asks. He replies: "Nothing! But to be thrown into prison at 65 and be humiliated is out of the question! [. . .] I'll never sell! The land belongs to Ma'loul." Khleifi later intervenes and asks: "So why did they [Jews] come?" Abu-Zaid, enraged, replies: "I didn't bring them! Ask the ones in America . . . In England, in Italy, in Belgium, in France, in Holland, in Poland, in Germany and Greece [. . .] I'm just an insect to be squashed!" Khleifi adds: "But they killed 6 million Jews." His reply conveys his rage against history: "I didn't kill them. Let them ask their tormentors to pay! I never hurt a fly." "So where's the solution," Khleifi broaches. The old man immediately replies: "In God's hands. If he wanted it that way! The solution is Justice. Let every man respect his neighbor's rights . . . Acknowledge mine, and I'll acknowledge yours."

This is the last statement made in the film. Dispossessed, oppressed, and negated, Abu-Zaid speaks in terms neither of hatred nor denial. Having been expelled, his property confiscated, livelihood taken away, and society destroyed, he remains a strong believer in equality and agreement. Significantly, he is also able to offer a clear alternative to present colonization: a just future based on mutuality and reciprocity. The victim is thus not only the subject of truth, but of justice as well. And herein lies the strength of *Ma'loul*. The journey to the past leads to the envisioning of a just and equitable future for both Palestinians and Israelis. Palestine has an alternative to colonization and dehumanization, *Ma'loul* concludes. And the route there, as the last shot of the road leading out of the forest shows, lies in real returns. It is a road not yet taken, however, as the shot of the "no turning" sign implies.

Ma'loul ends with a resounding reaffirmation of justice, especially powerful after the crushing defeat of Beirut. For Khleifi, legitimate rights can never be erased. If after Sabra and Shatila[19] Jean Genet pays homage to the Palestinians by remembering when "they have been dangerous for a thousandth of a second" in Jordan in 1970 (when a revolutionary overthrow of the monarchy was possible), then, after Beirut, Khleifi goes even further back to the original site of the tragedy, re-charts its scope and contours, and reaffirms the justice of Palestinian self-determination. Only a re-examination of the past can provide the necessary materials for a renewal of resistance and struggle in the present. Such a strategy was also adopted by Edward Said in his *After the Last Sky*, yet another post-Beirut text ruminating on a Palestinian existence torn between displacement and the wish for national renewal. As Said clearly states after underlying the objective difficulties of "an apparently unchanging abyss separating us from the national fulfillment we have not been able to attain": "I have never met a Palestinian who is tired enough of being Palestinian to give up entirely."[20] Between mourning and a sense of nagging irresolution, anticipation is thus renewed. Its note is even more strongly sounded in the last scene of Khleifi's subsequent post-Beirut film, *Wedding in Galilee* (1987): a child runs across the fields after curfew in order to sit on his favorite olive tree and look up at the star-filled sky in glee and wonder. The anticipatory power of this gesture is immense. Its value lies in its rootedness in the present: only from the ground of the colonial present can the future be made. Six months later the Intifada broke out: anticipation is realized. Crushed in Lebanon, the Palestinians rise up in the Occupied Territories. After Sabra and Shatila comes Jabalia refugee camp in Gaza. Defeat is yet again transformed into uncompromising defiance.

The Intifada broke out on December 9 1987, and lasted unevenly until the signing of the Washington Peace Accords in September 1993. A whole society mobilized and organized itself in revolt against the Israeli occupation resulting in what Edward Said has described as "one of the most extraordinary anti-colonial and unarmed mass insurrections in the whole history of the modern period."[21] The Intifada was spontaneous and on a vast scale, quickly organized by the left into People's Committees guaranteeing popular participation and control. It took the PLO and the whole world by surprise. Not since the rebellion of 1936–39 against the British Mandate and its policy of establishing a Jewish home in Palestine had occupied Palestinian society forged itself into such a unified fighting tool for national liberation. Forms of resistance were predominantly non-violent and included strikes, boycotts, civil disobedience, mass demonstrations, refusal to pay taxes, and stone-throwing. As a result, Israel lost control of the Occupied Territories. And its response was brutal: "might, force, and beatings," as Defense Minister Rabin stated, and "breaking their bones." Israel's colonial project was disrupted and needed re-establishing.[22] As Norman Finkelstein put it: "Israel aimed not merely to dominate and exploit Palestinians but to humiliate and denationalize them."[23]

The significance of the Intifada in the Palestinian national struggle is thus immense. For the first time in the history of the occupation, Palestinians felt that they were able to begin the process of decolonization. George Habash's sentiment was common: 'With the Intifada, I felt for the first time that it was possible to achieve freedom and independence in some part of Palestine.'[24] The apex of the Intifada was reached in its first year. In the process of national liberation, Palestinian society slowly began to reshape itself internally. Popular participation brought democratic organization and a massive women's mobilization in the political struggle. For many women the struggle for self-determination also meant an end to gender inequality. The momentum of internal change, however, was not to last. For women's organizations, decision-making power on the national level did not significantly improve, nor did the division of labour in society as a whole change. As Islah Jad argues: 'Overall, it may be concluded that a variety of popular committees played an important role in the Intifada during the year of 1988. But they were not new instruments through which the status of women was transformed.'[25] This point is also made by Eileen Kuttab: 'Although these activities [neighborhood cooperatives and group household production] revolutionized the household economy and transformed it into a political tool for steadfastness, the traditional role of women and the traditional division of labour remained untouched.'[26] With intensified Israeli repression, a lack of a clear social agenda on the part of the popular leadership, the emergence of Islamic fundamentalism, and the PLO's increasing control over the Intifada and its exploitation in the international arena for diplomatic gain, democracy and mass participation were stifled. The potential of national revolt turning into social liberation was thus severely curtailed. With that, the national initiative again returned to the PLO leadership, which reasserted its political dominance and its socially conservative agenda: the US's demands to recognize Israel and renounce 'terrorism' were seen by the PLO as more promising than the popular demands of struggle and resistance.[27] Democracy in the territories suffered, as did the nascent social radicalization of society, giving conservative forces the opportunity to regain the political and social momentum.[28] It is at this moment in history, as the tide was turning away from popular self-organization and control towards a disempowering diplomatic process, that Michel Khleifi goes to Palestine to film *Canticle of the Stones*.

Canticle is probably Khleifi's least understood and most experimental film to date. Its formal qualities are both uniquely Khleifi (mixing documentary and fiction, as in *Fertile Memory*) and part of a wider problematic of form in Palestinian cultural production. Since the *Nakba* of 1948, Palestinian culture has been faced with the difficult task of expressing the essence of a shattered, displaced, and scattered nation while showing how a disparate set of experiences and practices actually cohere. As a result, Said argues, Palestinian writing contains a certain 'formal instability' and a foregrounding of the specificities of form: 'But it is *form* that should be looked at. Particularly in fiction, the struggle to achieve form expresses the writer's efforts to construct a coherent scene, a narrative that might overcome the almost metaphysical impossibility of representing the present.'[29] This problematic was particularly poignant for Khleifi in *Canticle*: how to convey the immensity of collective suffering and dehumanization while overcoming the abstraction of media image?[30] His solution mirrors the innovative nature of the Intifada. Among the harrowing images of Israeli brutality and terror, Khleifi introduces a fictional love story in between. As he says in his 'Footnote' to the film: 'By juxtaposing elements of the real with a fictional love story at the heart of the painful and tormenting violence of Intifada, this became a filmic act aimed against the perception of the other as something abstract. It is against this perception that we wished to testify.'[31] Khleifi's dramatic re-conceptualization of his film, on direct encounter with the actuality of events of the Intifada, clearly conveys his commitment to articulate not only the daily reality of repression and domination but also the longer history of injury and injustice in Palestinian society. With the present conjuncture of the Intifada, then, the historical accumulation of denial and negation is conveyed.

Canticle begins with shots of the horizon followed by a scene of two lovers embracing. The centrality of the fictional element is immediately emphasized. It is, after all, the 'canticle of the stones' that Khleifi seeks to convey. As the lovers' story unfolds, shots from the Intifada are brought in. Amongst the occupation, a story of love, loss, and exile is told: the fast and intense pace of the Intifada scenes is contrasted with the tempo of a slowly evolving love story. Hospital scenes of death and injury are, for example, followed by shots of the two lovers reminiscing and reconnecting. In classical Eisensteinian mode, montage is conceived of as 'collision' and 'conflict.'[32] The result is a forced distancing: the viewer is constantly pushed back from the real to the fictional. This is also achieved on the level of linguistic register: the intellectualized love encounter is spoken in classical Arabic while the Intifada footage is in colloquial. Sounds are also contrasted: the pleasant musical piece in the love part is markedly different from the loud, screeching, and monotonous sounds of the Intifada scenes. The absence of connection and lack of fit is constantly being staged here. And that seems to be the point. *Canticle* becomes about the necessity of reconnecting both parts: fiction and reality, love and death, intellectuals and masses, and woman and society. To overcome the abstraction of image, the complexity of Palestinian life has to be conveyed—which is why, as I argue below, an 'internal front' within Palestinian society is opened and a history of personal injury and denial is recounted.[33]

The female lover has returned from exile in order to study 'sacrifice.' Her lover, who has just been released from prison, tells her from the outset: 'You shall see nothing else except our lost love.' Her struggle to see more is what the story is about: 'I want to clarify this secret obstinacy which pushes us to sacrifice in order to reach our ends.' 'Resistance is based on sacrifice,' she tells him. She should then, he insists, go to Gaza: 'Go, see the violence there. See what the children of the victims of Nazism are doing in Gaza, the gate of hell, the bride of the Arabs.' As she journeys across the West Bank and Gaza, the Intifada slowly unfolds: hospitals, cemeteries, and printing presses; demolished houses, curfews, and Israeli provocations; children shot and childhoods distorted and degraded. As one teenager, shot in the intestines, tells Khleifi: 'For the Israeli army, we are only animals: they beat and humiliate us and punish us on a daily basis. We have had enough of all that. Every person has the right to live with dignity on his land.' His companion adds:

> We are not asking for the impossible: like all the peoples of this world, we want to live without oppression or violence, without our people killed, without hearing the sounds of bullets everyday. But with the occupation you are forced to extract your freedom and independence because they will offer you nothing. The Intifada is the revolt of all those young people born under the occupation.

The colossal destruction of occupation is clearly visible: a father whose son is shot in front of his eyes screams: 'My life was destroyed by this state;' another father recounts in anguish how his son was assassinated in his presence; an Idna woman sits on the ground and wails as her house is being demolished by Israeli troops. Destruction is all around, as is the sheer determination to overcome the occupation. As one woman tells Khleifi: 'They think that by destroying our house, or by killing us we'll stop throwing stones. On the contrary!'

By reconnecting with the Intifada, the female lover's past gradually unfolds. She redeems her 'lost faith' and is able to tell her own personal story of injury and loss. The Intifada thus becomes not only the condition of her return to Palestine from the US but also a pre-requisite of her own expression as well. She recounts to her lover a story of past banishment and oppression. Despite trying to free herself from the confines of conservative social custom and tradition, her family punishes her severely for getting pregnant outside of matrimony: 'We learnt rebellion against the village, against power, occupation . . . at school nothing but demonstrations and strikes. We left our fears lying in the shadows of the poppies.' Her rebellion against society is thus stifled and contained, and her radicalism is crushed. Her lover first listens, and then begins complementing her narrative with his own words and imagined encounters, creating a deep sense of sympathy and identification. The significance of this episode for *Canticle*'s construction is crucial. Its force in the narrative is immense. During one of the most intense moments of national struggle in Palestinian history, Khleifi brings in the 'women's question.' The whole problem of gender inequality is raised. This is also reinforced in his interview with an old refugee woman from 1948, who tells him: 'I had to endure everything. I was the only one to sacrifice myself for them [her family].' Sacrifice thus gains an added dimension. And Khleifi's objective is immediately apparent: he opens up an 'internal front' of radical critique in order to remind Palestinian society of the meaning of liberation. For Khleifi, as for other radicals of the Intifada (on retreat after its first year), the requirements of social liberation should never be sacrificed to the demands of national struggle. Liberation is thus construed as a two-tiered process: as Palestinian society overcomes national subjugation it frees itself from internal forms of social oppression as well. Social emancipation is simultaneous with national liberation. Khleifi's conception of individual liberation, therefore, does not counter-pose the individual against society. For him, they are mutually constitutive. His radicalism entails conceiving of individual liberation as an outcome of collective struggle. It is, therefore, only when the individual becomes a self-determining agent that true liberation is achieved. The possibilities of this happening in Palestine are clearly signified at the end. After the journey of exploration, the lovers reconnect: the film ends with their embrace. The juxtaposition of love and occupation thus produces a regenerative space of possibility at the end. On the grounds of the present, the lovers can begin again to struggle for the future, and, in the process, reshape their own lives on the basis of justice and equality. *Canticle* is Khleifi's plea that Palestine deserves nothing less. The film stands as testimony to the Intifada's early spirit of social radicalism, which was in the process of being marginalized (by a combination of external and internal forces), leaving Palestinian society demobilized and susceptible to the vagaries of US–Israeli force and diktat. Oslo could well be predicted from this point onwards. The extent of the surrender, however, would come to horrify many, as Said's 'The Morning After' clearly shows: the PLO would become Israel's colonial enforcer in the Occupied Territories.[34]

As *Ma'loul* and *Canticle* show, the colonial present has always lead Khleifi back to the past and then propelled him forwards again to the future. For him, recognizing denied national rights has to involve an emancipatory project of restitution and rectification. It is only by understanding the *Nakba*, Khleifi insists, that we are able to move forwards to determine our future. Shunning both conformism and the banalization of reality characteristic of many recent Palestinian films, Khleifi advances a relentless critique of Israeli colonialism and its usurpation and alienation of Palestine. He also continues to affirm people's self-capacity to transform their own environment and to overcome exile, occupation, dispossession, and national and social inequalities. In times of capitulation and surrender, epitomized by Oslo, Khleifi's *oeuvre* therefore stands as an important reminder that a better future in Palestine-Israel is not only desirable but *possible* as well. And *that* is his single most important contribution to his people's struggle for justice and liberation.

FIVE

THE CINEMA OF DISPLACEMENT: GENDER, NATION, AND DIASPORA

Ella Shohat

At a time when the *grands récits* of the West have been told and retold *ad infinitum*, when a certain postmodernism (Jean-François Lyotard) speaks of an "end" to metanarratives, and when Francis Fukayama speaks of an "end of history," we must ask: Precisely whose narrative and whose history is being declared at an "end?"[1] Hegemonic Europe may clearly have begun to deplete its strategic repertoire of stories, but Third World peoples, First World diasporic communities, women, and gays/lesbians have only begun to tell, and deconstruct, theirs. For the "Third World," this cinematic counter-telling basically began with the post-war collapse of the European empires and the emergence of independent nation-states. In the face of Eurocentric historicizing, the Third World and its diasporas in the First World have rewritten their own histories, taken control of their own images, and spoken in their own voices, reclaiming and re-accentuating colonialism and its ramifications in the present, in a vast project of re-mapping and re-naming. Third-World feminists, for their part, have participated in these counter-narratives by insisting that colonialism and nationalism have impinged differently on men and women. All the re-mapping and re-naming, then, have not been without their fissures and contradictions.

Although relatively small in number, women in what has been termed the "Third World" already played a role as film producers and directors in the first half of this century: Aziza Amir, Assia Daghir, Fatima Rushdi, Bahiga Hafeth, and Amina Rezq in Egypt; Carmen Santos and Gilda de Abreu in Brazil, Emilia Santey in Argentina;

and Adela Sequeyro, Matilda Landeta, Candida Beltran Rondon, and Eva Liminano in Mexico. However, their films, even when focusing on female protagonists, were not explicitly feminist in the sense of a declared political project to empower women in the context of both patriarchy and (neo)colonialism. In the post-independence, or post-revolution, era, women, despite their growing contribution to the diverse aspects of film production, remained less visible than men in the role of film direction. Furthermore, Third-Worldist revolutionary cinemas, in places such as China, Cuba, Senegal, and Algeria, were not generally shaped by anti-colonial feminist imaginary. As is the case with First World cinema, women's participation in Third World cinema has hardly been central, although their growing production over the last decade corresponds to a burgeoning worldwide movement of independent work by women, made possible by new low-cost technologies of video communication. But quite apart from this relative democratization through technology, post-independence history, with the gradual eclipse of Third-Worldist nationalism, and growth of women's grassroots local organizing also helps us understand the emergence of what I call "post-Third-Worldist" feminist film and video.[2]

Here I am interested in examining recent women's positioning[3] within (neo) colonialist and racist systems. Feminist struggles in the Third World (including that of the First World) have not been premised on a facile discourse of global sisterhood, and have often been made within the context of anti-colonial and anti-racist struggles. But the growing feminist critique of Third World nationalisms translates those many disappointed hopes for women's empowerment invested in a Third-Worldist national transformation. Navigating between patriarchal nationalist ex-communicating denunciations as "traitors to the nation" or "betraying the race," and Western feminism's imperial rescue fantasy of veiled and clitoridectomized women, post-Third-Worldist feminists have not suddenly metamorphosed into "Western" feminists. Feminists of color have from the outset engaged in analysis and activism around the intersection of nation/race/gender. Therefore, while still resisting the ongoing (neo)colonized situation of their "nation" and/or "race," post-Third-Worldist feminist cultural practices also break away from the narrative of the "nation" as a unified entity so as to articulate a contextualized history for women in specific geographies of identity. Such feminist projects, in other words, are often posited in relation to ethnic, racial, regional, and national locations.

Rather than merely "extending" a pre-existing First World feminism, as a certain Euro-"diffusionism"[4] would have it, post-Third-Worldist cultural theories and practices create a more complex space for feminisms that do not abandon the specificity of community, culture, and history. To counter some of the patronizing attitudes towards (post)-Third World feminist filmmakers – the dark women who also do the "feminist thing" – it seems necessary to contextualize feminist work in national-racial discourses inscribed within multiple oppressions and resistances. Third World feminist histories can be understood as feminist if unearthed from the substantial resistance work these women have done within their communities and nations. Any serious discussion of feminist cinema must, therefore, engage the complex question of the "national." Third-Worldist films, produced within the legal codes of the nation-state, often in (hegemonic) national languages, recycling national intertexts (literatures, oral narratives, music), projected national imaginaries. But if First World filmmakers have seemed to float "above" petty nationalist concerns, it is because they take for granted the projection of a national power that facilitates the making and the dissemination of their films. The geopolitical positioning of Third World nation-states, even in the postcolonial era, implies that Third World film-makers cannot assume a substratum of national power.

This point about relative powerlessness is well illustrated in Youssef Chahine's film *Iskandariya Leh?* (*Alexandria Why?*, 1979). A semi-autobiographical film about an aspiring filmmaker haunted by Hollywood dreams, it offers an Egyptian perspective on the colonizing film culture of the US. Chahine's protagonist begins as a Victoria College student who adores Shakespeare's plays and Hollywood movies. The film is set in the 1940s, a critical period for the protagonist and for Egypt: Allied troops were stationed in the country then, and Axis forces threatened to invade Alexandria. Although *Alexandria Why?* focuses on the would-be filmmaker, its sub-plots offer a multi-perspectival study of Egyptian society, describing how different classes, ethnicities and religions – working-class communists, aristocratic Muslim homo-sexuals, middle-class Egyptian Jews, petit-bourgeois Catholics – react to Egyptian-Arab nationalism. The sub-plots stress the diversity of Egyptian experience, yet the unanimity of the reaction to European colonialism.[5] One story, for example, reaffirms the "Arabness" of Egypt's Arab-Jews, through a romance sub-plot involving a communist of Muslim working-class background and a Jewish-Egyptian woman, daughter of a middle-class anti-Zionist communist and sister of a Zionist.

Thus Chahine undoes the equation of Jews with Zionism, and with Europeanness.

Alexandria Why? weaves diverse materials – newsreels, clips from Hollywood films, staged reconstructions, Chahine's own youthful amateur films – into an ironic collage. The opening credit sequence mingles black-and-white 1940s travelogue footage of Alexandria beaches with newsreel footage of Europe at war, implementing a "peripheral" Egyptian perspective on Europe. In the following sequence, we watch a series of newsreels and Hollywood musicals along with the spectators in Alexandria. The musicals are subtitled in Arabic (Egypt was a translation center for the Middle East), while the newsreels have an Arabic voice-over suggesting a "return to sender" message from the "periphery." An anthology of musical clips featuring stars such as Helen Powell, and songs such as "I'll Build a Stairway to Paradise" are inserted into a reception context redolent of First World/Third World economic and military relations as well as of the worldwide hegemonization of the American Dream. The "Three Cheers for the Red, White and Blue" number, for example, at once charming and intimidating in its climactic image of cannons firing at the camera (here the Egyptian spectator), celebrates American power and renders explicit the nationalist subtext of First-World "entertainment."

The movie-going scenes suggest a kind of obsession, a repetitive ritual of film-going. Meanwhile, the Egyptian musical scenes clearly mock the protagonist's Americanizing fantasies. These numbers affect a kitschy, "underdeveloped" mimicry of Hollywood production values. As Egyptian performers emulate the formula of the Hollywood-Latino musical, they also point to Hollywood's role in disseminating imagery of the Third World. One Egyptian actor, sporting poncho and sombrero, plays a mariachi-style guitar, much as an earlier sequence featured the Argentinian song "Perfidia." It is Hollywood and its distribution network, we are reminded, that popularized Latin American performers such as Carmen Miranda, and dances such as the tango, rhumba, and the cha-cha, among the middle classes of the Middle East and the Third World generally. The final sequences mock the power that replaced European colonial powers in Egypt after World War II: The US, deriding the chimera of Americanization that enthralls the protagonist, and allegorically middle-class Egyptians generally. On arriving in the musical's national homeland, the protagonist is greeted by the Statue of Liberty transformed into a laughing, toothless prostitute. By 1979, when *Alexandria Why?* was made, the view of the US as a liberating force had given way to bitter disillusionment. The Statue of Liberty is shown via 1940s studio-style back-projection, but whereas Hollywood often exploited scenic matte shots to show exotic locales, the Egyptian film deploys the same technique to mock the industrialized fantasies of American mass culture. The tacky papier-mâché quality of Chahine's Statue of Liberty metaphorizes the factitious nature of Third World idealizations of North American freedom, particularly in the context of postwar Middle East, where the US has come to represent both an alluring model and a new imperialism supplanting European colonialisms.[6]

Here I am interested in examining the contemporary work of post-Third-Worldist feminist film/videomakers in light of the ongoing critique of unequal geopolitical and racial distribution of resources and power, as a way of examining the post-colonial dynamics of rupture and continuity in relation to the antecedent Third-Worldist film culture. These texts, I argue, challenge the masculinist contours of the "nation" in order to promote a feminist decolonization of national historiography. My attempt at a "beginning" of a post-Third-Worldist narrative for recent film and video work by diverse Third World diasporic feminists is not intended as an exhaustive survey of the entire spectrum of generic practices. Highlighting works embedded in the intersection of gender and sexuality with nation and race, this essay attempts to situate such cultural practices. It looks at a moment of historical rupture and continuity when the macro-narrative of women's liberation has long since subsided, yet where sexism and heterosexism prevail, and in an age when the metanarratives of anti-colonial revolution have long since been eclipsed, yet where issues of (neo) colonialism and racism persist. What then are some of the new modes of a feminist aesthetics of resistance, and in what ways do they simultaneously continue and rupture previous Third World film culture?

Third-Worldist films by women filmmakers within and outside the Middle East/ North Africa assumed that revolution was crucial for the empowering of women; that the revolution was integral to feminist aspirations. Sarah Maldoror's short film *Monangambe* (Mozambique, 1970) told the story of an Angolan woman's visit to her imprisoned husband, taken away by the Portuguese, while her feature film *Sambizanga* (Mozambique, 1972), based on the struggle of the M.P.L.A. in Angola, depicted a woman coming to revolutionary consciousness. Heiny Srour's documentary *Saat al Tahrir* (*The Hour of Liberation*, Oman, 1973) privileges the role of women fighters as it looks at the revolutionary struggle in Oman, and *Leile wal Dhiab* (*Leila and the Wolves*, Lebanon, 1984) focused on the role of women in the Palestine Liberation Movement. Helena Solberg Ladd's *Nicaragua Up From the Ashes* (US, 1982) focalizes the role of women in the Sandinista revolution. Sara Gomez's well-known film *De Cierta Manera* (*One Way or Another*, Cuba, 1975), often cited as part of the late 1970s and early 1980s Third-Worldist debates around women's position in revolutionary movements, interweaves documentary and fiction as part of a feminist critique of the Cuban revolution.

In their search for an alternative to the dominating style of Hollywood, Third-Worldist films share a certain preoccupation with First World feminist independent films, which have sought alternative images of women. The project of digging into "herstories" involved a search for new cinematic and narrative forms that challenged both the canonical documentaries and the mainstream fiction films, subverting the notion of "narrative pleasure" based on the "male gaze."

As with Third-Worldist cinema and with First World independent production, post-Third-Worldist feminist films/videos conduct a struggle on two fronts, at once aesthetic and political, synthesizing revisionist historiography with formal innovation.

The early period of Third-Worldist euphoria has since given away to the collapse of communism, the indefinite postponement of the devoutly wished "tricontinental revolution," the realization that the "wretched of the earth" are not unanimously revolutionary (nor necessarily allies to one another), the appearance of an array of Third World despots, and the recognition that international geopolitics and the global economic system have forced even the "Second World" to be incorporated into transnational capitalism. Recent years have also witnessed a terminological crisis swirling around the term "Third World" itself, now seen as an inconvenient relic of a more militant period. Some have argued that Third World theory is an open-ended ideological interpolation that papers over class oppression in all three worlds, while limiting socialism to the now non-existent Second World.[7] Three worlds theory flattens heterogeneities, masks contradictions, and elides differences. Third World feminist critics such as Nawal el-Saadawi (Egypt), Vina Mazumdar (India), Kumari Jayawardena (Sri Lanka), Fatima Mernissi (Morocco), and Leila Gonzales (Brazil) have explored these differences and similarities in a feminist light, pointing to the gendered limitations of Third World nationalism.

Although all cultural practices are, on one level, products of specific national contexts, Third World filmmakers (men and women) have been forced to engage in the question of the national precisely because they lack the taken-for-granted power available to First World nation-states. At the same time, the topos of a unitary nation often camouflages the possible contradictions among different sectors of Third World society. The nation-states of the Americas, Africa, and Asia often "cover" the existence of women as well as of indigenous nations (Fourth World) within them. Moreover, the exaltation of the "national" provides no criteria for distinguishing exactly what is worth retaining in the "national tradition." A sentimental defense of patriarchal social institutions simply because they are "ours" can hardly be seen as emancipatory. Indeed, some Third World films criticize exactly such institutions: films such as *Allah Tanto* (Guinea, 1992) focus on the political repression exercised even by a pan-Africanist hero such as Sekou Toure, Kamal Dehane's *Assia Djebar: Between Shadow and Sun* (Algeria, 1994) and *Guelwaar* (Senegal, 1992) critiques religious divisions, *Al Mara wal Qanun* (*The Woman and the Law*, Egypt, 1987) focuses on the legal discrimination against women, *Xala* (Senegal, 1990) criticize polygamy, *Finzan* (Senegal, 1989) and *Fire Eyes* (Somalia/US, 1993) critique female genital surgeries, *Mercedes* (Egypt, 1993) satirizes class relations and the marginalization of gays, and *The Extras* (Syria, 1994) focuses on the intersection of political and sexual repression within a Third World nation.

All countries, including Third World countries, are heterogeneous, at once urban and rural, male and female, religious and secular, native and immigrant, and so forth. The view of the nation as unitary muffles the "polyphony" of social and ethnic voices within heteroglot cultures. Third World feminists especially have highlighted the ways in which the subject of the Third World nationalist revolution has been covertly posited as masculine and heterosexual. The precise nature of the national "essence" to be recuperated, furthermore, is elusive and chimerical. Some locate it in the precolonial past, or in the country's rural interior (e.g. the Palestinian village) or in a prior state of development (the pre-industrial), or in a religion and ethnicity (e.g. the Copts in Egypt or the Berbers in Algeria), and each narrative of origins has its gender implications. Recent debates have emphasized the ways in which national identity is mediated, textualized, constructed, "imagined," just as the traditions valorized by nationalism are "invented."[8] Any definition of nationality, then, must see it as partly discursive in nature, must take class, gender, and sexuality into account, must allow for racial difference and cultural heterogeneity, and must be dynamic, seeing "the nation" as an evolving, imaginary construct rather than an originary essence.

The decline of Third-Worldist euphoria, which marked even feminist films such as *One Way or Another*, *The Hour of Liberation*, *Lila and the Wolves*, and *Nicaragua Up From the Ashes*, brought with it a rethinking of political, cultural, and aesthetic possibilities, as the rhetoric of revolution began to be greeted with a certain skepticism. Meanwhile, the socialist-inflected national liberation struggles of the 1960s and 1970s were harassed economically and militarily, violently discouraged from becoming revolutionary models for post-independence societies. A combination of IMF pressure, co-optation as well as "low-intensity warfare," as suggested earlier, have obliged even socialist regimes to make a sort of peace with transnational capitalism. Some regimes grew repressive toward those who wanted to go beyond a purely nationalist bourgeois revolution to restructure class, gender, region, and ethnic relations. As a result of external pressures and internal self-questioning, the cinema, too, gave expression to those mutations, as the anti-colonial thrust of earlier films gradually gave way to more diversified themes and perspectives. This is not to say that artists and intellectuals became less politicized, but that cultural and political critiques have taken new and different forms. Contemporary cultural practices of post-Third World feminists intervene at a precise juncture in the history of the Third World.

A FEMINIST CRITIQUE OF NATIONALISM

Largely produced by men, Third-Worldist films were not generally concerned with a feminist critique of nationalist discourse. It would be a mistake to idealize the sexual politics of anti-colonial Third-Worldist films such as *Jamila al-Jazairiya* (*Jamila, the Algerian*, Egypt, 1958) and the classic *La Battaglia de Algeria* (*The Battle of Algiers*, 1966), for example. On one level it is true that Algerian women are granted revolutionary agency. In one sequence, three Algerian women fighters are able to pass as Frenchwomen and, consequently, to pass the French checkpoints with bombs in their baskets. The French soldiers treat the Algerians with discriminatory scorn and suspicion but greet the Europeans with amiable "*bonjours.*" And the soldiers' sexism leads them to misperceive the three women as French and flirtatious when, in fact, they are Algerian and revolutionary. *The Battle of Algiers* thus underlines the racial and sexual taboos of desire within colonial segregation. As Algerians, the women are the objects of a military as well as a sexual gaze; they are publicly desirable for the soldiers, however, only when they masquerade as French. They use their knowledge of European codes to trick the Europeans, putting their own "looks" and the soldiers "looking" (and failure to see) to revolutionary purpose. (Masquerade also serves the Algerian male fighters who veil as Algerian women to better hide weapons.) Within the psychodynamics of oppression, the colonized woman knows the mind of the oppressor, while the converse is not true. In *The Battle of Algiers*, they deploy this cognitive asymmetry to their own advantage, consciously manipulating ethnic, national, and gender stereotypes in the service of their struggle.

On another level, however, the women in the film largely carry out the orders of the male revolutionaries. They certainly appear heroic, but only insofar as they perform their sacrificial service for the "nation." The film does not ultimately address the two-fronted nature of their struggle within a nationalist but still patriarchal revolution.[9] In privileging the nationalist struggle, *The Battle of Algiers* elides the gender, class, and religious tensions that fissured the revolutionary process, failing to realize that, as Anne McClintock puts it, "nationalisms are from the outset constituted in gender power" and that "women who are not empowered to organize during the struggle will not be empowered to organize after the struggle."[10] The final shots of a dancing Algerian woman, waving the Algerian flag and taunting the French troops, is superimposed on the title "July 2, 1962: The Algerian Nation is born." Here a symbolic woman carries, as it were, the allegory of the birth of the Algerian nation. But the film does not bring up the contradictions that plagued the revolution before and after victory. The nationalist representation of courage and unity relies on the image of the revolutionary woman, precisely because her figure might otherwise evoke a weak link, the fact of a fissured revolution in which unity *vis-à-vis* the colonizer does not preclude contradictions among the colonized.

The Third-Worldist films often factored generic (and gendered) space of heroic confrontations, whether set in the streets, the Kasbah, the mountains, or the jungle. The minimal presence of women corresponds to the place assigned to women both in the anti-colonialist revolutions and within Third-Worldist discourse, leaving women's home-bounded struggles unacknowledged. Women occasionally carried the bombs, as in *The Battle of Algiers*, but only in the name of a "Nation." Gender contradictions have been subordinated to anti-colonial struggle: women were expected to "wait their turn." More often women were made to carry the "burden" of national allegory (the image of the woman dancing with the flag in *The Battle of*

Algiers is an emblem of national liberation, while the image of the bride who deflowers herself in *Urs fil Galil* (*Wedding in Galilee*, Palestine/Belgium, 1988) allegorizes the failure of an impotent patriarchy to lead toward national liberation.[11]

A recent Tunisian film, *Samt al Qusur* (*The Silence of the Palace*, 1994) by Moufida Tlati, a film editor who had worked on major Tunisian films of the post-independence "Cinema Jedid" (New Cinema) generation, exemplifies some of the feminist critiques of the representation of the "Nation" in the early anti-colonial revolutionary films. Rather than privilege direct, violent encounters with the French, necessarily set in male-dominated spaces of battle, the film presents the 1950s' Tunisian women, at the height of the national struggle, as restricted to the domestic sphere. Yet it also challenges the middle-class assumptions about the domestic sphere as belonging to the isolated wife-mother of a (heterosexual) couple. *The Silence of the Palace* focuses on working-class women, the servants of the rich pro-French Bey elite, subjugated to hopeless servitude, including at times sexual servitude, but for whom life outside the palace, without the guarantee of shelter and food, would mean the even worse misery of, for example, prostitution. Although suffering under a regime of silence in terms of what they know about the palace, the film highlights their survival as a community. As an alternative family, their emotional closeness in crisis and happiness, and their supportive involvement in decision-making, shows their ways of coping with a no-exit situation. They become a non-patriarchal family within a patriarchal context. Whether through singing, as they cook once again for an exhibitionist banquet, or through praying, as one of them heals one of their children who has fallen sick, or through dancing and eating in a joyous moment, the film represents women who did not plant bombs but whose social positioning turns into a critique of failed revolutionary hopes as seen in the postcolonial era. The information about the battles against the French are mediated through the radio and by vendors, who report on what might lead to a full, all-encompassing national transformation.

Yet this period of anti-colonial struggle is framed as a recollective narrative of a woman singer, a daughter of one of the female servants, illuminating the continuous pressures exerted on women of her class. (With some exceptions, female singers/dancers have been associated in the Middle East with being just a little above the shameful occupation of prostitution.) The gendered and classed oppression she witnessed as an adolescent in colonized Tunisia led her to believe that things would be different in an independent Tunisia. Such hopes were encouraged by the promises made by the middle-class male intellectual, a tutor for the Bey's family, who suggested that in the new Tunisia not knowing her father's name would not be a barrier to establishing a new life. Their passionate relationship in the heat of revolution, where the "new" is on the verge of being born, is undercut by the framing narrative. Her fatherless servant-history and her low status as a singer haunts her life in the post-independence era; the tutor lives with her but does not marry her, yet gives her the protection she needs as a singer. The film opens with her singing with a sad, melancholy face a famous Um Kulthum song from the 1960s, "Amal Hayati" ("The Hope of My Life".) Um Kulthum, an Egyptian, has been the leading Arab singer of the twentieth century, who through her unusual musical talents – including her deep knowledge of *fusha* (literary) Arabic – arose from her small village to become *kawkab al-sharq* (the star of the East). Her singing accompanied the Arab world in its national aspirations, and catalyzed a sense of unity throughout the Arab world, managing to transcend, at least on the cultural level, social tensions and political conflicts. She had been especially associated with the charismatic leadership of Gamal Abd al-Nasser and his anti-imperial pan-Arab agenda, but the admiration, respect, and love she exerted has continued after her death (in 1975) to the present day. Her virtual transcendental position, however, has not been shared by many female singers and stars since.

The protagonist of *The Silence of the Palace* begins her public performance at the invitation of the masters of the palace, an invitation partly due to her singing talent, but also symptomatic of the sexual harassment she begins to experience as soon as one of the masters notices that the child has turned into a young woman. The mother who manages to protect her daughter from sexual harassment is raped herself by one of the masters. On the day of the daughter's first major performance at a party in the palace, the mother dies of excessive bleeding from medical complications caused from aborting the product of rape. In parallel scenes of the mother's shouting from her excruciating pain and the daughter's courageous crying of the forbidden Tunisian anthem, the film ends with the mother's death and with her daughter leaving the palace for the promising outside world of young Tunisia. In post-independence Tunisia, the film implies, her situation has somewhat improved. She is no longer a servant but a singer who earns her living yet needs the protection of her boyfriend against gender-based humiliations. Next to her mother's grave, the daughter, in a voice-over, shows her awareness of some improvements in the conditions of their life in comparison with her mother. The daughter has gone through many abortions, despite her wish to become a mother, in order to keep her relationship with her boyfriend – the revolutionary man who does not transcend class for purposes of marriage. At the end of the film, she confesses at her mother's grave that this time she cannot let this piece of herself go. If in the opening, the words of Um Kulthum's song relay a desire for a state of dream not to end – "*Khalini, gambak, khalini/fi hudhni albak, khalini/ oosibni ahlam bik/ Yaret Zamani ma yesahinish.*" ("Leave me by your side / in your heart / and let me dream / wish time will not wake me up") – the film ends with an awakening to hopes unfulfilled with the birth of the nation. Birth here is no longer allegorical as in *The Battle of Algiers*, but rather concrete, entangled in taboos and obstacles, leaving an open-ended narrative, far from the euphoric closure of the Nation.

In contrast to the Orientalist harem imaginary, all-female spaces have been represented very differently in feminist independent cinema, largely, but not exclusively, directed by Middle Eastern women. Documentaries such as Attiat El-Abnoudi's *Ahlam Mumkina* (*Permissible Dreams*, Egypt, 1989) and Claire Hunt and Kim Longinotto's *Hidden Faces* (Britain, 1990) examine female agency within a patriarchal context. Both films feature sequences in which Egyptian women speak together about their lives in the village, recounting in ironic terms their dreams and struggles with patriarchy. Through its critical look at the Egyptian feminist Nawal el-Saadawi, *Hidden Faces* explores the problems of women working together to create alternative institutions. Elizabeth Fernea's *The Veiled Revolution* (1982) shows Egyptian women redefining not only the meaning of the veil but also the nature of their own sexuality. And Moroccan filmmaker Farida Benlyazid's feature film *Bab Ila Sma Maftouh* (*A Door to the Sky*, 1988) offers a positive gloss on the notion of an all-female space, counterposing Islamic feminism to Orientalist fantasies.

A Door to the Sky tells the story of a Moroccan woman, Nadia, who returns from Paris to her family home in Fez. That she arrives in Morocco dressed in punk clothing and with a punk hairstyle make us expect an ironic tale about a Westernized Arab feeling out of place in her homeland. But instead, Nadia rediscovers Morocco and Islam, and comes to appreciate the communitarian world of her female relatives, as well as her closeness with her father. She is instructed in the faith by an older woman, Kirana, who has a flexible approach to Islam: "Everyone understands through his own mind and his own era." As Nadia awakens spiritually, she comes to see the oppressive aspects of Western society, and sees Arab/Muslim society as a possible space for fulfillment. Within the Islamic tradition of women using their wealth for social charity, she turns part of the family home into a shelter for battered women. At the same time, the film is not uncritical of the patriarchal abuses of Islam such as, for example, the laws which count women as "half-persons" and which systematically favor the male in terms of marriage and divorce. The film's aesthetic, meanwhile, favors the rhythms of contemplation and spirituality in slow camera movements that caress the contoured Arabic architecture of courtyards and fountains and soothing inner spaces. The film begins with a dedication to a historical Muslim woman, Fatima Fihra, the tenth-century founder of one of the world's first universities, envisioning an aesthetic that affirms Islamic culture, while also inscribing it with a feminist consciousness. In this way, *A Door to the Sky* offers an alternative both to the Western imaginary and to an Islamic fundamentalist representation of Muslim women. Whereas contemporary documentaries show all-female gatherings as a space for resistance to patriarchy and fundamentalism, *A Door to the Sky* uses all-female spaces to point to a liberatory project based on unearthing women's history within Islam, a history that includes female spirituality, prophecy, poetry, and intellectual creativity as well as revolt, material power, and social and political leadership.[12]

A number of recent diasporic film/video works link issues of postcolonial identity to issues of post-Third-Worldist aesthetics and ideology. The Sankofa production *The Passion of Remembrance* (1986) by Maureen Blackwood and Isaac Julien thematizes post-Third-Worldist discourses and fractured diasporic identity, in this case Black British identity, by staging a "polylogue" between the 1960s Black radical, as the (somewhat puritanical) voice of nationalist militancy, and the "new," more playful, voices – gays and lesbian women – all within a de-realized reflexive aesthetic. Film and video works such as Assia Djebar's *Nouba Niza al Djebel Chenoua* (*The Nouba of the Women of Mount Chenoua,* 1977), Lourdes Portillo's *After the Earthquake* (1979), Mona Hatoum's *Measures of Distance* (1988), Pratibha Parmar's *Khush* (1991), Trinh T. Minh-ha's *Surname Viet Given Name Nam* (1989), Prajna Paramita Parasher and Den Ellis' *Unbidden Voices* (1990), Indu Krishnan's *Knowing Her Place* (1990), Christine Chang's *Be Good My Children* (1992), and Marta N. Bautis" *Home is the Struggle* (1991) break away from earlier macro-narratives of national liberation, reinvisioning the Nation as a heteroglossic multiplicity of trajectories. While remaining anti-colonialist, these experimental films/videos call attention to the diversity of experiences within and across nations. Since colonialism had simultaneously aggregated communities fissured by glaring cultural differences and separated communities marked by equally glaring commonalities, these films suggest that nation-states were in some ways artificial and contradictory entities. The films produced in the First World, in particular, raise questions about dislocated identities in a world increasingly marked by the mobility of goods, ideas, and peoples attendant on the "multi-nationalization" of the global economy.

Third Worldists often fashioned their idea of the nation-state according to the European model, in this sense remaining complicit with a Eurocentric enlightenment narrative. And the nation-states they built often failed to deliver on their promises. In terms of race, class, gender, and sexuality in particular, many of them remained, on the whole, ethnocentric, patriarchal, bourgeois, and homophobic. At the same time, a view of Third World nationalism as the mere echo of European nationalism ignores the international Realpolitik that made the end of colonialism coincide with the beginning of the nation-state. The formation of Third World nation-states often involved a double process, on the one hand of joining diverse ethnicities and regions that had been separated under colonialism, and on the other, of partitioning regions in a way that forced regional redefinition (Iraq/Kuwait) and a cross-shuffling of populations (Pakistan, India, Israel/Palestine). Furthermore, political geographies and state borders do not always coincide with "imaginary geographies" (Edward Said), wherein the existence of internal émigrés, nostalgics, and rebels, i.e. groups of people who share the same passport but whose relations to the nation-state are conflicted and ambivalent. In the postcolonial context of constant flux of peoples, affiliation with the nation-state becomes highly partial and contingent.

While most Third-Worldist films assumed the fundamental coherence of national identity, with the expulsion of the colonial intruder fully completing the process of national becoming, the post-nationalist films call attention to the faultlines of gender, class ethnicity, region, partition, migration, and exile. Many of the films explore the complex identities generated by exile – from one's own geography, from one's own history, from one's own body – within innovative narrative strategies. Fragmented cinematic forms come to homologize cultural disembodiment. Caren Kaplan's observations about a reconceived "minor" literature as de-romanticizing solitude

Lubna Azabal (as Suha) in Hany Abu Assad's *Paradise Now* (2005).
(Courtesy of Augustus Film.)

Mai Masri, *Frontiers of Dreams and Fears* (2001). (Courtesy of Mai Masri.)

and rewriting "the connections between different parts of the self in order to make a world of possibilities out of the experience of displacement"[13] are exquisitely appropriate to two autobiographical films by Palestinians in exile, Elia Suleiman's *Homage by Assassination* (1992) and Mona Hatoum's *Measures of Distance* (1998). *Homage by Assassination* chronicles Suleiman's life in New York during the Persian Gulf War, foregrounding multiple failures of communication: a radio announcer's aborted efforts to reach the filmmaker by phone; the filmmaker's failed attempts to talk to his family in Nazareth (Israel/Palestine); his impotent look at old family photographs; and despairing answering-machine jokes about the Palestinian situation. The glorious dream of nationhood and return is here reframed as a Palestinian flag on a TV monitor, the land as a map on a wall, and the return (*awda*) as the "return" key on the computer keyboard. At one point the filmmaker receives a fax from a friend, who narrates her family history as an Arab Jew, her feelings during the bombing of Iraq and the Scud attacks on Israel, and the story of her displacements from Iraq, through Israel/Palestine, and then on to the US.[14] The communications technologies become the imperfect means by which dislocated people retain a national imaginary, while also fighting for a place in a new geography (the US, Britain), nation-states whose foreign policies have concretely impacted their lives. *Homage by Assassination* invokes the diverse spatialities and temporalities that mark the exilic experience. A shot of two clocks, in New York and in Nazareth, points to the double time-frame lived by the diasporic subject, a temporal doubleness underlined by an intertitle saying that the filmmaker's mother, due to the Scud attacks, is adjusting her gas mask at that very moment. The friend's letter similarly stresses the fractured space-time of being in the US while identifying with both Iraq and Israel.

In *Measures of Distance*, the Palestinian video/performance artist Mona Hatoum explores the renewal of friendship between her mother and herself during a brief family reunion in Lebanon in the early 1980s. The film relates the fragmented memories of diverse generations: The mother's tales of the "used-to-be" of Palestine, Hatoum's own childhood in Lebanon, the civil war in Lebanon, and the current dispersal of the daughters in the West. (The cinema, from *The Sheik*, through *The King and I*, to *Out of Africa*, has generally preferred showing Western travelers in the East rather than Eastern women in the West). As images of the mother's hand-written Arabic letters to the daughter are superimposed over dissolves of the daughter's color slides of her mother in the shower, we hear an audiotape of their conversations in Arabic, along with excerpts of their letters as translated and read by the filmmaker in English.

The voice-over and script of *Measures of Distance* narrate a paradoxical state of geographic distance and emotional closeness. The textual, visual, and linguistic play between Arabic and English underlines the family's serial dislocations, from Palestine to Lebanon to Britain, where Mona Hatoum has been living since 1975, gradually unfolding the dispersion of Palestinians over very diverse geographies. The foregrounded letters, photographs, and audiotapes call attention to the means by which people in exile maintain cultural identity. In the mother's voice-over, the repeated phrase "My dear Mona" evokes the diverse "measures of distance" implicit in the film's title. Meanwhile, background dialog in Arabic, recalling their conversations about sexuality and Palestine during their reunion, recorded in the past but played in the present, parallels photos of the mother in the shower, also taken in the past but viewed in the present. The multiplication of temporalities continues in Hatoum's reading of a letter in English: to the moments of the letter's sending and its arrival is added the moment of Hatoum's voice-over translation of it for the English-speaking viewer. Each layer of time evokes a distance at once temporal and spatial, historical and geographical; each dialog is situated, produced, and received in precise historical circumstances.

The linguistic play also marks the distance between mother and daughter, while their separation instantiates the fragmented existence of a nation. When relentless bombing prevents the mother from mailing her letter, the screen fades to black, suggesting an abrupt end to communication. Yet the letter eventually arrives via messenger, while the voice-over narrates the exile's difficulty in maintaining contact with one's culture(s). The negotiation of time and place is here absolutely crucial. The videomaker's voice-over reading her mother's letters in the present interferes with the dialogue recorded in the past in Lebanon. The background conversations in Arabic give a sense of present-tense immediacy, while the more predominant English voice-over speaks of the same conversation in the past tense. The Arabic-speaking voice-over labors to focus on the Arabic conversation and read the Arabic scripts, while also listening to the English. If the non-Arabic speaking spectator misses some of the film's textual registers, the Arabic-speaking spectator is overwhelmed by competing images and sounds. This strategic refusal to translate Arabic is also echoed in Suleiman's *Homage by Assassination* where the director (in person) types out Arabic proverbs on a computer screen, without providing any translation. These exiled filmmakers, thus, cunningly provoke in the spectator the same alienation experienced by a displaced person, reminding us, through inversion, of the asymmetry in social power between exiles and their "host communities." At the same time, they catalyze a sense of community for the diasporic speech community, a strategy especially suggestive of diasporic filmmakers, who often wind up in the First World precisely because colonial/imperial power has turned them into displaced persons.

Measures of Distance also probes issues of sexuality and the female body in a kind of self-ethnography, its nostalgic rhetoric concerning less the "public sphere" of national struggle than the "private sphere" of sexuality, pregnancy, and children. The women's conversations about sexuality leave the father feeling displaced by what he dismisses as "women's nonsense." The daughter's photographs of her nude mother make him profoundly uncomfortable, as if the daughter, as the mother writes, "had trespassed on his possession." To videotape such intimate conversations is not common practice in Middle Eastern cinema, or for that matter, in any cinema. (Western audiences often ask how Hatoum won her mother's consent to use nude photographs and how she broached the subject of sexuality.) Paradoxically, the exile's distance from the Middle East authorizes the exposure of intimacy. Displacement and separation make possible a transformative return to the inner sanctum of the home; mother and daughter are together again in the space of the text.

In Western popular culture, the Arab female body, whether in the form of the veiled bare-breasted women who posed for French colonial photographers or of the Orientalist harems and belly dancers of Hollywood film, has functioned as a sign of the exotic.[15] But rather than adopt a patriarchal strategy of simply censuring female nudity, Hatoum deploys the diffusely sensuous, almost pointillist images of her mother naked to tell a more complex story with nationalist overtones. She uses diverse strategies to veil the images from voyeuristic scrutiny: already hazy images are concealed by text (fragments of the mother's correspondence, in Arabic script) and are difficult to decipher. The superimposed words in Arabic serve to "envelop" her nudity. "Baring" the body, the script metaphorizes her inaccessibility, visually undercutting the intimacy verbally expressed in other registers. The fragmented nature of existence in exile is underlined by superimposed fragmentations: Fragments of letters, of dialogue, and of the mother's *corps morcelle* (rendered as hands, breasts, belly). The blurred and fragmented images evoke the dispersed collectivity of the national family itself.[16] Rather than evoke the longing for an ancestral home, *Measures of Distance*, like *Homage by Assassination*, affirms the process of recreating identity in the liminal zone of exile.[17] Video layering makes it possible for Mona Hatoum to capture the fluid, multiple identities of the diasporic subject.

A discourse which is "purely" feminist or "purely" nationalist, I have tried to argue, cannot apprehend the layered, dissonant identities of diasporic or post-independence feminist subjects. The diasporic and post-Third-Worldist films of the 1980s and 1990s, in this sense, do not so much reject the "nation" as interrogate its repressions and limits, passing nationalist discourse through the grids of class, gender, diasporic, and sexual identities. While often embedded in the autobiographical, they are not always narrated in the first person, nor are they "merely" personal; rather, the boundaries between the personal and communal, like the generic boundaries between documentary and fiction, are constantly blurred. The diary form, the voice-over, the personal written text, now bear witness to a collective memory of colonial violence. While early Third-Worldist films documented alternative histories through archival footage, interviews, testimonials, and historical reconstructions, generally limiting their attention to the public sphere, the films of 1980s and 1990s use the camera less as revolutionary weapon than as monitor of the gendered and sexualized realms of the personal and the domestic, seen as integral but repressed aspects of collective history. They display a certain skepticism toward metanarratives of liberation, but do not necessarily abandon the notion that emancipation is worth fighting for. But rather than fleeing from contradiction, they install doubt and crisis at the very core of the films. Rather than a grand anti-colonial metanarrative, they favor heteroglossic proliferations of difference within polygeneric narratives, seen not as embodiments of a single truth but rather as energizing political and aesthetic forms of communitarian self-construction.

SIX

PALESTINIAN EXILIC CINEMA AND FILM LETTERS

Hamid Naficy

Today's exilic and diasporic cultures tend to coalesce around certain ideological and narrative discourses and media uses that both express and constitute the postcolonial displacements and the postmodern scatterings that characterize our era. In an earlier work, I focused on a single group of exiles and immigrants, the Iranians in Los Angeles – forming the largest population outside the country of origin – which created an Iranian national identity by means of its vibrant pop culture, particularly television, in the entertainment capital of the world.[1] Like its Hollywood big brother, this exilic pop culture was exported worldwide – to Iranians in the diaspora and sporadically to those back home. It was during this project that I became keenly aware not only of the singularity and specificity of each exile and diaspora, but also of the multiplicity and universality of exilic and diasporic conditions worldwide. Having examined one displaced community and culture in depth, I became interested in investigating what the various diasporic and exilic cultural producers worldwide, particularly filmmakers, had in common. In the course of the project, it became evident that although there is nothing common about deterritorialization and there are profound differences among displaced filmmakers, their films, made since the 1960s, shared certain common features – an accent – that constituted a new global cinema – an accented cinema. This shared accent signifies upon both the deterritorialized existence of the filmmakers and the films' artisanal and decentered conditions of production and consumption.[2]

This accented cinema is by no means established or cohesive, since it has been in a state of preformation and emergence in disparate and dispersed pockets across the globe. It is, nevertheless, an increasingly significant cinematic formation in terms of its output, which reaches into the thousands, its variety of forms and diversity of cultures, which are staggering, and its social impact, which extends far beyond exilic and diasporic communities to include the general public as well. For example, an earlier survey of Middle Eastern and North African filmmakers, which included Palestinians, showed a surprising number of filmmakers, 321 in all, from sixteen sending countries, making 920 films. Palestinian filmmakers made thirty-five of these films.[3] However, the real figures are higher since there is no central clearing-house or research institute that regularly collects and disseminates data on them. By way of comparison, a more thorough survey of Iranian filmmakers in exile, conducted only a few years later, showed a significant rise in the number of films they had produced. While the first survey had pegged the number of films they had made at 307, the later survey showed 538 films. The same rise in the number of films would be detected if a thorough survey of the Palestinian films and filmmakers were conducted.

PALESTINIAN CINEMA AS AN ACCENTED CINEMA

Palestinian cinema is one of the rare cinemas in the world that is structurally exilic, as it is made either in the condition of internal exile in an occupied Palestine or under the erasure and tensions of displacement and external exile in other countries. The historical factors causing the migration and displacement and the density, variety, and cultural and economic capital of the displaced populations in the receiving countries are factors that favor accented filmmaking. Displaced Algerian filmmakers, for example, have made their films (collectively called *beur* cinema) almost exclusively in France, the country that until 1961 colonized Algeria and to which Algerians emigrated in massive numbers after their independence. Likewise, the majority of Turkish filmmakers have worked in Germany, where historical and political relationships have favored Turkish guest-workers. On the other hand, Palestinians have made films in a number of Middle Eastern, European, and North American countries, commensurate with their worldwide diaspora.

Palestinian films also form a highly diverse corpus, ranging from amateur films to fiction feature films, from documentaries to experimental films, and from art video to video installations and television shows. Many are interstitially made and transnationally funded, and are multinational, multilingual, and intercultural – all of which contribute to their accent. Michel Khleifi's films are a case in point. For example, his French–Belgian co-production *Wedding in Galilee* (1987), spoken in Arabic and Hebrew, received funding from multiple sources. Thanks to its activist governmental policies, France has the largest film industry in Europe. Since the end of World War II, the Centre Nationale de la Cinématographie (CNC) has been shoring up French cinema against both the war's destruction and the postwar competition from US imports. The CNC film fund is continually replenished by taxing the box office receipts of moviehouses and TV networks that broadcast films. All films produced in France are entitled to some CNC support, which partially shields the filmmakers from the vagaries of the market, allows alternative artists to obtain sufficient funds to begin their films, and injects capital into the film industry in general. This support takes the form of a production advance, considered a loan that must be paid back, should the films make a profit. Khleifi received 1,600,000 French francs for his production advance. CNC support also takes the form of distribution assistance, for which Khleifi received 175,000 francs, and direct payment to film laboratories to strike film prints, whereby Khleifi received three such prints. On the Belgian side, in addition to obtaining aid from commercial entities, Khleifi received financial assistance from the Ministry of the French Community, which is a Belgian government agency supporting French cultural forms.[4]

Khleifi also obtained private capital from film and TV agencies of several countries, including Belgium, France, Britain, and Germany, and relied on legal agreements between France and Belgium, which support film co-production and co-distribution. As the number of television channels and networks increased due to privatization of the former state monopolies in Europe, the need for programming increased, turning television into a key supplier of funds for alternative and exilic filmmaking. These entities sometimes pay for the production of films and sometimes for the rights to broadcast them. Khleifi received the latter support from ZDF in Germany and Canal Plus in France.

In addition to obtaining funds, accented filmmakers such as Khleifi obtain assistance by in-kind arrangements with a variety of businesses, including airlines, national and local tourism boards, multinational companies, film distributors, film labs, and ethnic businesses. Sometimes, too, the performers, musicians, and technical crew donate all or part of their services to the film out of national or exilic solidarity.

The ending credits of accented films are filled with the names of such benefactors as well as those of family members, friends, non-profit agencies, and the like.

Accented filmmakers are also often forced to invest in their own films heavily. Khleifi did so, turning his *Wedding in Galilee* into a Belgian, French, and Palestinian co-production. As a person born in Israel, he could have applied for Israeli funding, as well. However, apparently he refrained from doing so because he feared either contamination or co-optation. His fears were strong enough to refuse to show the film at the Jerusalem Cinematheque. Its commercial release in Israel also encountered obstacles. One distributor who expressed interest in it wanted to cut it down by fifteen minutes and shorten its title to *The Wedding*. Although the distributor cited commercial reasons for demanding these modifications, Khleifi surmised that they were political, stemming from the distributor's objection to the film's display of Shimon Peres' official portrait and its foregrounding of Israeli military's occupation of Arab villages. The film's reception among the Arabs in North Africa was also controversial. In certain Egyptian and Moroccan circles, *Wedding in Galilee* was considered a shocking film for its extensive female nudity (the actresses were Tunisian and French-Armenian), the impotence of the Palestinian groom, and the village headman's invitation to Israeli military to attend the wedding as guests. In essence, the interstitial production mode, which gives accented filmmakers the flexibility to play funding agencies of different nations against each other and to take advantage of the anomalies and contradictions of the various film culture industries, can sometimes become a liability. As a result, accented films are structurally political and controversial, during both production and reception.

If the dominant cinema is considered universal and without accent, the films that diasporic and exilic subjects make are accented. However, this accent emanates not so much from the accented speech of the diegetic characters as from the displacement of the filmmakers and their interstitial and sometimes collective production modes. Although many of their films are authorial and autobiographical, both authorship and autobiography must be problematized because the filmmakers' relationship to their films and to the authoring agency within them is not only one of parentage but also one of performance. These are especially true of the works of avant-garde artists such as Elia Suleiman, particularly his *Chronicle of Disappearance* (1996) and *Divine Intervention* (2001), in which he appears as a character known as ES, his ironic but mute alter ego. However, it is also important to put the author back into authorship to counter a prevalent postmodernist tendency, which either celebrates the death of the author or multiplies the authoring effect to the point of de-authoring the text. Accented Palestinian filmmakers, such as Suleiman, Khleifi, and Hatoum, are not just textual structures or fictions within their films, but are also displaced empirical subjects, situated in the interstices of cultures and film practices, who exist outside and prior to their films. As such, they are presumed to be more prone to the tensions and hesitations of exile, diaspora, and transnationalism, and their films should and do encode these tensions. These are important factors that set apart the recent postmodern exilic filmmakers from the modernist European émigré filmmakers of an earlier era, who were often absorbed by the studio system and were in fact instrumental in its consolidation as a hegemonic transnational cinema of another kind.

Accented films are characterized by a highly complex "accented style," as well, consisting of many shared features, only one of which, epistolarity, is examined.

EPISTOLARY MODE

Epistolarity is defined as "the use of the letter's formal properties to create meaning."[5] This is an ancient and rich genre of imaginative and critical literature producing works that range from Ovid's *Heroides* to Goethe's *The Sorrows of Young Werther*, from Montesquieu's *Persian Letters* to Viktor Shklovsky's *Zoo, or, Letters not about Love*, from Doris Lessing's *The Golden Notebook* to Roland Barthes' *A Lover's Discourse: Fragments*, and from Vladimir Nabokov's *Lolita* and *Ada or Ardor* to Jacques Derrida's *The Post Card: From Socrates to Freud and Beyond*. Epistolarity is a mode of cine-writing that inscribes both as icons and narrative agents the means of communication that link people across time and space. It involves the acts and events of sending and receiving, losing and finding, and writing and reading of letters. It also involves the acts, events, and institutions that facilitate, hinder, inhibit, or prohibit such acts and events. In the classical fictional cinema, letters figured large and a number of films can be classified as epistolary films.[6] The critical literature on the epistolary mode has chiefly focused on the use of letters and the postal system. However, in a highly technologized and diasporized world, letter-writing is increasingly being replaced, supplanted, or supplemented by other means of communication, including photographs, telephones, fax machines, audio- and videocassettes, email, and the World Wide Web. These means provide individual as well as group links, helping to close the spatial distance (between here and there) and the temporal gap (between now and then).

Epistolarity is a chief contributor to the accented cinema's style. There is an inexorable and constitutive link between epistolary literature and exile for both of them involve distance, separation, absence, loss, and the desire, however unfulfilled, to bridge the multiple gaps. Whatever form the epistle takes, whether it is a letter, a telephone conversation, or an email message, it becomes a "metonymic and a metaphoric displacement of desire" – the desire to be with an other and to re-imagine an elsewhere and other times.[7] Although epistolaries are usually addressing an absent interlocutor, the very fact of addressing someone turns the film letter into an act of creating the illusion of presence. At the same time, since it posits a dialog between an addresser and an addressee within the diegesis and between the film and its audiences in the theater, this form of cinema is structurally dialogical. Epistolary filmmaking also entails a dialog with the self and like all epistolaries it involves self-evaluation. In exile, where the traditional definitions and boundaries of selfhood, nationhood, and culture are brought under serious questioning or are blurred severely, the epistolary becomes an important strategy for self-expression and self-narrativization. That is why many exilic film letters are also autobiographical or contain elements of the autobiography and diary cinema. However, since in exile, personal identity is enmeshed more than ever with identities of other sorts, exilic autobiographical films are not concerned solely with the self and with the individual. Rather, they tend simultaneously to highlight elements on which group affiliation or division are based, such as, race, gender, class, ethnicity, nationality, religiosity, and political belief. As a result, exilic epistolary cinema is highly social at the same time that it is intensely personal. However, for a variety of reasons, such as their fragmented, non-linear, dialogic, self-reflexive, multivocal, multi-authorial, and defamiliarizing structures and narratives, the relationship in this cinema between authorship and authenticity, fictionality and nonfictionality is never a given. Instead, the relationship is posed continually as a question and, characteristically, it is often left unresolved. Exilic film letters have a number of characteristics, only one of which is examined below in the light of certain Palestinian documentary and avant-garde films.

PROHIBITIONS AND TRANSGRESSIONS

One of the fundamental characteristics of epistolarity is that it is produced under erasure of one sort or another. As such, epistolary narratives invariably spring from an injunction, a prohibition against writing, which may take several forms.[8] It may spring from amorous, personal, sociopolitical, financial, technological, exilic, or narrative prohibitions. Many amorous epistolaries are driven by an injunction against writing put into effect by one of the lovers. In certain circumstances, it is the familial and social norms that prohibit lovers from communicating with one another. Prohibition also may stem from personal refusal to engage in communication. In a number of scenes in Andre Tarkovsky's deeply exilic film *Nostalgia* (1983), the sound of the telephone ringing in some room is heard clearly but no one appears to answer it. The unanswered ring in this film, like the unanswered ring at the dawn of the telephone, invokes in the viewer questions and anxieties about the identity of the caller and the intended receiver and about the message that is not delivered or is refused. Elia Suleiman's *Homage by Assassination* (1992) provides a more extensive example of refusal to communicate. The filmmaker is on the screen throughout but he does not utter a single word. The dogged refusal to answer or to speak may have multiple empirical reasons and symbolic meanings and it is a feature that may turn the dialogic mode of epistolarity into a potentially monologic form, in this instance.

The injunction may be instituted by the state prohibiting its citizens from communicating with one another either internally or from exile. Exiles from repressive societies have learned to get around the censorship and surveillance of their native or host governments by developing private encryption procedures for communicating with each other and with their compatriots elsewhere. In written letters, audio letters, video letters, e-mail, and phone conversations certain words are used symbolically to mean certain other words. The term hospital, for example, may stand for prison. Thus, when speaking about the jailing of a family member who is a political activist, one may say that she has become sick and hospitalized. Such symbolic encryption is often multi-lingual and may be driven by shared group codes, if participants are members of an exile political party or internal opposition group. However, more often, it is highly private, drawing upon shared childhood, friendships, events, nicknames, jokes and references – all of which tend to befuddle the censors and eavesdroppers as well as confuse the participants about the exact meaning of what is said. Exilic epistolaries are, thus, hermeneutically very rich and ambiguous and they provide good examples of "writerly" communication (in the sense developed by Barthes.[9] Unpacking their connotation requires not only knowing coders but also knowing decoders. Dense epistolary texts such as the film *Calendar* (1993) by the Egyptian-born Armenian-Canadian director, Atom Egoyan, position each decoder to potentially become a coder, each viewer to become a maker of the film's meaning.

There are, of course, times when letters are intercepted and phone conversations disrupted by security agents or by a bad connection (the latter problem is prominently inscribed in *Calendar*). Prohibition also may be driven by economical and financial considerations, preventing the making of expensive international phone calls. It is the prohibitive cost of long-distance phone calls and the exiles' intense desire for lengthy and frequent contact that compels the Argentinian exiles in Paris in Fernando Solanas' film *Tangos: Exile of Gardel* (1985) to concoct their ingenious methods of rigging phone booths – a method learned from a Palestinian exile.

Because of its live ontology and the concomitant immediacy, intimacy, and intensity, the telephone is the most susceptible to both the prohibition and transgression of the prohibitions. The inability to contact via phone at critical moments and the overwhelming desire to do so turns the telephone into a highly cathected instrument, creating intense micro-narratives of desire, delay, disappoint-ment, and fulfillment. *Homage by Assassination* is partially driven by such narratives. It shows Suleiman cloistered in a claustrophobic apartment in New York City during the first Persian Gulf War with Iraq in 1991. Like a letter, the film self-reflexively reports and enacts the quotidian routines of Suleiman's day as he goes about writing and editing his film: He is seen tying on his bootlaces, boiling milk on the stove, watching from the window a couple's quiet quarrel in the street below, weighing himself on the scale, going to the bathroom, attempting to make phone calls, writing, xeroxing, faxing, and video-editing. Throughout all these activities, the filmmaker is waiting and is mute, but the audience hears on the answering machine the voices of a number of people attempting to reach him by phone: a talk-radio host interested in obtaining a "Palestinian angle" on the Gulf War, his friend telling him of his success at reaching their hometown, Nazareth in Israel, and another one telling the latest joke about Palestinians. In a humorously touching sequence, Suleiman picks a bouquet of flowers from a vase, places it on the copy machine, and faxes the copied flowers to an Iraqi Jewish friend. The friend is not identified, but it is film scholar Ella Shohat, whose response to Suleiman also arrives by fax.[10] In it, she recounts (in her own voice) the story of her family's displacement from Iraq, years of living with a split identity in Israel/Palestine, and finally her arrival in the United States.[11]

Although Suleiman is silent in the film and there are various impediments to his communication with the outside world, he is at the nexus of a highly technologized epistolary and communication network consisting of computer, copier, fax, telephone, answering machine, radio, and television that can put him in touch with the world. Yet he refuses to speak and cannot be reached easily. Like Amir Naderi in *Manhattan by Numbers* (1993) and Atom Egoyan in *Calendar*, Suleiman is worried and pessimistic about the affiliative potentials of telecommunication media in this era of exilic fragmentation and media manipulation. Ensconced in his claustrophobic safe zone of an apartment where all the shades are drawn and in the darkened editing bay, he is producing his epistolic film, like all epistolaries, in a state of anomic separation and deep loneliness. Exilic loneliness, like amorous loneliness that forces epistolary writing, can be solipsistic. However, since exile structurally involves questions of collective belonging as well, exilic epistolary is less prone to this affliction. Despite Suleiman's refusal, silence, and loneliness within the film's diegesis and despite the film's austere, even pessimistic, tone, *Homage to Assassination* is an impassioned epistle from Suleiman to the world, giving voice to a few moments, perhaps typical, in the life of Palestinian exiles.

Mona Hatoum's experimental film *Measures of Distance* (1988) is made not only under patriarchal erasure but also under the prohibitions imposed by dual exile.[12] It consists of a series of letters from her mother in Lebanon sent to the filmmaker in Canada (away from her two previous homes, Palestine and Lebanon). Both the visual and the sound tracks are richly textured, palimpsestical, and multi-lingual. Throughout the film, portions of the mother's handwritten letters in Arabic are superimposed on the stills of her nude body, while on the soundtrack they are read in English by the daughter. In addition, under the voice-over of the letters is a series of impromptu conversations and phatic banter in Arabic between mother and daughter about intimate matters of sexuality, family relations, and childhood experiences. The prohibition against the transmission of the letters takes two forms: one patriarchal, the other political. In one of the letters, Hatoum's mother gives her artist daughter permission to use in her work their tape-recorded conversations and photos but asks her (twice) not to share them with her father. Several years earlier he had become angry when he had discovered them naked, taking photographs and talking about intimate matters (these stills and recordings form the documentary material of the film). It is as though, the mother tells her daughter, that by baring her body and soul to her daughter she had given her something that rightfully belonged only to him. The mother's prohibition against making public those photos and taped conversations serves patriarchal purposes, something that the filmmaker subverts by making her film public. The boldness of her transgression becomes more evident if one takes into consideration the sociocultural contexts of Middle Eastern, Arab, Palestinian, and Muslim societies that place a high value on the clear demarcation and separation of the private from the public. Beyond these culture-specific violations, Hatoum's transgression is in line with what Derrida has called the "postcard structure," a structure that raises questions about what is public or private, inside or outside, real or fictional.[13]

The political prohibition against the transmission of the letters is brought on by the chaotic conditions of the civil war and the Israeli occupation of Lebanon. The last letter, which brings the film to a close, bears the news about this prohibition. Over the darkened screen Hatoum's voice reads her mother's letter about the destruction of the local post office by a car-bomb and the resulting suspension of their vital emotional link of letters (a friend hand-carries the last letter out of Lebanon). Hatoum's mother says that from now on the only link between them must be the telephone, even though they may have trouble getting through or having a proper talk. The film ends at this point. Without letters there is no epistolary film.

Military censorship provides another form of prohibition for filmmakers living in societies that are wracked by war, revolution, and occupation. Jean Khalil Chamoun and Mai Masri's documentary *Wild Flowers: Women of South Lebanon* (1986) is about the Shi'i women's resistance against the Israeli military occupation of south Lebanon whose censors systematically prevented Israeli, Palestinian, and other journalists and filmmakers from taping and transmitting materials without prior military censorship. One harrowing sequence demonstrates the length to which rebels and revolutionaries go to violate such repressive injunctions. Filmed clandestinely by a cameraman other than the filmmaking team, this sequence shows a suicide car-bomb, driven by a Palestinian rebel, creeping up to an Israeli military vehicle. Anxious moments pass as one waits for the bomb either to go off and take the driver with it or for the driver to be discovered and arrested. The bomb does go off, blowing up the driver and the Israeli vehicle. This is what is seen on the screen. What the film does not show or tell, however, is that the videographer, who taped the scene from a building overlooking the street, was arrested and jailed by the Israeli security forces soon after the bombing. As the filmmakers told me, when he was released several months later, he was able to retrieve the tape of the incident, which he had hidden ingeniously and hurriedly somewhere in the building before his arrest. Subsequently, the tape was shown on Lebanese television.[14]

War conditions, like exile, tend to increase peoples' distrust of journalists and filmmakers at the same time that these professionals may be the only ones able to carry out to the world the voices of the ordinary people from war-torn regions. Because of their intimate contact with the women and villagers, however, this Lebanese and Palestinian husband-and-wife team was able to gain their trust. In exilic epistolary films, trust between the addresser and the addressee, the subject and the filmmaker, and the film and its audience is crucial. It becomes particularly so if the film uses the trial motif – another important feature of amorous epistolary literature.[15] The trial motif involves lovers and former lovers invoking some of the following discourses in their own defense: use of laws and the legal language, direct address to the jury, invocation of legal precedents, confession, bearing of witness, expression of suffering and lamentation, appeal for justice, confrontation, self-justification, accusation, threat, and seeking of revenge. As an amorous epistolary for the homeland, *Wild Flowers* invokes many of these trial motifs. In several sequences women (and a few children and elderly men) take the filmmakers into their confidence and recreate for their camera (as though for the jury) the guerrilla tactics they have used against the Israeli occupation forces. The detailed recreations are staged for the purpose of providing evidence to the court of world public opinion that despite the arrest and incarceration of much of the young male population, Palestinians, particularly women, have not given up resistance. Trusting that the filmmakers accurately will transmit their stories, women – young and old – directly address the camera as though facing a jury, accusing, bearing witness to, and defiantly and tearfully lamenting about what they claim the occupying forces have done to them and how they have lost their lands, houses, jobs, and loved ones to the revengeful tactics of individual and collective punishment. By guiding the camera to specific sites, ruins of houses, prisons, farmlands, and roads and by identifying

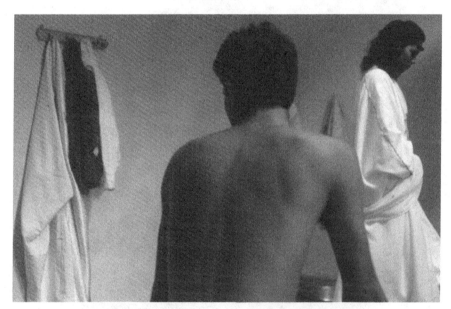

Michel Khleifi's *Wedding in Galilee* (1987).
(Courtesy of Omar al-Qattan, Sindibad Films.)

Mai Masri, the co-director of *Wild Flowers: Women of South Lebanon* (1986) and other documentary films.

Mai Masri, *Children of Shatila* (1998). (Photo courtesy of Mai Masri.)

certain specific events, individuals, and victims, they back up their accusations with documentary evidence. The women's testimonials and Masri and Chamoun's film itself are epistles that not only document fleeting history but are also themselves acts of resistance in history.[16]

To summarize, the exilic epistolary cinema, like other discourses of desire, is inherently critical and political. It involves writing under the threat of erasure imposed by lovers, dominant social orders, social upheavals, military and political occupation, economic hardship, technological inefficiency, political censorship, surveillance, and exile. One cinematic response in exile to these threats of erasure has been the invocation of liminal panic and claustrophobic spaces, which I have elaborated upon extensively elsewhere.[17] The epistolary mode is a response of the opposite kind to same set of threats. It is not so much about coiling back upon the self, about silence and loneliness – although it includes some of that also – as it is about breaking out of the loneliness and isolation that exile imposes. It is about expansiveness not closedness; it is about immensity not claustrophobia. Whatever the threat, the injunctions often serve to intensify the desire to violate it, for it is the human's lot to want to live free and to connect. As a result, epistolarity is characterized not only by the threat of erasure but also by the desire to transgress and to remove the threat. The epistolary is thus always already a genre of desire.

SEVEN

A LETTER FROM THE REST OF THE WORLD OR "THE AFGHAN ARABS"

Nizar Hassan

At the beginning of 2004, I received an email from a person I don't know, who had seen my latest movie *Ijtiyah* (*Invasion*). He said that he would like to recommend it to be screened in the next Input conference, which would be held in Barcelona at the end of that month. Input is an international, independent organization that deals with independent television and film production and encourages high quality. After I gave my initial consent, I received an email from the organization asking me to fill out a participation form. I provided all the required information: Director: Nizar Hassan, Address: Nazareth, Palestine, Producer: Raed Anduni, Ramallah, Palestine, etc. I immediately received an automatic answer saying, "Your form has fulfilled all the requirements, and since Palestine and some other Arab countries are not members of the organization, and since we require that every country have a representative who would carry out all the necessary paperwork and preparation, we have appointed a special representative for you called The Representative of 'the Rest of the World.' Thus the place (country) of production is 'the rest of the world' (Palestine)." At the bottom of the email was also written, 'We will inform you later whether your film is accepted or not.'

A week later, I received an email from the organization saying, "I put your film under the category 'the rest of the world' and thus I made a big mistake, for according to the application you had sent and the information you wrote down, your movie should be under the category 'Israel' and therefore you should contact your representative, Ms. Naomi . . ." I wrote the following response:

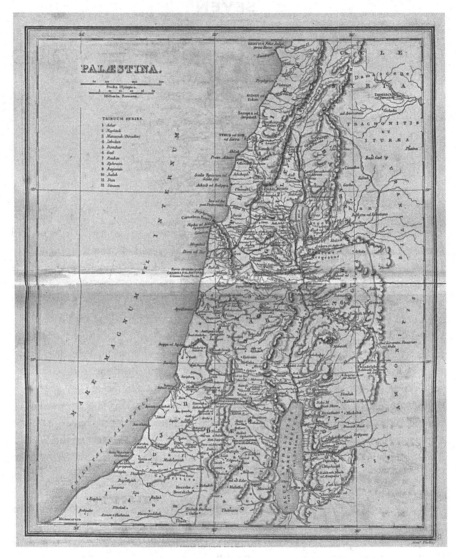

An old map of Palestine.

Dear Sirs,

I did not mention the name of Israel in my application, not even once, and if you had been struck with blindness when you read my application or afterwards, then I cannot cure you. If one of you concluded that it was a grave mistake when I wrote "Nazareth, Palestine," then I am not responsible for all the stupidity in the world. My homeland is called Palestine. A Jewish gang from all over the world with the help of an insolent gang of Europeans and Arabs seized my homeland to erect on it a state they called Israel. Information published by humanity did not mention that this gang brought with them a piece of land from somewhere and put it in a vacuum somewhere on the surface of planet Earth and later called it Israel! Even their information says that it is Palestine, promised to them by God as a land for Israel, and I personally don't believe that God is a real estate agent! I don't want to deal with you. Drop my film from your program and remember that *you* requested my participation in your conference. Withdraw it immediately!

Toward the end of March, I received an email from the Input organization saying, "We are happy that your film *Ijtiyah* (*Invasion*) was chosen to participate in our conference, and evidently the film and the director will represent Palestine under the category 'the rest of the world.'" At the bottom of the letter, I was asked to register my participation electronically on the organization's website, with a reminder that travel and accommodations costs will be covered by the participant and the representative and will be in fact paid for by one of the institutions of the government, such as the ministry of foreign affairs or ministry of culture or a private television channel.

Since then, the movie and its Palestinian director appeared on the official website and documents of Input thus: a name in big letters, followed on the same line by the name of the country in small print.

I started making arrangements and contacted Input's representative, who carries an Arab name, was born and raised in Europe, and belongs to a non-Arab minority, which constitutes an organic part of an Arab country.

She was trying to alleviate the burden of costs on me and had an understanding of my life and the problem of my citizenship to which I don't belong. She took upon herself securing accommodations and contacting the Palestinian embassy in order to guarantee a plane ticket. Later, the ambassador called me and we agreed that I would contact the Palestinian Authority ministry of culture, and so it was.

No sooner had a week passed than I received another email from the organization sent to all participants carrying the good news that 700 people will be attending the conference and offering the possibility of checking all their names on their website. I entered the site and found it to be designed differently: this time, the names of the countries were put first (this has nothing to do with "Jordan First" nor with "Gaza and Jericho First")[1] in large blue print and on a separate line the names of the participants in fine black print were arranged by country. Countries were listed in alphabetical order starting with Afghanistan, then Argentina, etc. I scrolled down quickly to find Palestine and make sure that everything was in order.

I was so shocked when I didn't find it [Palestine] on any of the pages of the website! Soon enough, this shock turned into apprehension and suspicion that they tricked me and that I would find my name under the name of that state (Israel). I scrolled down wearily. I didn't find my name there, so I sighed in relief. I was confused: what happened this time? Where did they put me? Where did I disappear to?

I sent an email asking for an explanation and received the following response: "No, your name has not disappeared. It is on the page and here is what happened: Input organization does not recognize Palestine and such matters cannot be changed overnight. Thus we put your name under the state of Afghanistan." I was dumbfounded. I immediately went to the website and found that it was as they said. With the power of a wicked mind, I was transformed into an Afghan and the sole representative of Afghanistan!

I immediately looked for a way to contact the embassy of Afghanistan in Madrid and soon discovered that the only embassy they have is located in Washington DC. They told me from there that they were hoping for Afghan participation in the conference, and they did not believe that I am Afghan.

So, I would not get the money for a plane ticket from the Afghans!

I sent an email to the conference organizers: "The Afghans will not pay for my ticket. They didn't take me seriously or perhaps were afraid when they heard my Arab name. As for the Palestinian ministry of culture, they will not finance my travel expenses because I am an Afghan." I made a quick call to a friend of mine who practices law and spoke to him about the stalemate in which I found myself. He at once wrote a letter to Input warning them that they are exposing the life of his client, Nizar Hassan, to great danger, for he now lives in a state of extreme peril after they listed his name under the state of Afghanistan. He fears that the United States or an

Arab regime will intercept him, thinking that he belongs to the Afghan Arabs. Two days later, I sent a serious letter to Input saying that I would never participate in their conference because there were two things I will neither compromise nor forsake: my Palestinian identity and my homeland, Palestine.

The end?

> "Dear Nizar, congratulations. We are very pleased. Finally, they recognize Palestine. It is now on our website and official documents."

Afghanistan disappeared, and in its stead appeared Palestine!

Translated by Taoufiq bin Amor

EIGHT

THE CHALLENGES OF PALESTINIAN FILMMAKING (1990–2003)

Omar al-Qattan

> On dirait que toute la mémoire du monde se pose sur chaque peuple opprimé . . .
> [It is as if all the world's memory resides within each oppressed people]
>
> Gilles Deleuze[1]

One of the things that I have learnt over the last fourteen years making films as a Palestinian is how organically linked are the subjective and the objective, metaphor and militancy, the aesthetic and the political, indeed the struggle for Palestine and the strategies deployed for making films on and in it. Perhaps this realization arises from the fact that I have worked both as director and producer. It seems, though, that there may be other reasons: in any artistic project, boundaries become even more intolerable than they usually are. For Palestinian filmmakers, often having to work from exile, straddling, as it were, different borders and markets, negotiating one's way across different languages and in the midst of polemic, these boundaries are a concrete reality rather than a theoretical problem.

What, though, is a Palestinian? I begin with this question because it seems to me as crucial to the making of a film on Palestine as the positions one chooses for one's camera. Naturally, I am only able to ascertain that it is crucial *as far as I am concerned*. I hope, however, that others will see some use in my posing it. I have struggled with this issue because of my personal history: I was born into a wealthy family, to Palestinian parents, in Beirut. I came to the UK at the age of 11 and have been here ever since. I think and write in three languages. More importantly, I have never lived in a refugee camp, have never been hungry, have never personally been dispossessed, have never suffered physical injury as a result of military oppression and so on. It is also fair to say that I am well integrated in British society and that I have sometimes been tempted by the possibility of erasing any connection I have to Palestine and the Arab world, if only for my peace of mind and, perhaps, an improvement in my career! So what makes me a Palestinian filmmaker – my family origins, nostalgia, political commitment?

It's become clear to me over the years that none of these elements on their own are adequate to help me find my bearings. After all, if political commitment were sufficient, it would mean that many people would be politically active on behalf of Palestinian rights, but does this make them Palestinian? Many others have fond memories of a beautiful past or a lost home, yet there is nothing especially Palestinian about nostalgia; and finally, many people are ethnically Palestinian through their parents, but some are collaborators! So though I may feel Palestinian because of these elements, on their own they are inadequate to formulate an artistic programme, let alone a politically committed one. I have therefore gradually come to simplify my relationship with Palestine as, first and foremost, an ethical imperative for which I happen to be equipped because of the objective conditions of my family history, my cultural heritage and the friendships I have developed with other Palestinians. This means that my own preference is to call Palestinian any film engaged with Palestine, and not to limit the name to narrow nationalist boundaries. More importantly, being Palestinian or engaging with the Palestinian cause has been and continues to be a process, not an absolute given, where I as an individual am constantly reviewing and revisiting my relationship with the Palestinian people, their struggle, their land, their memories, and so on. This relationship is always problematic.

My own maiden discovery of Palestine on film occurred when I saw Michel Khleifi's *Fertile Memory* for the first time in early 1985. I became aware of the beauty of the people and the land from which my parents had been expelled – not as a slogan, or a political aspiration, or a symbol, not as a place in the past, but as a revelation of an extraordinarily sensuous, rebellious, funny, and living reality, full of hope and possibility. This experience allowed me slowly to find my way to Palestine – in the sense of physically going there, which I did for the first time six months later, and also inasmuch as it raised the possibility for me to begin building my own relationship with Palestinian reality.

I am aware that this may sound, in a paradoxical way, like a young man or woman enthusing about the State of Israel and rushing to serve in a kibbutz, as many did in the 1960s and 1970s – or perhaps as a sort of postcolonial Orientalist urge for new, undiscovered territory. Certainly, as a 21-year-old, the romance of discovery permeated my uncertain first steps into Palestine as a subject as well as a reality. But *Fertile Memory*, with all its wonderful lyrical elegance, is also a film about the conflicts between individuals and their society – in this case, the novelist Sahar Khalifa and Khleifi's own aunt, a working-class woman who refuses to sell her land to the Israeli authorities. It is also a film about the struggle of these two women against the oppression of a male-dominated society. So although the film is overwhelmingly tender about Palestine, it poses questions that leave little space for romanticizing Palestine as a reality, and actually opens a chasm between me as a viewer/individual and Palestinians as a people, just as it describes the chasms between its characters and their surroundings. Indeed, it seems to ask: where am I in this struggle? Where are the Palestinian people and what relationship do I have/can I have with them?

In other words, rather than confirming a sort of blind kinship with Palestine, the film opened my eyes to the necessity of developing a point of view, a position, an affiliation, without which I would indeed have been a naïve and romanticizing tourist of Palestine. From then on, to different degrees of consciousness, the challenge of making films on Palestine posed a variety of complex and difficult questions for me, as I am certain it does, in different forms, for my colleagues. What relationship do I have with the collective Palestinian experience? Where is that collective to be found? Is it in the generally powerless and silent existence of an oppressed people? Do I have a right to speak on behalf of a collective when I am on its margins? As a Europeanized Palestinian, am I an agent of colonial narrative or am I uniquely placed to oppose it? These questions, as we shall see, acquire very concrete dimensions as soon as one begins to make a film.

The year after my first visit to Palestine, I joined the INSAS film school in Brussels, where Michel Khleifi was teaching. One of his nephews, a student in physiotherapy, was a close friend, so I became familiar with Michel's difficulties in putting together the funding for his next film project, a fictional film entitled *Wedding in Galilee*. For several months prior to the planned start of production in the spring of 1986, he had been trying to secure enough funding to cover a considerable gap in his budget, which consisted until then of commitments from the Belgian Ministry of the French-Speaking Community, German television ZDF and the French National Center for Cinema (Centre National de la Cinématographie, CNC). The PLO had tentatively promised to help, but several attempts to lobby various PLO dignitaries had so far been unsuccessful. This may have been due to Michel's communist politics or it may simply have been the result of short-sightedness or incompetence. Whatever the case, here was an opportunity to make the first Palestinian feature film inside historical Palestine and there were no Palestinian takers. I suspect also that for the Palestinian leadership, with their inherited history of colonial oppression, it was inconceivable that a Palestinian could actually make a film meeting international artistic standards.

A chance encounter between my mother and Michel was to lead to a solution. Outraged by his account of a visit to Tunis, at the time the PLO's headquarters, where an official had boasted his love for cinema by assuring Michel that he had a video machine in every room of his sumptuous villa, my mother promised to do what she could to help. As a result, my father and uncle, successful contractors and long-time philanthropists living in Kuwait and Saudi Arabia respectively, agreed to provide a guarantee for the film's budget shortfall.

I recount this story because, in an accidental way, it led to one of the first serious alliances in modern Palestinian history between capital and a progressive notion of cultural production, an alliance that was to be replicated over the following years in many other areas, particularly through the work of Arab- or Palestinian-funded non-governmental organizations. Michel Khleifi was an articulate, indeed militant, proponent of a progressive culture and one of the first Palestinian intellectuals to defend culture's importance as a tool of resistance, as well as to call for its disenfranchisement from the grip of party-political sloganeering. In particular, he strongly argued for a cinema of the poor. What did this actually entail?

I would summarize it as follows: faced with the overwhelmingly powerful and hostile forces of mainstream filmmaking, in a situation of conflict with a disdainful and generally unsympathetic neocolonial culture, such as the one in Israel, and emerging from a history of dispossession, humiliation and defeat and a society with very limited means of production and a barely existent skill base, the progressive filmmaker must first and foremost find a way of hijacking the technology and capital of his or her "masters" to make films. The model here is not the émigré artist who integrates into a host society and is more or less able to express an *individual* voice. It is on the contrary the individual artist who appropriates the tools of the colonial or postcolonial master to express a *collective* voice. This involves redirecting knowledge and capital to his or her country and there making rich films with poor means, to use Khleifi's own terms, not the poor films made by rich means which many in dependent economies aspire to make as a result of their sense of inferiority or their wish to imitate the powerful (until this day, I hear Palestinian dignitaries and some members of the Palestinian elites huffing and puffing about why we still haven't made a Palestinian *Exodus!*) What I mean by rich films is those works that enjoy the plenitude of ideas, the freedom of imagination, the lucidity of argument and the artistic achievement of any accomplished work of art – not rich in the sense of well-funded.

In some ways, there was a danger that the relatively high cost of *Wedding in Galilee* (at least as far as Arab film budgets were concerned) would undermine these principles, or that this alliance with enlightened capital, even if "nationalist" in nature, would somehow impose a less progressive tone on the film. This did not happen, thanks to Khleifi's tenacious and rigorous aesthetic program. In fact, despite the film's international success, it proved to be deeply provocative – to the Israelis, because here was an example of a living and dynamic Palestinian culture exposed to the world (we must not forget that for long Israeli society as a whole was in denial of the very existence of the Palestinians as such); and to Arab audiences, because of its nuanced depiction of Palestinian society and its internal contradictions.

Wedding in Galilee became the first Palestinian feature film to enjoy international acclaim and success and won the International Critics' Prize in the 1987 Cannes Film Festival. More importantly, though, it created a precedent for the transfer of European investment and technical know-how to a tiny, barely nascent film community *by means of a Palestinian project*. Until 1986, Palestinians inside Palestine/Israel had worked, if at all, in the Israeli or visiting foreign film industry as second- or third-tier technicians. Their skills and experiences were very limited. Suddenly, it became possible for a film to be initiated and made by a Palestinian. Rashid Masharawi, who later went on to become a prolific director, worked as the set carpenter on the film. His brother Saado was the film's props master and later worked as such on several other films. For many actors, it was their first experience acting in a Palestinian-directed film. As for me, working as a trainee (and occasional tea-boy!), it was my first taste of the wondrous world of filmmaking.

Little did we know then that those heady days were soon to be overshadowed by the tragic realities of the first Intifada and a completely changed environment which would make it impossible for a feature-film crew to shoot in the Occupied Territories, where half of *Wedding of Galilee* was filmed. It is important to note here that we had some Israelis, including actors and technicians, working in the West Bank locations without much ado. A year or so later, this became virtually impossible. Although we were harassed by a group of local thugs whom we suspected of being sent by the Israeli military, there were very few, if any, logistical problems caused directly by the Israeli authorities. It is also important to note that this lack of interference, and the relative peace of the early 1980s, were due to a strategy of occupation which was soon to be overhauled with the start of the popular uprising in late 1987 (the first Intifada), a strategy of attempted economic appease-ment towards the Palestinians in the Occupied Territories coupled with political oppression. It was a time when (cheap) Palestinian labor could freely move in and out of Israel but where politically active Palestinians were being imprisoned or exiled.

Wedding in Galilee describes this untenable situation with an eerie foresight. A troublesome village is under curfew but its *Mukhtar*, or headman, wants to marry off his son in traditional pomp. The military governor decides to allow him to do so, on condition that he and his officers are invited as guests of honor. The *Mukhtar* accepts, stipulating that they stay until the end of the celebrations. But many in the village are outraged and some young men plot to kill the governor during the wedding. At the same time, the groom resents his father's stubbornness and is unable to consummate the marriage. As the celebrations deteriorate into chaos and anger, the villagers line up the main street of their village and throw, rather than give away, their parting gifts at the departing soldiers. "If you want to join the celebrations," says the groom's sister to one of the Israeli officers, "you must take off your military uniform." In other words, coexistence is not possible under military occupation.

The rapturous reception that the film received on its first screening in Cannes was overwhelming. Here at last was an instance of a proud and accomplished Palestinian talent, unafraid of expressing itself and confidently sitting side-by-side with its peers in the world of filmmaking. No longer the cowed, hesitant and humiliated Palestine, but a living, dynamic, and inescapable culture making itself heard. Perhaps it is important to note that this was also the beginning of a new dynamic that persists, against the odds, until today, where the struggle for Palestinian freedom is often most successfully conducted through Palestine's living culture, a peaceful but determined effort to introduce Palestine to the world not as a negative force, but one full of challenges and complexities and beauty. The Israeli critics were generally sarcastic, or else preferred to remain silent. Some tried co-optation: an Israeli distributor with strong US connections proposed to Michel a "firm" promise of an Oscar if he agreed to call the film Israeli! Distribution offers abounded; more prestigious prizes followed too. The film was even theatrically distributed in the US and continues to this day to enjoy a reasonable home video career. But this euphoria was short-lived.

In December 1987, when the Intifada erupted first in Gaza then in the West Bank and Jerusalem, it no longer became possible to represent the Middle East conflict as a series of military confrontations between states. The world now saw a popular, unarmed rebellion live on its television screens and a brutal military repression by Israel's occupation army. An unprecedented number of journalists and television crews began to arrive in the Occupied Territories. For filmmakers, this created two interesting new realities: it became virtually unthinkable to produce a film like *Wedding in Galilee* since the security situation would have made the movement of a large crew and numerous pieces of equipment all but impossible. At the same time, it brought a flood of "news money" to the area. Local fixers, translators and drivers were now needed to help foreign journalists on their hungry quest for Intifada stories. With the introduction of the portable Super-VHS camera into the market, someone came up with the idea of commissioning Palestinian cameramen (and later women) to film in areas too dangerous for a foreign journalist. The fixer business became increasingly competitive, as it grew more and more lucrative. This was not always a positive development: it created a generally well-paid body of "para-journalists" and camera operators, without contributing to their technical knowledge in anything more than a shambled manner. From the point of view of the rapacious news organizations, this did not much matter as long as they could get the images they needed for their "stories." I believe that we are in some ways still paying the price for these distortions.

During the period 1987–93, I was unable to visit Palestine, since it became increasingly difficult to obtain the temporary permits which had allowed me to travel there as an Arab national. Michel Khleifi, however, made the powerful docu-drama *Canticle of the Stones,* which came out in Cannes in 1990. The experience of this film's release, when compared with *Wedding in Galilee*, was difficult indeed. The Israeli embassy in Paris threatened to withdraw the only Israeli film in the festival; the press was hostile or simply cold, and even the Arab press, which had so enthused about *Wedding*, was reticent. One could explain this as the usual political hostility, amplified now that we were in a situation of actual conflict rather than those brief days of relative peace in 1987. It might also be very the innovative form of the film, its original use of Classical Arabic in the dialog, its extraordinarily powerful portrayal of Palestinian suffering, using an unusual combination of observational documentary and the lyrical, mournful poetry of its editing. Perhaps this reticence was also due to certain developments in world cinema in the late 1980s and early 1990s, which were to lead to the emergence of a simple (simplistic) aesthetic and a preference for individual(istic), harmless and generally apolitical and sanitized subject matters. Even at its most gruesome, Tarantino's violence, for example, is a *performance*, for humorous, gratuitous consumption, not designed to make you *feel* violence – whereas the violence of *Canticle* was true to life and overpowering.

One certain gain from this period of upheaval was the increased contact between Palestinians in the Occupied Territories and the international media. Even in a country as notoriously insular and self-centered as Britain, several brave television executives began to take interest in Palestinian films. *Canticle of the Stones* was partly funded by a pre-sale to the Independent Film and Video Department at Channel 4, headed at the time by Alain Fountain; it was also during the first Intifada that Mai Masri was first able to secure commissions from the BBC or Channel 4. Later, in 1992 or 1993, Channel 4 commissioned a series of "video diaries" by Israeli and Palestinian filmmakers (until today, television executives in Europe are always careful to program Palestinian films (if at all) with a suitably "balancing" Israeli counterpart – as if the former were simply too dangerous to be allowed on public television without some sort of hand-holding by the latter). But throughout the 1990s and until today, this new relationship, with all the major steps it achieved to the advantage of the nascent Palestinian film *corps de métier*, was fundamentally unbalanced and flawed.

The case of *Canticle of the Stones* is an interesting early example. The film was delivered to Channel 4 in Britain soon after its release in 1990. It was not until late 1992 however that it was broadcast, and even then at midnight and in the suitably safe framework of an Israeli–Palestinian film season. For a film about an urgent and topical phenomenon like the Intifada to be shelved for two years is extraordinary. When we protested to Channel 4, we were told that this was a programming coincidence and that they were waiting for a suitable "slot" to show it. It is of course very difficult to answer these positions because a channel executive can find a thousand reasons for postponing a film, or not programming it at all. I have no doubt whatsoever, though, that this form of self-censorship was a result of fear – that the violence of the Israeli occupation and the sympathy generated by the Palestinian victims were politically unpalatable – *especially since they were being shown through the work of a Palestinian*. This is an irony: if an Israeli Jew or (a non-Arab) British director had made the same film, which is quite possible, it may well have been shown. After all, we are democracies. It just happens that the Palestinian is not part of this "we" club.

The imbalance between a European broadcast market and Palestinian and Arab filmmakers was, and still is, principally a financial rather than a purely political one. It is a sad and maddening fact that there is no market for films or documentaries in the Arab world of more than marginal value. Distribution channels are weak, copyright laws hardly respected, cinema networks barely emerging after decades of closure and state control, and of course the inescapable censor. One could go on making films with European funding for European consumption but it is a deeply frustrating and unsatisfactory process to do so while being almost completely severed from your natural market. This is a problem faced by all filmmakers emerging from developing or weak economies, with the possible and interesting exception of Iranian cinema, although I wonder how many Iranian films we would have been able to see in Europe (or would have been made at all) were it not for the extraordinary economic and political investment that certain European countries, particularly France and Germany, have been making in Iran in the last ten years or so, an investment that I dare say is far from innocent! The distortions produced by this particular relationship bear interesting comparison with the most contemporary Palestinian filmmaking and I shall come back to this point later.

In 1990, having just completed my studies at the Institut national supérieur des Arts du Spectacle (INSAS), I started my first professional film project. After a short visit to Jordan and Kuwait, I had been overwhelmed by the now pervasive dominance of religious ideology in societies that had, until the late 1970s, been relatively secular, if traditional and conservative. It was not possible for me to enter

Palestine at the time but more importantly, it seemed to me that the increasingly intrusive and oppressive presence of religious political ideology in the lives of the Arab people was almost as alarming a threat as Israel! I therefore decided to make a film about this phenomenon. Why is this happening? How do individuals deal with it, how are they integrating it into their lives and why? Are there any forms of resistance to its presence? Indeed, could it be a liberating force that I, hailing from a secular and liberal background, simply had not understood? I had no clear idea of the form the film would take, but I was hoping to find a family which contained within it contrasting and conflicting voices and points of view.

A few years previously, on my first visit to Palestine, I had stayed with a wonderful family (friends of my parents) in Ramallah, which I had come to consider almost as a microcosm of Palestinian experience. There were two sets of elderly brothers who had married sisters, and a second and third generation of young men and women, some of whom had married their cousins or outsiders. The parents were refugees from the village of Lifta (now expropriated by Israel) outside Jerusalem and were simple, generous folk. Their children though had all been educated abroad or at Birzeit University in the West Bank. The eldest had studied medicine in Moscow and had come back with his young Russian wife. Two other brothers had also studied in the Soviet bloc. All three were more or less Communist Party or Popular Front for the Liberation of Palestine (PFLP) sympathisers, while their younger brother, who had studied locally, had become close to the Muslim Brotherhood. One sister had married and lived in Kuwait, where her husband's situation was very comfortable. In addition to the generational contrasts, there were very lively political differences and debates which I thought, five years later, would make wonderful material for a film on the rise of religious ideology and its effects on a community. The fact that they all lived in the same house made this model seem even more appealing.

I researched the film for a whole month in Jordan, hoping in vain to find a similar family. In the end, I came across a wonderfully articulate and rebellious middle-aged woman and her small family in the Hussein refugee camp in Amman. Haifa' El-Samhouri (Um Mahmoud) lived in a tiny house with her husband and youngest son, an unemployed 24-year-old with ambitions to become a painter. Her next-door neighbor was an active member of the very conservative local mosque and the butt of Um Mahmoud's scathing jokes (Jordan's king had recently allowed the practice of a limited form of parliamentary democracy following violent food riots which gripped the whole country in late 1989 and as a result, a number of religious movements had won parliamentary seats and public attention). But it was Um Mahmoud's incredibly rich and sarcastic internal world which interested me most: her dreams, her homesickness for Jaffa, the hometown in Palestine from which her family had been expelled in 1948, the frustrations of a loveless marriage which she expressed without reserve, and the biting wit with which she spoke about the world and the people surrounding her.

A couple of days after I returned to Belgium to start fundraising for the film, Saddam Hussein invaded Kuwait and everything in the region was thrown into disarray and confusion. Whatever one was to do for the following months, perhaps years, would now have to take into account this appalling new reality of military escalation and war. It was also a time of extreme irrationality, which was to witness a dramatic conflation of ideology in the region – nationalist and religious, personal and public, local and regional. The film I went on to make, *Dreams and Silence*, was deeply marked by this new reality full of anxiety and uncertainty, compounded by an increasingly obscurantist public discourse of pandemonium. In the middle of all this, my main character was to attempt to trace her way back to a meaningful reality, although she too, on and off the camera, was often the victim of the same fantasy and wishful thinking so common in the Arab world prior to the humiliating defeat of Saddam Hussein's troops.

Palestine as a theme was now dominated by a religious ideology and political significance far beyond the limits of the injustice suffered by its people, and, more importantly, a significance that reached deep into the everyday lives of citizens of the Arab world in ways previously unfamiliar. Courtesy of CNN, this process was now on display to an international audience.

Like all major historical events, the Gulf War was to produce a surprising, if deeply ambiguous outcome. In some ways, it led to the recognition of Palestinian rights in ways that had previously been unthinkable, through the Madrid Peace Conference. In other ways, it created an entirely new dynamic of conflict, the results of which we are witnessing to this day – the quasi-total decimation of Iraqi society of course but also direct, long-term American intervention in the region, the rise of "Islamic" resistance to this intervention, and, paradoxically, the emergence of what I would call grocery-shop notions of Palestinian nationhood – isolationist, narrow, and deprived of the strategic depth of the Arab world. It also eventually led to the reinforcement of Israeli racial and national separatism.

What significance did all this have for making Palestinian films? Let us return for a moment to the idea of the cinema of the poor. This idea is inspired by and dependent on the principle that the question of Palestine – the struggle for Palestinian rights – is a struggle for freedom from oppression, whether Israeli or otherwise, for the right to self-determination and self-expression, for the right to live safely and freely in one's homeland or anywhere else in the world for that matter and *that it is one we share with the rest of the oppressed peoples of the world.* This universality was and remains of the utmost importance, especially from the point of view of an artist wishing to express a point of view to as wide an audience as possible. We thought of ourselves as agents of communication between realities, which we interpreted to an audience anxious to discover and understand those realities. The universality of our subject matter was therefore essential, as was that of our own and our protagonists' points of view. But during the first Intifada, which persisted until late 1993, a new Palestinian agent of communication emerged: the "commando" cameraman/woman delegated by Western news agencies to film stories. Audiences around the world were able to see more of Palestine, though almost exclusively in the context of the uprising. This led to an almost universal sympathy for the Palestinians and probably contributed significantly to forcing the great powers to at least seriously address the Palestinian problem. Sadly, though, the tangled realities behind the events shown on television, let alone the voices of Palestinians involved in the conflict, were gradually to become almost entirely subordinated to the terminology of news reports and their reflection of international political priorities: first Palestinian "autonomy" and recently the "fight against terrorism" and "statehood." So while there was an extraordinary proliferation of images from Palestine, there was rarely a corresponding understanding of what lay behind those images. (Godard, in his magisterial film on the Palestinian resistance *Içi et ailleurs*, as well as the rest of his work, has taught us that there is a fundamental difference between seeing and looking, *voire et regarder.*)

This meant that, as filmmakers, we could expect support from our mostly European sources of funding within the limits of this new outlook. During Oslo and until the outbreak of the second Intifada in the autumn of 2000, it was virtually impossible to get any kind of European backing for a film if it dared to step outside these strictures, strictures that were pleasantly disguised behind the apparent

A scene from Michel Khleifi's *Tale of the Three Jewels* (1994).
(Courtesy of Omar al-Qattan, Sindibad Films).

euphoria of peace which followed the handshake of Yitzhak Rabin and Yasser Arafat on the White House lawn in September 1993. It is in this context that Michel Khleifi's *Tale of the Three Jewels* (1994) and *Forbidden Marriages in the Holy Land* (1995), as well as my own *Going Home* (1995), should be seen as belonging to a particular historical period coming to an end.

Tale of the Three Jewels was commissioned in the winter of 1993 by the BBC and the One World Group of Broadcasters for a series of films which was to be shown during a UN-sponsored international conference on population and immigration due to be held in Cairo in the summer of 1994. Written in about fifteen days, it was shot in nine extremely difficult and cold weeks in the Gaza Strip in the winter of 1994, a few weeks before the arrival of the Palestinian Authority. It is a feature film, the first ever to be entirely filmed in Gaza, which tells of a boy's dream to emigrate to South America to find three lost jewels, which would win him the hand of a Gypsy girl whom he has met by chance and with whom he has fallen in love. Despite its fairy-tale nature, the film is firmly anchored in Gaza's realities of poverty and violence, especially the suffering endured by its children, but like all of Khleifi's work, it is full of the detail and observation which give his films their beauty and vitality.

During our second day of filming, a deranged Jewish settler walked into the Abraham mosque in Hebron and massacred twenty-eight people as they prayed. The whole of the Occupied Territories erupted in protest and it became clear that our project could well be jeopardized. Yet thanks to the brave determination of our Belgian and local crew, we all voted to stay. I remember telling a French television crew who were making a report on our filming, that while we had come to Gaza with a desire to support its people it was they who in fact were supporting us – despite the fact that they, like the rest of the Palestinians in Gaza, had been under night-time curfew for seven years; had not been allowed to use Gaza's beaches during that period; had been living under the arbitrary regime of sudden all-day curfews or the equally erratic public strikes declared by the unified command of the uprising. Yet still, we were able to film all over the Gaza Strip (something no longer possible today since Israel divided the north from the south and confiscated or razed whole areas of Palestinian land to "protect" its illegal settlements. Much of the film takes place in an orange grove – today, there are almost no orange groves left in Gaza, most of them uprooted by the Israeli Army). Of course, with hindsight, it was crazy to do some of the things we did with a thirty-strong crew and equipment, but at the time, we were all possessed with a powerful sense of commitment and defiance, almost as if making the film was an act of resistance in itself.

Sadly, though, the sense of triumph that followed the film's completion was not matched by its reception in the 1995 Cannes Film Festival. By then, Oslo was the dominant buzzword and suddenly almost anything to do with Palestine had to be seen within its limited parameters. In *Tale*, the horrific violence suffered by Gaza's children is inescapable, as is the cruelty of the Israeli occupation. For a world now blinded by the euphoria of the moment, these seemed like aspects of a period past. Never mind that violence continued to haunt both Palestinian and Israeli societies during and after the Oslo years. In the new rosy atmosphere of "coexistence" and peace, there was no place for dark realities. So even though *Tale* went on to enjoy a very successful festival and (a relatively good) television career, it was the victim of this new mood of peace hysteria.

Forbidden Marriages and *Going Home*, both in their own way unfashionable treatments of very unfashionable themes, met with similar fates. In the first, a documentary examining mixed-background marriages between Arab Muslims and Christians and Israeli Jews (and one Arab and Arab-African mixed-race marriage), the viewer is confronted not with the rosy picture of Palestinian–Israeli bed-partners looking toward a problem-free future, but with the fundamental injustices of all religious codes of marriage and citizenship, including Israel's abhorrent law of return, which allows immigration and full citizenship to the state only for Jews. Again, this brave film had a wonderful grassroots and festival success, but to this day it still remains to be widely broadcast on television. *Going Home* suffered a similar fate: following the journey of a British officer who had served in the last days of the Palestine mandate to present-day Israel and the Occupied Territories, it is a reflection on one of the most difficult and complex problems at the heart of the Palestinian tragedy: the right of return for Palestinian refugees and the right to remember the past and to demand official and public Israeli reparation and recognition of the injustices perpetrated against the Palestinians as a fundamental step towards eventual reconciliation.

Two events in the careers of these three films are worth recounting here. First, *Tale* was rejected by the London Film Festival even though it was the first ever Palestinian–British co-production of a feature film. A year later, the festival wanted to show *Forbidden Marriages*, perhaps because of its more "palatable" subject matter for those heady "peace" days. Khleifi agreed, on the condition that the festival also show *Tale* and *Going Home*. They refused and accused us of "censorship." As a result, *Tale* has only been shown in the UK in a reduced format on BBC 2 as well as on video and in festivals, while no broadcaster has bought *Forbidden*. It also took three years and considerable protest to get *Going Home* shown late one evening on Channel 4 – in the context, of course, of an Israeli–Palestinian film season.

This leads me to the next episode: in April 1998, I was approached by a British producer, through Channel 4, with the idea of reformatting *Going Home* for a season of films coinciding with Israel's fiftieth anniversary. The producer had previously made a couple of television series in which filmmakers in certain countries were given a fixed amount of money and asked to shoot rushes on a specific theme or situation. The rushes were then sent to London, where they would be edited by the producer and shown on television. This seemed at first like an interesting way to proceed, but on reflection, I became outraged by its fundamental propositions. First of all, it meant that the London producer would make a killing, having to forego the big expense of organizing and doing the shoot him or herself. Secondly, it struck me as an incredibly spurious economic model, reminiscent of the colonial practices of the nineteenth century, where the dominated economies provided cheap raw material, which was then shipped to Britain, manufactured and sold at a massive profit, often back to the poorer colonial markets.

It was only after I protested to the Channel 4 commissioning editor that the producer backed off and I was "allowed" to show a slightly updated and revised version of my film. More interestingly though, this episode is revealing of the fundamental imbalances and distortions which we have inherited from the days of the first Intifada: a local, generally poorly skilled and trained workforce dependent almost entirely on the demands and whims of a European broadcast market whose priorities very rarely coincide with those of that workforce. During the Oslo years, the continuing problems, contradictions and ugly realities of Palestine and Israel were subordinated to the "peace" message so avidly desired by the Western powers, until of course those realities finally exploded in their face.

After these bitter experiences, it became gradually clear to us that we were out of sync with the times, and that we if were to carry on making films on Palestinian themes we needed to develop not only a new approach, but an entirely new formal language to do so. The Oslo phase was one in which people who had suffered almost three decades of occupation were tired of political pressure and wanted, naturally, to start building their lives and livelihoods again. There was much talk at the time of "nation-building." Public and private institutions needed to be launched; educations resumed, individual lives repaired and enjoyed. It was a time of (temporary) forgetfulness and a genuine desire to believe that the future held good things for the Palestinians, at least for those living in the West Bank and Gaza Strip. On an international level, it is important to remember that the collapse of the Soviet bloc and the gradual dominance of liberal capitalism produced its own brand of cultural euphoria. It would be difficult to summarize the effect this had on cinema in these pages, but there are several developments that I believe had a direct influence on the Palestinian cultural scene, particularly its filmmaking.

In the 1980s and the 1990s, a preference for depoliticized and simple (simplistic?) aesthetic form manifested itself in world cinema. In some cases, this was evident in an anxiety to make commercially successful films and often led to an over-enthusiasm for imitating Hollywood. In other cases, there was a tendency toward films focusing on psychological situations that mistook intimacy for passion and navel-gazing for introspection. There were of course exceptions: the baroque, epic scale of Emir Kusturica's work is one, or Van Trier's cruel, lyrical landscapes of human suffering, or, on an entirely different scale, the deeply humane irony and political acuity of the Finnish director Aki Kaurismaki. But even Ken Loach, once a progressive observer of political realities, began producing simplistic and often frivolous work, which at its best smacked of political tourism and was deeply conventional in form. Slim, often tedious work from Iran or Taiwan and elsewhere was condescendingly declared as ingenious (exotic?); it seemed, and continues to seem, as if cinema, entering its second century, had lost its bearings.

While Palestinian society was undergoing a temporary lull in its struggles (or at least so it seemed to the outside world), a gradual emptiness and banalization began to seep into the artistic expression it was producing. Rather than agents of communication, artists and writers and filmmakers were becoming themselves the subject of their work, hence the frequent appearance in the last few years of the director in his or her films, often doing little more than vainly trying to make sense of the realities around them. Yet rather than posing this process as the complex and dialectical struggle (which it is), often these films are satisfied to chart their author's itineraries – a passage through a checkpoint, a conversation with the local children, or, in fiction, staring at an imagined reality (or fantasized reality rather) without providing the slightest handle for the spectator, an emptiness of observation, a narcissistic vision and a poverty of reference that is remarkable for a people living under occupation. In the process, and until the last year or so, we were witness to an extraordinary evacuation of political reality in many of our works of artistic expression, although the real disappointment with film is that other artforms were doing this while producing original and sometimes powerful work: Ala' Hlehel's caustic stories full of social sarcasm; Adania Shibli's lyrical elegies of childhood and love; and, most of all, the extraordinary work of the young artist Raeda Saadeh, who uses herself as a subject/object in provocative, deeply ironic and violent reflections on womanhood and sexuality.

During the Oslo years, and following our bitter disappointments and anger regarding *Tale of the Three Jewels, Forbidden Marriages*, and *Going Home*, we engaged with several different projects ranging from Michel Khleifi's adaptation to the cinema of the life story of the legendary Syrian film star Asmahan, to my own of Toni Hanania's novel *Homesick* (a lyrical account of his childhood in war-torn Beirut and his arrival in an English boarding school) neither of which ever found the necessary financing to be filmed; to an unsuccessful attempt to make a feature film around the theme of Jerusalem with the Palestinian ministry of culture, after it had rejected all the twelve treatments presented to it by Michel; and in 2000, I was hired to work as director on a two-hour documentary life of the Prophet Muhammad for the American Public Network (PBS) – it was as if we simply could not adapt ourselves to the new reality of banalization of those wasted years and seemed to be drifting away from our most cherished preoccupations. This is an unbearable failure to admit to: however prescient (or misguided) one's criticisms of what others have been doing, or what the world has been up to, inaction is itself utterly inadequate!

Fortunately, the explosion of the Oslo fanfare into the second Intifada has changed things considerably for filmmakers interested in Palestine, although it is of course painful to note that so many lives had to be lost and ruined for the world to be disabused of its Oslo delusions. I would like here to pay tribute to those courageous correspondents, journalists, and activists of the International Solidarity Movement, who have braved danger and (in the tragic case of James Miller and several Palestinian journalists) lost their lives to document the atrocities of Israel's social genocide against the Palestinians in the last eighteen months or so, as well as to those

Palestinian and Israeli filmmakers who have done the same – Muhammad Bakri, Nizar Hassan, Eyal Sivan, Anat Even, among others. They have inspired people to remember the importance of bearing witness as an essential part of any filmmaker's work and have, in an often sporadic way, done enormous service to the dissemination of the justice of the Palestinian struggle, with the help of the lightweight and inexpensive Mini-dv camera. Yet naturally, this development will not on its own lead to a revolution in Palestinian filmmaking.

Palestinian filmmaking has never been as prolific nor has enjoyed as much attention and success as it does today. But I think that we must ask ourselves whether this is the result of genuine recognition or whether there are other reasons for this success. Is the recognition due to Palestinian film's universal artistic and intellectual value or is this a momentary phenomenon, which will disappear as soon as Palestine disappears from the television screens or as soon as international solidarity with the Palestinian people begins to wane? Is there an element of tokenism and condescension about some of the over-enthusiasm in the West for some Palestinian films? Are they appreciated *because they are Palestinian* or because they are good films? Moreover, can we fairly speak of a Palestinian film industry and, if not, what can we do to create one?

Although there are today more and more Palestinians working in film and television, it is still very difficult to find experienced and highly skilled Palestinian technicians. Sound engineers are one example, as are directors of photography or indeed screenwriters. Directors and producers themselves still struggle to find production funding for their films, despite the one or two exceptions who do. Even then, it is difficult to speak of a generally cultured body of artists (this is true of all the artforms) simply because of the lack of reference materials (films, theoretical works, etc.) inside Palestine and an absence of locally available learning opportunities. This calls for a considerable investment in training and film education.

Second, there are virtually no distribution channels available in Palestine itself and those available in the Arab world, through one or other of the satellite channels, are meager indeed.

Finally, and perhaps most importantly, there are no locally accessible public or private investment sources for film (except, ironically, Israeli funds, which have been used by several Palestinian filmmakers in the past). This investment, as we have seen, is absolutely essential if there is ever going to be a proper balance between the local and international markets.

There are two ways possible for addressing these fundamental problems – a major public investment programme by the Palestinian Authority or a private-sector initiative funded and managed by a local non-governmental organization (NGO). Given its record in the past years as far as arts funding is concerned, it is very unlikely that the Palestinian Authority will engage in anything more than the occasional investment. However, there have been some cases of successful funding by the independent sector in the other arts and it is time to create an independently run Palestinian film fund dedicated solely to training and education, distribution, development and production in the film and television industry. I believe that this should be open to any filmmaker wishing to make a film on or in Palestine, regardless of nationality, in order to create new opportunities of mutual exchange with other industries and to lay the ground for a better equipped, more exposed and more generously funded film culture.

It is thus essential to remember that there will never be a truly vibrant and confident film industry as long as we depend almost entirely on the erratic funding of foreign broadcasters and as long as our technical skill base is weak. There may be individual successes, but these will never amount to more than temporary phenomena, as I hope has been shown from our own experience.

The immediate outlook today is not a happy one. It seems likely that it will become more, rather than less, difficult for Palestinian filmmakers to make films in their country. Rashid Masharawi, who is from Gaza, has not returned to his home in Ramallah for several months because of the possibility that the army will deport him to Gaza where he will be virtually a prisoner. Mohammad Bakri's film *Jenin, Jenin* continues to be banned in Israel. Three months ago, and for the first time since I have been traveling back to Palestine, I and my (Belgian) two-man crew were denied entry at Ben Gurion Airport and summarily deported the following day. We were planning to make a short film on the journey to Palestine of the writer John Berger and the photographer Jean Mohr, but it seems that our presence was deemed a security risk for Israel! Many foreign journalists and filmmakers are facing similar difficulties (the BBC, for example, has just been boycotted by the Israeli government for showing a program about Israel's nuclear arms industry).

Yet the struggle goes on. Michel Khleifi has almost completed, with his co-director Eyal Sivan, a three-part documentary of historical testimonies taken along the border that was to divide Palestine according to the 1947 UN resolution 181, his first film in eight years. It is a wonderfully rich and provocative work in which the calamitous absurdity of the partition is exposed. I am also aware of several other projects being made despite Israeli strictures and so, however hard it tries, the Israeli government will find it impossible to repress all and every film coming out of Palestine. Yet the difficulty now is not simply to persist with our filmmaking, but to rise to the most daunting challenges of this dark period: to continue to build our technical and artistic capacity while at the same time reaffirming the universal values of the Palestinian struggle through film by drawing on our people's extraordinarily rich personal and collective experiences.

NINE

IN PRAISE OF FRIVOLITY:
ON THE CINEMA OF ELIA SULEIMAN

Hamid Dabashi

> *What strange magic is it*
> *That in a broken mirror unbroken*
> *Appears the image?*
> Mehdi Akhavan Sales

On Sunday 23 May 2004, I joined a small band of demonstrators protesting against the obscenest public spectacle I have witnessed in my life. "Salute to Israel Parade" is "the single largest gathering in the world in support of Israel," according to its organizers. The area of Manhattan surrounding Fifth Avenue, the principal route of the parade, was an eerie scene straight out of Costa-Gavras' 1973 masterpiece *État de siege*. Police cars, trucks full of sandbags parked in the middle of streets as barriers, barely restrained German shepherds (the same dog, I believe, used by the US army in the US torture chambers in Abu Ghraib prison in Iraq), police officers in riot gear, plainclothes security, more police officers riding on horses, still more police officers guarding the parade route, empty streets and allies leading to the parade route, closed doors, closed shops, hushed hotel entrances, metal traffic barriers subdividing the streets into weird passageways that looked like an insoluble jigsaw puzzle. An overwhelming sense of fear was thick in the air as a few solitary souls dared the elements and walked the stretch on 58th Street between subway station 1/9 on Columbus Circle and Plaza Hotel on Fifth Avenue, where a handful of pro-

Palestinian activists had gathered to protest this parade. For about three hours, from 11.00 a.m. to 2.00 p.m., I stood there aghast at the terror of the spectacle, on the same day as one of the most brutal massacres of Palestinians at Rafah in Gaza by the Israeli army – shooting rockets from Apache helicopters at people protesting the destruction of their homes.[1]

How could these people be so vulgar in their criminal appropriation of another people's homeland and flaunt it so blatantly – and do so in the name of a people who themselves have been the victims of the most egregious injustices in history? What depth of human depravation would turn a human being into a criminal colonizer of another nation – stealing their land, destroying their homes, appropriating their wealth, murdering their men, raping their women, slaughtering their children – all not in any distant point in the forgotten past, all in the broad daylight of history, all indeed at the very same moment when this obscene parade was in progress. There was a small group of anti-Zionist Hassidim, the Neturei Karta, to our right as we stood at the corner of 58th Street and Fifth Avenue, and ten times as many Zionist hoodlums screaming at us from across the street – and in between us was the vast expanse of Fifth Avenue, right in front of the Plaza Hotel, on one side and behind the pro-Palestinian activists, and FAO Schwartz toystore on the other, and behind the Zionists. And then for hours upon interminable hours marched the closest thing I have seen to a caricatured version of Leni Riefenstahl's *Triumph of the Will* (1934) – flaunting in odious shades and ominous shadows the power of commanding the center of this empire's attention.

The victims of this parade were not just the millions of Palestinians robbed of their homeland in the broad daylight of history, but also the moral authority of Judaism, as the ennobling religion of the most savagely persecuted people in history.

I stood there for three hours – carrying a Palestinian flag in one hand and alternating between a picture of Rachel Corrie[2] and a sign that read "Free Palestine!" in the other – until I got tired and hungry, and could barely speak from screaming "Free, Free, Palestine," and still the parade was progressing, led by senators, congressmen, city council members, real-estate magnate thieves, firefighters, ambulance chasers, physicians, lawyers, musicians, and even airline pilots, who jumped into a Hava Nagila right in front of us – the gentle Neturei Karta were not amused.

They kept coming up – highschool bands, travel agents inviting people to go to "Israel," even an Irish band. Among the myriad colorful curiosities coming our way on the corner of 58th and Likud, was a massive group of kids wearing blue T-shirts on which was depicted a complete map of Palestine in white, on which their parents had superimposed the following letters, also in white capital letters: ARE WE THERE YET? – meaning, "have we captured the entirety of Palestine yet?"

In addition to Leni Riefenstahl's *Triumph of the Will*, the "Salute to Israel Parade" reminded me of the famous march of Cleopatra to meet Julius Caesar in Joseph Mankiewicz's spectacular 1963 extravaganza, *Cleopatra*. Who was the Cleopatra of this parade? Israel? Who was Julius Caesar? George Bush? Any need to guess what had a claim to be the Roman Empire these days? Why is it that except in the realm of fantasy and film, dreams and nightmares, the obscenity of the US–Israeli liaison to dominate and control the world and its strategic regions is impossible to fathom?

THE UNBEARABLE BANALITY OF THE OBSCENE

When I woke up from a necessary short nap in the afternoon of that blasted Sunday, I looked up the synonyms for the word "obscenity," and noted that most of them had something to do with incomprehensibility, incongruity of sanity and sight, of a vast discrepancy between what one sees and what one reasons. Now suppose, for the sake of argument, that the *obscenity* in question is the very idea of "Israel" – where a succession of white colonial settlers first from Europe, then from the US, and now from Russia, moving to a people's homeland, murdering or maiming them, forcing them to flee their land, destroying or else confiscating their houses, and then for a period of more than half a century continuing to do more of the same, and then extending their power and influence to inhabit the most dangerous organs of the most dangerous predatory empire Planet Earth has ever seen to persuade them to come and protect and sustain the barbarity of their armed robbery of a people – and then on top of it all mobilizing a massive parade smack in the heart of the mendacious arrogance of this empire, boasting of their power, flexing their financial muscle, flaunting their political might. It is unimaginable – and there is the rub.

THE CREATIVE CRISIS OF MIMESIS

The obscenity of what I witnessed that day at the corner of 58th and Ben Gurion in New York gradually mutated into an abiding sense of absurdity. There was something seriously silly, altogether hilarious, about the "Salute to Israel Day." One would not know whether to laugh or to get angry at the spectacle. Between laughter and anger there suddenly developed a mild, mutational, manner of conversion, conversation, affinity even. The link between "frivolity" and "obscenity," between the most fearful streak of the collapse of all serious discourse and the ability to show the obscenity of this spectacle and what it represented, now seemed to me thematic, structural, organic. It then occurred to me that somewhere in the cool navigational detour of *obscenity* into *frivolity* dwelled the seed of Elia Suleiman's cinema. A Palestinian filmmaker of ingenious creative frivolity, Elia Suleiman has succeeded, in the course of the ten years that he wasted in New York, and the lifetime he endured in his occupied homeland, to figure out a visual vocabulary with which he can frighten the colonial occupiers of his homeland out of their customary wits and thus leave a record for posterity.

I thought that the closest language corresponding to the barefaced *obscenity* of the Zionist armed robbery of a nation of its territory was in fact *frivolity*. I thought if *obscenity* was the will to power and domination undoing reason *ad nauseam*, then *frivolity* was taking that *ad nauseam* transgression of reason and turning it, *ad absurdum*, to a will to resist power. Being a "Palestinian" filmmaker posited myriad challenges (and thus possibilities) to an artist – and Elia Suleiman's sense of nonsense, absurdity, and above all his playful, frolicsome, and frivolous pathway from destabilizing anger to spectacular victory, from incapacitating frustration to a triumphant exposition of the barefaced reality, was one most worthy of a closer examination.

In the first scene of Elia Suleiman's now signature film, *Yadun 'Ilahiyya (Divine Intervention, 2002)*, a man is driving a car. The camera is mounted on the passenger side. The man is silent, observant of the road. He eventually reaches for something to his right and picks up what looks like a peach or an apricot, holds it in his hand and starts eating it. The act is innocent, inconspicuous. The camera is attentive, recording the act dutifully, motionless, emotionless, slightly curious. The man, Elia Suleiman, ES as we call him, finishes the fruit and has its pit in his right hand, wondering what to do with it. He gently reaches for a button in his car and pushes it, pulling down the window to his left. The window is now completely down. The camera is still – and suddenly cuts for a split second to a long shot where we can see that this car is driving on a highway, at the side of which an Israeli tank is parked idly. The camera cuts back quickly to the interior of the car, in time to catch the poker-faced driver throwing the pit out, and then cuts back to the exterior where we saw the passing car and the parked tank, and in a moment of stupendous cinematic wonder and joy, the tank blows up and lands in bits and pieces of its debris on the highway. The car proceeds on the highway calmly – leaving the tank debris, the bewildered camera, and all of us mortals behind. Rarely in the history of cinema has a cinematic will to resist and subvert power so joyously dismantled the entire machinery of a state apparatus (colonial or otherwise) – by definition an institutional monopoly on violence.[3]

At the heart of Elia Suleiman's cinema dwells a dark humor, the frivolity of a pointed anger mutated into laughter, a crisis of mimesis (how and with what language can one speak of the despicable thievery of Zionism) uplifted to the creative core of a visual artistry.[4] What we witness in Elia Suleiman's cinema is the precise critical moment when the depth of tragedy mutates into the height of comedy, comedy meets absurdity, and then absurdity remembers the dark dread at the heart of its own memory of the terror it must, and cannot but, remember. Keeping the memory of the cruel past alive, out-foxing the clumsy occupier (all occupiers are clumsy, for they are, *ipso facto*, not at home), and holding a fire of hope, a ray of purposeful intelligence, for the future of Palestine is what holds the cinema of Elia Suleiman together, a cinema that is the magic of anodyne emotive motions conjugated in an endless succession of visual defiance of the metaphysical violence at the roots of any mimetic narrative of a colossal injustice. In the non-narrative lineage and visual staccatos of his cinema, Elia Suleiman has finally found a way of telling the Palestinian tale of dispossession and despair without interruption or denial, with a hope that speaks of hopelessness, with a laughter that hides the anger, a serious frivolity that overcomes the somber hilarity of robbing a people blind and terrorizing a people out of their homeland and then calling them violent and terrorist. Elia Suleiman's cinema is the revenge of joyous laughter on obscene mendacity.

That cultivated light-heartedness is definitive to Elia Suleiman's creative process. In one of his most perceptive comments about his own filmmaking techniques, he has said:

> I never really come to a film through the structure. I simply jot down notes and build a story through them. Then I compose tableaux. When I get a tableau that stands by itself, it becomes an image. Later, when you shoot, there are a lot of ever-present possibilities. I

write a very precisely structured script, but then I leave that work alone and start the process again. I want to avoid archiving images. I always want to make the creative process continue and not simply shoot what I've written on the set. Also, something else happens through the montage. In terms of narrative structure, it's because I see them in poetic montage. Even my shorts continue this process . . . *Chronicle of a Disappearance* was a document about the time that I shot it. For me, it was the silence before the storm. This one [*Divine Intervention*], which also follows some of the same individuals, shows all hell breaking loose.[5]

This purposeful frivolity is substitutional narrative, a manner of storytelling when all else has failed. Elia Suleiman does with his camera what the Palestinian fighters do with their mutilated bodies. They both find ways of telling their stories – one with exploded bodies, the other with disjointed staccatos of narrative stutters that magically mutate into coherent statements, with pitiless precision. As suicidal violence means denying the colonial state the very last (bodily) site of violence by a violence that out-explodes the institutionalized violence of the state, as Weber theorized it, disjointed narrative amounts to the discursive dismantling of that state, and of the violence that brought about and sustains it.

Frivolity is the noble version of obscenity, as obscenity is the degenerate version of frivolity. There is a correspondence between the degenerate obscenity of something that defies reason and sanity, and the ennobling frivolity that similarly defies the boundaries of reason and sanity – but from the graceful side of that disgraceful act. Consider the scene in Elia Suleiman's *Divine Intervention* when a tourist approaches an "Israeli" police officer and asks for directions to go to see the historic sites of Jerusalem. The "Israeli" officer has no clue where they are. He gets out of his driving seat, goes to the back of his truck, produces a blindfold Palestinian incarcerated in there, and asks him to tell the tourist where the Palestinian historic sites are. The Palestinian, blindfold and handcuffed, starts giving the woman directions, motioning with his head as to where she ought to go. Blindfold and handcuffed, unable to see or motion, the Palestinian (obviously) knows his homeland better than the "Israeli" police officer who has captured and incarcerated him on the charge of protesting against his claim that he (the "Israeli" police officer) owns that land and he (the Palestinian) does not. With that single sequence, Elia Suleiman has permanently incarcerated the term "Israel" inside the confining mandates of two

Ola Tabari (as Adan) in Elia Suleiman's *Chronicle of a Disappearance* (1996).

Elia Suleiman (as himself) in Elia Suleiman's *Chronicle of a Disappearance* (1996).

Elia Suleiman (as himself) with a Yasser Arafat balloon
in Elia Suleiman's *Divine Intervention* (2002).

Elia Suleiman, Cannes 2006, where he was a member of the jury.

critically compromising sets of double quotation marks. The term just sits there and no military machinery, no matter how powerful, no "Israeli" lobby, no matter how resourceful, can get it out. Stealing other people's homeland is obscene, occupying it and denying the thievery trespasses the limits of obscenity – and here is where logic and argument fails and frivolity (a handcuffed and blindfold guide telling a tourist where she needs to go while the gun-carrying colonial officer denies him the fact that that knowledge entails) prevails.

There is another short sequence in *Divine Intervention* that does a similarly compelling job, but this time by placing a question mark in front of "Israel." This is the famous staring-down scene, where ES is driving his car in a street, comes to a stop at a traffic light, and notices an "Israeli" settler coming to stop right next to him, hoisting the Israeli flag over his car. ES has the famous driver-side window of his car completely down, from which he is blasting out-loud Arabic pop music – from here ensues a staring-match between ES and his "Israeli" contender. The camera sides with ES and the audience roots for him – and he wins. The quotation mark remains permanently abiding by "Israel."

Generations of Zionist colonial settlements in Palestine have systematically and persistently dispossessed Palestinians of their homeland. Almost a century after the commencement of this act of colonial thievery, Europeans (Germans in particular) engage in a horrid act of unfathomable barbarity and murder millions of innocent Jews in one of the most savage acts of genocide in human history. But what did Palestinians have to do with that criminal act? Palestinians – Jewish, Christian, Muslim, or otherwise – have had an historical claim on Palestine long before and entirely independent of European colonial thieveries around the globe or savage acts of ethnic cleansing inside Europe itself. Jews are as much entitled to Palestine as Christians and Muslims – and all of them as Palestinians, not as Jews, Muslims, or Christians. The idea of an exclusively Jewish state in Palestine is as ludicrous in Palestine as that of an Islamic republic or a Christian empire. Palestine belongs to Palestinians – all of them – and no particular group of Palestinians has an exclusive right to the whole land, nor did they before a band of European colonial adventurers descended upon Palestine. It is the absurdity of that historical fact that remains definitive of the Palestinian predicament, and thus at the root of the national trauma sustaining the creative energy of artists such as Elia Suleiman.

The cinema of Elia Suleiman does not work reactively, however. It is proactive and emancipatory. Its language is not determined by the militant vulgarity of the occupiers of his homeland. He sets the discourse. The way Elia Suleiman's frivolity works is by creatively retrieving the forsaken layers of memory and re-arranging them stylistically as if with Tourette's syndrome, where the subconscious begins to speak its anxieties out loud, with no control. What I saw on the corner of 58th and Menachim Begin was a Tourette's syndrome of obscenities. The problem is not that the Zionists do not know that they have stolen a people's homeland. The problem is that *they do know it.* In fact they flaunt it. I once read in a detective story that the best place to hide a stolen item is in the police station. The Zionists re-stage their heist in the most famous street of the most famous city of the most notorious empire in the world. This is how they hide it. The miracle of Elia Suleiman's cinema is in his art of frivolously reformatting the layers of self-erasing memories so that instead of being concealed they are actively exposed – but exposed in a liberating and emancipatory, and not in a vindictive and self-victimizing, language, and that is precisely where Zionism has categorically failed to procreate its own kind of enemies.

As a project, Zionism failed not because the injustice it sought to address was not there. It was there. Generations and histories of European pogroms testify to a legitimate concern for the collective fate of European Jewry. Zionism failed because it sought to redress a grave historical injustice by perpetrating another injustice – and they thus turned Palestinians into the moral equivalents of the European Jewry – victims of a monumental act of injustice. It is that profound act of historical irony, of a people who should have remained the moral measure of truth and perseverance, because of the horrors that history had inflicted on them, turning around and becoming the victimizers of yet another people, that remains definitive to the Israeli–Palestinian predicament today, and is best captured in Avi Moghrabi's ingenious documentary, *Avenge but One of my Two Eyes* (2005).

The failure of reason to grasp the terror of that irony in art mutates into a radical reconsideration of form. The narrative destruction of form is the key factor in Elia Suleiman's aesthetic anti-formalism, a feature of his cinema that is as much eclectic and accidental to his history as it is actively cultivated in his art. In his own estimation, this is how Elia Suleiman formulates the nature of this eclectic aesthetics:

> I think that I have recently caught the thread of what it is that I should rely on to make a good image or a punch line to deliver a comic moment. You obviously gain experience in

trying to translate and express yourself both filmically and technically, though I still envy some of the shots I made in *Homage by Assassination* (1992), one of my earliest shorts. When it came to *Divine Intervention* I felt very confident in terms of expressing myself totally uncensored. So, in this film there is a minimalist choreography and static framing but also the appropriation of commercials. There is also obviously the action scene at the end of the film so I approached the film from a variety of angles.[6]

These are of course entirely *ex post facto* and fabricated narratives – mere reflections on telling a coherent story of an otherwise incoherent set of images, magically appearing coherent in the broken mirror of his manner of storytelling. Nevertheless, what Suleiman reveals here is the mechanics, not the dynamics, of his cinema.

In the dynamics of his kinetic vision, the peculiar character of Elia Suleiman's portrayal of *frivolity* is that it is neither satirical nor farcical. It does not harbor ridicule, nor does it ascribe asininity. It does not bank on inanities of conquest, nor does it expose the idiocy of those who have stolen his homeland. His frivolity operates on an entirely different register. It is first and foremost sardonic, bitter and biting, angry but subdued, mordant yet meandering, scornful but not in a defeated way. It is defiantly sarcastic, creatively derisive, joyously flamboyant. It is mannered, stylized, graceful. As the embodiment of this frivolity, ES, the central character at the heart of Elia Suleiman's films so far, is poised, seasoned, elegant, and somber, and yet he manages to be also curiously conscious of the audience he has invited to observe his frivolities. His is a frivolity with a tad of arrogance, a smidgen of condescension, a flair, a pride, a pleasure in posing – and yet there is something bitter in his sweetness, something dark in the light of his countenance, something imperceptibly angry in the playfulness of his stratagems, something inexplicably barren in the opacity of his eroticism.

In detecting these uplifting aspects of Elia Suleiman's cinema, he stands in sharp contrast to the banality of the later cinema of Steven Spielberg, most unbearably in his *Munich* (2005). This comparison is a lesson in how the primacy of a political agenda has a catalytic effect on the art it produces, while an emancipatory aesthetics opens up political venues unimagined before. The more over the years Elia Suleiman's cinema has become aesthetically elegant, sleek, graceful, and precise, the more Steven Spielberg's cinema over as many years has degenerated into a cliché-ridden, boring, and clumsy infomercial. In *Munich* in particular, Spielberg uses the most tired and old clichés in trying to humanize the Israeli terrorists by having them always portrayed at a dining table eating, joking, frolicking, and conversing (while getting ready to go to kill people). The problem with Spielberg's *Munich*, which *ipso facto* marks Elia Suleiman's superior sense of cinema, is that the Hollywood tycoon wants to have his cake and eat it too: both sending a gang of Israeli assassins to haunt and murder Palestinians with or without any connection to the Olympic event, and yet do it in a way that Golda Meir's presumed oracular statement stands tall and proud: "Every civilization finds it necessary to negotiate compromises with its own values." It does not matter whether Golda Meir did or did not say this (she did say that Palestinians do not exist). Spielberg wants her to have said that because that is where he wants to play – where Black September guerrillas are faceless terrorists and this gang of Israeli assassins are moral agents of a civilization doing dirty things against its own principles – pretty much the same way that the US military conducts its "war on terrorism" – which of course reveals the real purpose of Spielberg's *Munich*, a post–9/11 re-enactment of the Israeli assassins,' murdering of Palestinians in the 1970s by way of justifying the US criminal atrocities in Afghan and Iraqi torture chambers early in the twenty-first century. In openly calling for torturing people, Alan Dershowitz and Michael Ignatieff could not have agreed more with Spielberg's motto that "every civilization finds it necessary to negotiate compromises with its own values."[7]

Elia Suleiman's cinema, however, emerges from an entirely opposite set of sensibilities – finding emancipatory aesthetic solutions to otherwise debilitating political dead-ends. After a long and arduous early history, Palestinian cinema came to specific visual registers in the works of Michel Khleifi – to this day the most eloquent, imaginative, daring, and defiant vision that put the plight of Palestinians on the map of world cinema. Elia Suleiman, however, is the harbinger of a whole new generation of a far different vision of reality and how to convey it. As he emerges as one of the most mysteriously imaginative young filmmakers of his generation, the task of present and future critics is to keep it grounded in Palestine. The world of cinema will soon claim Elia Suleiman in the way the republic of letters has claimed Edward Said. The unique, unparalleled, and ingenious aesthetics of Elia Suleiman addresses and adds a new manner of seeing in Palestinian cinema. In other words, the more he becomes a globally celebrated filmmaker the more he will have universalized the particulars of Palestine. With the same speed that Steven Spielberg, once a young filmmaker of exquisite emotive power, is getting lost in the labyrinth of a lucrative but banal cinema, Elia Suleiman is sublimating his creative entanglement with the plight of his people into a cinema of universal appeal. To the same degree that a fanatical commitment to the Zionist (or any other unexamined) project has been instrumental in degenerating Spielberg's cinema to unabashed acts of propaganda for both Israel and the US militarism (from *Saving Private Ryan* in 1998 to *Munich* in 2005), Elia Suleiman's sublimation of his historical dispossession as a Palestinian in far more emancipatory aesthetic terms has become the harbinger of not just a superior art but also of a more ennobling politics.

To see the pain at the heart of that ennobling effect of Elia Suleiman's cinema, it is imperative to keep the thin fragility of his frivolity squarely in sight, lest it will feign formal mannerism and metaphysical certainty. The sardonic disposition of (Suleiman's cinematic) frivolity can collapse, lose its creative control, and expose the terror that is at its heart. In the course of an interview, the schizoid nucleus completely breaks down into nervous, terrifying, laughter:

> When Elia Suleiman brought his film *Divine Intervention* to Ramallah he found the Israeli soldiers had got there first. The entrance to the cinema had been bombed, the cashtill rifled, the Dolby stereo stolen. Storming the adjacent "house of culture," the soldiers proceeded to gun down a row of costumed mannequins and shoot holes in a canvas that hung on the wall. "They executed a painting," Suleiman says, before dissolving into giggles. "I thought that was so funny. I mean, it's depressing when you're there. I was in Ramallah only yesterday and I was completely devastated. But we all have our own mechanism to lift us up again. Yesterday was a nightmare. Today I'm laughing."[8]

In another interview, with Jason Wood, published in *Artificial Eye*, Elia Suleiman reports of his having screened *Divine Intervention* in Ramallah:

> I have actually just come back from a screening in Ramallah, which I think is one of the most memorable screenings and moments in my life. The people there are living a similar and much worse experience to that depicted in the film. They are privileged in that their laughter and angst is much more intense than that experienced by anyone anywhere else in the world. It is the only place in all the screenings that I have attended that the audience begins to clap at the exact moment that Manal's foot crosses the checkpoint; for them it is

a very intense and physical experience. When the tower falls they are in euphoria. I wrote this scene ten years ago inspired by a moment when Manal and I had a rendezvous to have a coffee in Jerusalem. She wanted to defy the checkpoint and a soldier pointed a rifle at her, she said go ahead and shoot, I'm crossing. They didn't shoot. She is not an actress; she is a journalist who told me many of the stories and incidents that you see in the film. Ninety per cent of the people that you see are non-actors. When I first asked her to be in the film her initial reaction was that I must have been joking.[9]

The catharsis is communal, liberating, counter-intuitive. Because Elia Suleiman's dark sense of frivolity (through a nervous laughter that finds a way into the moment of the absurd) works through an inventive retrieving of his people's collective memory, where the conniving subconscious speaks its obscenities out loud, then his sardonically sedated anger will remain the single most reliable energy charging the phantasmagoric fury of his art. It is towards a reading of the theatricality of that absurdity, and a mapping out of the way that that phantasmagoric fury works, that one must read Elia Suleiman's cinema and its root in Palestinian experiences.

IN PRAISE OF FRIVOLITY

Born in Nazareth on July 28 1960 and raised under Zionist occupation, Elia Suleiman grew up under Israeli political and cultural domination. His childhood and teenage years were replete with wars, occupations, expulsions, revolutions, massacres, massive refugee crises, betrayals, and corruptions; perhaps the most traumatic of them all was the 1982 massacre of Palestinians in Sabra and Shatila refugee camps – a massacre conducted by the principal Israeli ally in Lebanon, the Christian Phalangists, under the direct supervision of the Israeli general in charge of the Lebanese invasion, Ariel Sharon.[10] The world looked aghast at the Sabra and Shatila massacre of Palestinians. Jean Genet, among the first to visit the site of the horrid crime, captured the unrepresentability of the terror: "A photograph doesn't show the flies nor the thick white smell of death. It does not show how you must jump over bodies as you walk along from one corpse to the next."[11] This is just about the time that Elia Suleiman began his exilic life in the United States, reading and watching the US media distort this and every other world event to suit their collective interests. Frightening and forcing a people out of their homeland, cramming them up in dehumanizing slums of refugee camps all around their country, then unleashing a savage army to murder them en masse right there inside those refugee camps, and if they dared to utter a word or to pick up arms and defend themselves branding them vile, violent, and terrorist – that is the history of Zionism in Palestine in a nutshell, and that is the debilitating knot at the heart of the Palestinian national trauma, informing everything Palestinian artists and intellectuals have said and done, or not said and not done, over the last half-century.

Before he came to the US and as he was growing up in occupied Palestine, the world around Elia Suleiman was marked by the liberation of Algeria in 1962, offset by the failure of Ayatollah Khomeini in Iran to dethrone Mohammad Reza Shah Pahlavi in the June 1963 uprising. The cracking down on the 1963 rebellion strengthened the Shah and increased the power and presence of the US in the region – with Iran, Israel, and Turkey emerging as the main strategic cornerstones of the US regional interests in its Cold War with the USSR. Elia Suleiman was still a toddler when the Palestine Liberation Organization was founded in Cairo in 1964, and had just entered Israeli primary school when the June 1967 War took place, leading to the Israeli military occupation of the rest of Palestine. The Black September of 1970, in which thousands of Palestinians were massacred by the Jordanian King Hussein – who had requested help from Israel and the US in this royal endeavor – occasioned yet another massive forced migration of Palestinian refugees to Lebanon, and ushered Elia Suleiman into his teenage years, in the same year that Gamal Abd al-Nasser died of a heart attack, striking a major blow against the troubled cause of Arab nationalism. Three years later, the October 1973 War further isolated Palestinians trapped inside their own homeland, within the Israeli borders. In August 1976, the Lebanese Christian Phalangist forces, brandishing arms still bearing Israeli insignias, massacred thousands of Palestinian refugees living in the Tel al-Za'atar camp outside Beirut. Elia Suleiman was a rabble-rousing teenager growing up in Nazareth, when on November 19 and 20 1977, Egypt's President Anwar Sadat visited Israel – and thus the normalization of the relationship between the two states began, with the fate of millions of Palestinians in and out of their homeland left entirely to their own non-existent devices. Before Elia Suleiman's teenage years were over in Nazareth, the Israelis would move to occupy southern Lebanon, on 15 March 1978, as far as the River Litani, murder thousands of Lebanese and Palestinian civilians, and create an allied Christian army under Major

Saad Haddad.[12] As Elia Suleiman was becoming a young man, the Iranian Revolution of 1978–79 was a major moral boost for the wretched of the earth in the region, before it degenerated into a tyrannical theocracy and betrayed the hopes and aspirations of millions of Iranians who participated in it and even more people around the world who had wished it well. The life around Elia Suleiman's childhood and youthful memories was quite "nasty, brutish, and short."

During the 1980s, Elia Suleiman left his homeland first for Europe and then for the United States, where he spent twelve of his most formative years, between 1981 and 1993, in New York. Eight years of fratricida war between Iran and Iraq (1980–88) and then the first Gulf War (1990–91) began and ended Elia Suleiman's sojourn in the United States. Halfway through Elia Suleiman's time in the United States, the first Intifada (1987–93) commenced – a spontaneous act of popular uprising against the military occupation of Palestine by the Israeli forces and the systematic appropriation of land by colonial settlers (mostly from Brooklyn, NY). After enduring decades of savage violence, mass detentions, house demolitions, indiscriminate torture, and deportations, the Palestinians revolted as a nation, independent of their corrupt leadership. Meanwhile, Elia Suleiman was tucked away in the anonymity of his life in the United States, watching on US television his fellow Palestinians fighting the terror of the Israeli occupation of Palestine. A sense of kinetic distance will thus always characterize Elia Suleiman's cinema – segregated from the communal solidarity of Palestinians once by being born and raised inside "Israel" and then by living for more than a decade inside the United States, now the principal imperial hubris behind the Zionist occupation of Palestine – manipulating and abusing the post-Holocaust fears and anxieties of the Jewish community in the United States for its own imperial designs in the region.[13]

By the late 1980s, two paramount features defined Elia Suleiman's vision of Palestine – first, that its pain and suffering was inexplicable; and second, that this inexplicability was mediated by and integral to the layers of collective amnesia generated and sustained by the globalized obscenity of the US media. In his cinema, he will invert despair and duplicity, put the world to shame, and find a way out of the *cul-de-sac* of representing the unrepresentable.

INTRODUCTION TO THE END OF AN ARGUMENT (1990)

In the early 1990s, Elia Suleiman had lived in New York for about a decade. His very first film (co-directed with the Canadian-Lebanese filmmaker Jayce Salloum), *Muqaddimah li-Nihayat Jidal* (*Introduction to the End of an Argument*, 1990), was an inconspicuous announcement of a filmmaker who had things to say. Of the origin of his initial interest in filmmaking, Elia Suleiman once told me that it was rooted in his anger and frustration with the way Palestinians were being portrayed in not just the mass media, but in fact in the work of the most liberal-minded filmmakers – that his problem was in fact with narrative filmmaking:

> After being disgusted with . . . misrepresentations of the Palestinians, I decided to go and get my tools and equipment and learn something about how to defend this gut feeling. So I asked my brother who was teaching at Haifa University to get me theory books. He said come and take whatever you want . . . So I went and picked up all the film books that were collecting dust on the shelves and I started to read Godard for example and suddenly I felt that I was not a lonely voice, that I belonged to a sect of people who were rebellious against narrative structure as such, and that they were there in force and that I could belong, and I could nourish myself. So I started to read, and I didn't know who the heck Godard was, but I saw an utter and immediate affiliation with what he was saying. Godard, Bresson, Antonioni, I started reading all the interviews I could manage to get hold of and I started to see that there was another way of telling, that these people all stood on my side so I started reading and to replete myself with all this language and literature so that I could come back and . . . and out of that came something, years and years later, and I made the first work, which was *Introduction to the End of an Argument*. It was a counter-attack.[14]

A 45-minute gem of a docu-satirical pastiche that Suleiman and Salloum shot on video, *Introduction* is a mélange of footage from Hollywood films and American television shows and news programs, interspersed with cartoons – coming together to configure a menacing figure of "the Arab," systematically fabricated and demonized, precisely at a moment when Palestinians were being robbed of their homeland. The hilarity at the center of *Introduction* is spontaneous, snatched from the US mass media, effectively showing that whether they make movies in Hollywood or report what is happening in the world in the news, the ruling elite of the United States is a banal band of self-delusional entertainers, capable of inflicting unfathomable pain, suffering, and terror on the world and yet calling their own counterparts in the rest of the world terrorists. Through their successful collapse of news and entertainment, Suleiman and Salloum are able to expose the metaphoric musings that are the very alphabet of the US global charlatanism – using the misrepresentation of other people's noble struggles for freedom and dignity to construct an accurate representation of the pathology at the heart of imperial and colonial imagination.

What emerges from this Tourette's syndrome of visual and sound-clips is a new register on absurdity. The result is an uncanny mutation: the idea of "the Arab" as vile, violent, primitive, erotic, exotic, and ultimately evil is thus turned against itself. The *Introduction* is not only an example of what cultural critics call "problem of representation." It is also an examination of the psychopathology of those who are responsible for such representations. The film reverses the gaze by looking at the way American media look at the world. The paramount absurdity of that vision becomes its own undoing – not by analyzing it, but by merely (creatively) staging and framing it. What Salloum and Suleiman have done is simply (but ingeniously) clipping out the most absurd moments of a collective will to ridicule and demonize a people, framing them together, and thus turning them into a reflective mirror, projecting the image back to the image-maker, and thus exposing the deranged disposition of the propaganda machinery itself.

HOMAGE BY ASSASSINATION (1992)

It was not until the first Gulf War – commenced on August 2 1990 – that Elia Suleiman found his signature visual vocabulary of absurdism in his second short film. *Homage by Assassination* (1992) was part of *Harb el Khalij . . . wa Baad* (*The Gulf War, What Next?*, 1993), a collection of five short films commissioned by the BBC. Five Arab directors were asked to reflect on the first Gulf War (1990–91). Borhane Alaoui's *Black Night Eclipse* is the depiction of the predicament of a Lebanese filmmaker living in Paris baffled as to how to make a short film about the war. Nouri Bouzid's *It is Scheherazade They're Killing* shows a family feud in Tunisia as they watch the events of the war unfold. Mustapha Darkaoui's *The Silence* is a meditation on a theater and film group disheartened by the events in Iraq. Nejia Ben Mabrouk's

Research of Shaima traces the filmmaker as she looks for a girl whose face she has seen on television. And Elia Suleiman's *Homage by Assassination* is the story of a young filmmaker who is trying to write a script as the war rages. All these films begin and end foregrounding their own narrative devices – particularly the paralyzing fact of filming one's own predicament.

From *Homage by Assassination* forward, this self-consciousness of the storyteller becomes definitive to Elia Suleiman's cinema. Once I asked him to explain to me the origin of his narrative techniques, the way he puts stories together, and this is what he said:

> I can tell you one thing that I remember, because sometimes I don't have the right response to what eventually drove me to make films, and how. No education. No background. No cinephile. No film buff. No culture of cinema. Why film? . . . I can tell you one thing that is as close as possible to some memory that I have. I don't know where it comes from, because it's not from literature because I didn't read books when I was young. When I used to tell a story, when I was young, and it sort of developed very well in my teenage years, I knew very well how to plot it and how to narrate it, and it was true make-believe, sometimes from true stories, the mode of storytelling, I knew how to impress people. I knew how to make people cry, and I got into the act. I was not distant either, I wasn't just the hakawati, you know. Sometimes I was emotionally involved with whatever fiction I created and believed. Sometimes to make them laugh, and this I remember very well, I had the capacity to make people giggle very fast, I knew how to get that gag in the storytelling and I knew how to make them cry. This much I can tell you without any hesitation.[15]

This very self-consciousness has now become the staple of Elia Suleiman's cinema – whereby the medium itself becomes the key category in introspection. In *Homage*, Elia Suleiman depicts the solitary meditation of a man, Elia Suleiman (ES) himself, having sought refuge from the vulgarity of the US media coverage of the first Gulf War inside an almost barren apartment, while keeping his connection with the outside world with phone and fax, and through internet and television. There is an eerie sense of solitude about ES's presence in his apartment. He seems to recede into the inconspicuous domain of a spectator. He sees, hears, and knows everything – but no one sees, hears, or knows him. We see his silent and (to the outside world) invisible observations precisely at the moment that he is gathering his wits to register the meaning of war – who is murdering, who is suffering, who pays the price? He listens to Arabic music, he composes Arabic phrases on his desktop computer, he waits for faxes and phones, and he listens to his phone messages. What does it mean when a Jewish friend from Israel calls to share her worries about her relatives in Iraq?[16]

In *Homage by Assassination*, Elia Suleiman keeps the camera at a distance, registering the solitary vigilance of ES. Equally evident is his dark sense of humor, playing with the fact that he never speaks. A journalist is trying to get hold of him on the phone – if he did we would hear ES talk. We won't. ES's life is completely digitized. Even his romantic life: he is shown making a Xerox copy of and then faxing a bouquet of flowers to someone he loves. We hear a clock ticking in the apartment. We see ES standing in his kitchen staring at a kettle of water, waiting for it to boil. The water boils and spills over. He keeps staring at it. ES is an insomniac, an isolated spectator lost inside his computer. He is no longer in-the-world. His apartment is a cell, a chamber of pure (disembodied) intelligence. He, ES, the Palestinian, has become an icon, insolated, cybernated, paid homage to by assassination, assassinated by homage. He is a commercial break running loose, refusing to end, preventing the regular programming to resume. He is a commercial break becoming regular programming. *Homage by Assassination* is a highly stylized visualization of impotence in face of overpowering banality, an introverted look at the facile docility of power, its matter-of-factness, its indifference, its anonymity, its artificial intelligence. *Homage by Assassination* is Kafka's *Metamorphosis*, updated and postmodernized.

CHRONICLE OF A DISAPPEARANCE (1996)

At the dawn of 25 February 1994 – coinciding with Friday, 14 Ramadan, 1414, a Jewish American Zionist physician, Baruch Kappel Goldstein, passed through two Israeli army checkpoints around the al-Ibrahimi Mosque in Hebron and proceeded to murder as many Muslims as he could in a massive Friday prayer in one of the holiest months on the Islamic calendar. Since then he has become a Zionist hero, at whose grave there are annual pilgrimages and celebrations. His gravesite reads:

> Here lies the saint, Dr. Baruch Kappel Goldstein, blessed be the memory of the righteous and holy man, may the Lord avenge his blood, who devoted his soul to the Jews, Jewish

religion and Jewish land. His hands are innocent and his heart is pure. He was killed as a martyr of God on the 14th of Adar, Purim, in the year 5754.

In the year of the Hebron massacre, Elia Suleiman returned to Palestine and through a grant from the European Community worked towards the establishment of a Film and Media Center at Birzeit University. His first feature film, *Sijil Ikhtifa'* (*Chronicle of a Disappearance,* 1996), made after and about his return to Palestine, established him as a rising star in Palestinian cinema and won him the Luigi de Laurentis award for the best first film at the Venice Film Festival.

Chronicle is by far the most successful account of the disjointed memories of a generation of Palestinians growing up inside the Zionist occupation of their homeland. It is the story of a "return" that dismantles the very idea of return. Elia Suleiman goes back to Palestine after a sojourn in Europe and the United States. But what does that return mean exactly? Nothing. There is nothing to return to, there is nothing to return from. Time and space begin to collapse in Elia Suleiman's vision of his homeland and in its place a furious frivolity begins to take over. The result is a reflection on the texture of a manner of exile that no longer means anything – because there is no home to claim, because the world has in its entirety become Palestine.

Chronicle of a Disappearance refuses to submit to a consistent narrative (Palestinian or otherwise): it is a celebration of the vignette – of the intransigent transient, of the flamboyant fleeting moment – as the only solid claim to truth. It is a counter-narrative, a counter-dream – it refuses to tell (anything). It is a dream that resists a beginning, a middle, and an end. It is uttered in staccatos: fantastic, phantasmagoric, nonsensical, seductive.

In *Chronicle*, Elia Suleiman posits himself as a misfit insider. We see ES, the screen persona of Elia Suleiman himself, trying to give a talk on his cinema and the microphone beginning to act up. While the technician scrambles to fix it, he loses his audience, who are receiving incessant calls on their cellphones. The return of the misfit (filmmaker) questions both the departure and the return, ES having effectively never left Palestine, and thus having effectively never returned – thus dismantling the very idea of location and space, and with it the Israeli claim on having occupied it. The space is reclaimed visually, by virtue of filming, populating, and humoring it. But the spaces of Elia Suleiman, as best exemplified by the surreptitious camera looking over the shoulder of a bomb-maker, are always inconspicuous and displaced.

From *Chronicle* forward we note the singular significance of spatial and temporal rhythm in Suleiman's cinema – a rhythm that hinges on the centrality of silence in his sequences. Everything in Suleiman's cinema seems to work around silence and it's a peculiar kind of silence. His are not silent movies, but silence is integral to the choreography of his sequences. Silence punctuates and narrates his films. Once I asked him specifically about the significance of silence in his cinema:

> The fact is that I did not academically know, chronically know, what the silence did. I was calculating today how many silent films did I see in my life . . . Usually you would cut things out that you do not need to see. But I happen to be obsessive with the whole thing. You take the glass and you put it there and if you tell me there's an illusionary gap, sometimes I cannot even cohesively understand where that gap is. I want to open the door and I want to see the continuity of going outside . . . Of course I can tell you that intellectually that silence is very close to death, and maybe there is an unconscious insistence on my part that there is a death in every image that I see. There is that potentiality. There is also the fact that in silence there is a vacuum, and that this vacuum, this empty space, is the potentiality of filling the blank, which in turn raises the question of what is to be filled in the blank. In other words, not too much polluted rigor or speech or that which can be preachy to the spectator, and thus the spectator has that meditative capacity or role or space to actually fill in or participate with the image. This is not a strategy at all. I am saying that this potentially maybe there. I think that silence is also resistant to the passage of time passing, in a sense. You know, it somehow roots you in the present.[17]

WAR AND PEACE IN VESOUL (1997)

That ennobling sense of silence, and an overriding awareness of its both strategic and aesthetic necessity, is categorically absent in *War and Peace in Vesoul* (1997), a documentary that Elia Suleiman and the prominent Israeli filmmaker Amos Gitai shot together when they were both invited to attend a film festival in Vesoul, France. Half of the film is shot on the train from Paris to Vesoul and the rest on the site of the festival. Gitai is from Haifa and Suleiman from Nazareth – and much of the film is a conversation about their lives as an Israeli and a Palestinian. While the first half of the film is quite self-indulgent on part of both directors, who, tongue in cheek, cater to their liberal audience in Europe and the United States, the second part, when the press and the festival officials begin to demand positions from the two directors, exposes the political predictability of this liberal audience but also implicates the documentary itself.[18]

ARAB DREAM (1998)

Commissioned on the fiftieth anniversary of what the Zionists call their "War of Independence" (independence from whom?) and the Palestinians consider their catastrophe, Elia Suleiman's *Al-Hilm Al-Arabi* (*Arab Dream*, 1998) narrates the story of a Palestinian filmmaker revisiting Palestine. In a review of this film by Rotterdam Film Festival, someone observed:

> Is there a future with so much past? The Palestinian filmmaker Elia Suleiman goes in search of his past and possible future in occupied territory. Wherever he looks, he feels surrounded by images and places that have a political significance. Can a landscape be free of meaning, is there any point in striving for an approach that transcends all ideology?[19]

A young white student once asked Malcolm X, "What can I do?" to help the cause of the civil rights. "Nothing," responded Malcolm.[20] By the year 2000 and the end of *Arab Dream*, it was all but evident in Elia Suleiman's cinema that central to the predicament of the Palestinian narrative, as he saw it, was that it could never be told. The enormity of the thievery that Zionism had committed required a different manner of telling it.

CYBER-PALESTINE (2000)

The Second, or al-Aqsa, Intifada commenced on September 28 2000, after Ariel Sharon, at the head of a massive military force, stormed into al-Haram al-Sharif, proclaiming that it was part of "the eternal capital of Israel." Sharon intensified a second round of Palestinian uprising against the systematic occupation of their homeland, the criminal appropriation of their territories, and the ineptitude and corruption of the late Yasser Arafat's leadership. Following Sharon's visit, massive riots broke out around Jerusalem, in the course of which the Israeli armed forces yet again opened fire into the rows of protestors, killing, among others, the 12-year-old boy Muhammed al-Durra, whose brutal murder was captured on camera and broadcast around the world. Even the pictures of the innocent boy and his desperate father trying to hide behind a barrier failed to jolt the world into anything other than a perfunctory condemnation.

Premiered in the Directors' Fortnight at Cannes, and released at the commencement of the Second Intifada, Elia Suleiman's *Cyber-Palestine* (2000) is part of a quintet feature commissioned by the Bethlehem 2000 Project on the occasion of December 31 1999. *Cyber-Palestine* is an experimental film with a sardonic sense of despair: the story of Joseph and Mary, ordinary Palestinians living under a brutal colonial regime. As Joseph drives the pregnant Mary, now in labor, on his motorcycle to the hospital, the couple runs into myriad Israeli checkpoints. One Israeli officer asks Mary who the father of her child is. Joseph is infuriated. As the Israeli soldier beats him up, the scene is intercut with images of Intifada kids throwing stones and being shot at. Mary finally delivers her baby, sits at the computer, a key to her home at hand, searches for "Cyber-Palestine" on the Internet, and hits "home." She gets on her motorcycle, her baby on her back, her key in her hand, and heads home – to Palestine.

"Is there a place you call home?" I once asked Elia Suleiman in the course of a conversation in New York. "No," he said. "And how does that make you feel?" I wondered:

> Not so great . . . I would like to have all my books in one place, and I would like to have the familiarity, and I would like to have the dog that goes down the slope. I would like that very much, and I would like to have it at least as a base. But I don't see that possibility, and I am not the only one who feels that way, because I speak to many people who seem to have the same question, it seems to me that no one place is now sufficient for all the desires and the needs. I can see that, for example, Paris is enhancing me culturally, aesthetically and on many other levels as well. But I also need to be enhanced by things I don't get in Paris – blue sky, Arabic food. I want to hear Arabic, I want to be able to wake up in the morning with a particular smell of the sweat in the bed. I don't know how else to describe it. I want to get off the bed and I want to go extremely slowly and clumsily to the store on the corner and buy the Arabic paper and sit so lazily in the café and read it and not read it. I like to do that. And this very motto is a temporality by itself. I need this

temporality as the dance of my life. As of now, there is a place, it's not yet really credible, but it's in the experimental level. It's Beirut.[21]

DIVINE INTERVENTION (2002)

With *Yadun 'Ilahiyya* (*Divine Intervention*, 2002), which won him the prestigious Jury Prize at Cannes, among many other prizes at other festivals, Elia Suleiman emerged as one of the principal Palestinian filmmakers of his generation. His films were now featured in film festivals around the world.

Divine Intervention is a non-linear narrative about three characters: ES (Elia Suleiman), the woman he loves (Manal Khader), and his troubled father (Nayef Fahoum Daher). A young Palestinian living in Jerusalem loves a woman who lives in Ramallah. They meet at the Israeli military checkpoint, where their encounter is punctuated by the overwhelming power of the colonial officer occupying their homeland. His father, who lives in Jerusalem, is about to retire. Financially in trouble, he is forced to sell his car-repair business. He suddenly suffers a heart attack. He is taken to Jerusalem for treatment. His son has to take care of him. The Israeli creditors take the business from him and come to make an inventory of his belongings at home. The young man is plotting to see more of the woman he loves. He finally manages to sneak her into Jerusalem by distracting the soldiers with a red balloon with Yasser Arafat's face on it. There is a suggestion that they actually sleep together; and when they do, she leaves him sleeping in a bed in a fetal position, goes out to the street and casts a admonitory glance at a Palestinian collaborator, as the man's father dies, and she turns into a *fedai/ninja* – wreaking havoc on Israeli soldiers.

Divine Intervention was premiered in the New York Film Festival of 2002, at the very same festival that the US authorities denied Abbas Kiarostami a visa to come for the US premier of his *Ten* (2002). Elia Suleiman decided to and was able to attend. "There is an ugliness in the US today," I remember Elia Suleiman telling me in the course of a conversation in New York, "which is identical to what one sees in Israel."[22] The film then hit the US market on January 17 2003. Of *Divine Intervention*, Anthony Lane wrote in the *New Yorker*: "That isn't becoming to Elia Suleiman, who as both actor and director can conjure up unforced, gag-strung surrealism all his own, and who might like to think twice before evolving into the Jeff Koons of the Occupied Territories." Where is this place called "Occupied Territories"? Golda

Meir said Palestinians do not exist. American film critics follow suit and cannot even bring themselves to say "Palestine." As for Elia Suleiman becoming the Jeff Koons of "the Occupied Territories," the comparison can only hold if York, Pennsylvania, where the American kitsch, post-pop artist was born and raised, is invaded and occupied by the Chinese for half a century.

Paramount in Elia Suleiman's *Divine Intervention*, evident from the very first scene when he appears on screen and wills, by a mere pit of a fruit he is eating, to blow up an Israeli tank to smithereens, is his cinematic will to resist power. This rebellion begins with a radical defiance of time and narrative, a denial of placing truth inside a teleological tale.[23] His frivolous counter-narrative *ipso facto* resists the power of a singular story to show or tell any history – Palestinian or otherwise. *Divine Intervention* is at once ecstatic and fractured. Its episodic vignettes are connected not via a thematic unity or narrative trajectory, but through the relentless gaze of a defiant witness.

In the last scene of *Divine Intervention*, we see ES seated with his mother in the same spot in the kitchen as his father sat at the beginning of the film, although now it is not just a kettle that is boiling, but a big pot with its lid about to explode. I asked Elia Suleiman about this last scene when we had our conversation in October 2002:

> I can tell you what instigated it. Whenever I go to Nazareth, this is how all things begin with me, as flat and linear as you hear them. I sit with my mother on the sofa, always before lunch, and we have coffee and I hate this pressure cooker because it's very old and I am always begging her to buy another one and telling her I can bring her the best pressure cooker because I am always afraid that when she comes to touch it one day it's going to explode. Whenever it starts to make noise, and begins to escalate, I am always half-listening to her, and half-listening to the pressure cooker. I am always so happy when this happens. Sometimes I ask her, don't you think it's had enough? And she would tell me, no not yet, and it continues, and so there is that tension that I start to experience. I feel it's dangerous. This is the initial departure of an image like that. Then come the intellectual side of the image and the baggage of consuming so much of the culture and modernity that I live, that it can come to be what it can also mean in addition to what I just said. So it's not like I just put it in the film because of this initial suggestion. No, I put it in the film because of what you saw, because I wanted to actually signify that this could be lava exploding, but only after having gone through the film and seeing the beginning and the end, and having edited it . . .[24]

At the creative center of *Divine Intervention* is a cinematic will to resist power, and thus to violence, aesthetically sublated and yet palpably overriding the film, for "decolonization," as Frantz Fanon realized from the heat of the battle, "is always a violent phenomenon."[25]

THE END OF AN INTRODUCTION TO PALESTINIAN CINEMA

Perhaps the singular achievement of Elia Suleiman as a filmmaker is the dropping of a virtual, white, male European as the principal interlocutor of the Palestinian predicament – the presumption that unless "he" is convinced, the Palestinian dispossession has not happened. By refusing to succumb to a narrated past (a past predominantly fabricated by successive generations of Zionist propaganda now held by the self-delusional US media to be self-evident truth), a debilitating present (a present presided over by an obscene Israeli military machinery, ignorant of the violence it perpetrates on its own citizenry), or a sealed and foregone future (a future predicated on the same storyline), Elia Suleiman has effectively cut loose and let go of a white, male, European interlocutor at the presumed center of practically all hitherto failed attempts by Palestinians to convince the world as to what has happened to them. The world did not care – and the world was complicit in turning the victims of an obscene European colonial project into the bugbear of its own perturbed imagination – called "terrorism," while the Israelis perpetrated the gravest act of terrorism on earth. To a considerable and definitive degree, the non-linearity and anti-narrative disposition of Elia Suleiman's cinema are the effective outcome of this revolutionary breakdown of a mimetic crisis at the heart of Palestinian cinema. Elia Suleiman is the filmmaker of the future of Palestine, as Michel Khleifi is the chronicler of its present past – imperfect.

Beginning with *Introduction to the End of an Argument* (1990), Elia Suleiman studied carefully the absurdity that feeds the amnesia at the root of the propaganda machinery – chiefly stationed in the US mass media – that has categorically camouflaged a lie, fabricated a truth, and thus sold the historical thievery perpetrated on Palestinians as an act of emancipation for European Jewry – themselves the historical victims of European racism for centuries – from pogroms to the Holocaust. In *Homage by Assassination* (1992), Elia Suleiman discovered his self-conscious manner of storytelling, placing himself as a witness, very much like Naji al-

Ali's ingenious invention Hanzalah, at the center of his people's destiny.[26] By the time he made *Chronicle of a Disappearance* (1996), ES, Elia Suleiman's screen persona, had discovered the centrality of a syncopated sense of silence that sustained and informed all that needed to be told – giving an account of what had happened not just to the body of dispossessed Palestinians, but also to their meandering soul. When he made *Arab Dream* (1998), Elia Suleiman had once and for all retired the presumption of a white European male as the central interlocutor of the Palestinian catastrophe – and moved forward to tell the story of his people in a way that could no longer be denied, denigrated, or dismissed. By opting for an active dismantling of all teleological manners of storytelling, he disrupted all the stories that had ever been told – all resolutions, conclusions, certainties. He dismantled the very act of storytelling. From there, he went to *Cyber-Palestine* (2000) to claim a cyberspace where his homeland was (not) – and by the time he made *Divine Intervention* (2002), the fate of that homeland had become integral to a cinematic will to resist power, an aesthetic act of emancipation – where he could no longer be arrested, incarcerated, denied, denigrated, robbed. There is thus a lightness of purpose and practice in Elia Suleiman's dead-serious frivolity that flies in the face of trauma and tragedy, a flightiness that can no longer be captured, nailed, checkpointed, jailed, expelled, or called a terrorist. Even if ten million more people joined the "Salute to Israel Parade" in New York, Zionism would have miserably failed – and Elia Suleiman's cinema is the evidence of it.

Tomorrow, when Palestine is free: Elia Suleiman is already there.

Hanzalah keeping vigil – a witness to history.

NOTES

NOTES TO PREFACE

1 See Edward Said, *After the Last Sky: Palestinian Lives*. (New York: Columbia University Press, 1998).
2 John Berger's most famous book on visual art is *Ways of Seeing* (London: Penguin, 1990). For Jean Mohr's photographs on Palestine see ibid.
3 Amira Haas, "You can drive along and never see an Arab." *Haaretz*, January 23 2003.
4 Ibid.

NOTES TO CHAPTER 1

1 Israeli Military Order 101 was implemented on August 27 1967 and banned gatherings of people, as well as pictures, maps, and drawings of a political nature, and flags. It was stated that Israeli soldiers had the right to use any kind of force needed to carry out this order, including acting pre-emptively. Military Order 101 was amended on October 5 1981 with Military Order 938, which also made it illegal to listen to certain songs. On October 14 1983, the order was again amended and added recording, cinematography (including records and voices), and the broadcasting of films to its list of illegal activities with Military Order 1079. See *Israeli Military Orders in the Occupied West Bank 1967–1992*, Jerusalem Media and Communication Centre, 2nd edn. 1995, p. 15. For complete military order, see *http://muqtafi.birzeit.edu*, Military Order 101, p. 227.
2 Walid Khalidi, *All That Remains: The Palestinian Villages Occupied and Depopulated by Israel in 1948* (Washington, D.C.: Institute for Palestine Studies, 1992).
3 My own family house in Bethlehem, built in 1908, had its front entrance and surrounding walls bulldozed and destroyed by an Israeli army tank in 2001, with several bullets shot into the front door and kitchen windows. A few months later, across town, my mother's family house

suffered a similar fate when an Israeli missile was launched into the side of the house, driving a hole right through the bedroom wall into the house.

4 See "The Siege", *http://www.sakakini.org/siege/sakakini1.html*.

5 Israelis also carry blue cards. However, inside the identity cards of Palestinians with Israeli citizenship, it is clearly noted that they are "Arab" and therefore not Israeli Jews with full rights.

6 Checkpoints, a method of collective punishment, are points of control that circle every Palestinian town and village to prevent movement. Those Palestinians who are given permission to travel are typically delayed for hours at checkpoints, after which they may or may not be allowed to travel past a given checkpoint. All roads and the Palestinian living areas are controlled by a series of checkpoints.

7 Americans for a Safe Israel, press release on January 9 2003, (*http://www.afsi.org*).

8 Several sites featured a statement found on Frontpage.com (*http://www.frontpagemag.com/ Articles/ReadArticle.asp?ID=5738*).

9 This appeared on the website of a minor Israeli–American "folksinger". She goes on to talk about the doves that appeared on our poster, falsely stating that "in Palestinian culture, the doves flying in the foreground are not symbols of peace, but of the souls of 'martyrs' ascending to heaven." (*http://www.sandycash.com/jan22–2003.html*).

10 For me, the most meaningful part of curating the first Dreams of a Nation festival was working with the small group of volunteers who came together to make it all happen. The project had virtually no financial support or backing, little institutional support, and very few resources available to us. I especially extend my gratitude and admiration to Hamid Dabashi, Kamran Rastegar, Ahmed Issawi, Ghada Jiha, Kareem Fahim, and Golriz Dadedell for coming together to work on this project.

NOTES TO CHAPTER 2

1 This chapter is based on a lecture delivered at the Dreams of a Nation film festival held at Columbia University in January 2003. I would like to thank Hamid Dabashi for inviting me to deliver it and Neville Hoad for his comments on an earlier draft.

2 Amilcar Cabral, "National Liberation and Culture," in *Unity and Struggle, Speeches and Writings* (London: Heinemann, 1980), p. 140.

3 *Sunday Times*, London (15 June 1969).

4 Quoted in Cabral, "National Liberation and Culture."

5 See "Ramallah cultural centre destroyed by Israeli army," Agence France Press, April 13 2002, and Martin Merzer, "Israeli Soldiers Blamed for Vandalism Palestinian Venter for Arts Ransacked," *Miami Herald*, April 24 2002. [See also Annemarie Jacir's account of the same incident in her chapter in this volume. HD]

6 On the role of Palestinian literature, see the important collection edited and introduced by Salma Khadra Jayyusi, *Anthology of Modern Palestinian Literature* (New York: Columbia University Press, 1992). On Palestinian painting, see Kamal Boullata, *Istihdar al-makan: dirasah fi al-fann al-tashkili al-Filastini al-mu'asir* (Tunis: al-Munazzamah al-'Arabiyah lil-Tarbiyah wa-al-Thaqafah wa-al-'Ulum, 2000). See also his "Asim Abu Shaqra: The Artist's Eye and the Cactus Tree," *Journal of Palestine Studies*, vol. 30, no. 4 (Summer 2001): 68–82. On Palestinian theater inside

Israel, see Radi Shihadeh, *al-Masrah al-Filastini fi Filastin 48: bayna sira' al-baqa' wa-infisam al-huwiyyah* (Ramallah: Wizarat al-Thaqafah al-Filastiniyah, 1998). On Palestinian songs, see my "Liberating Songs: Palestine Put to Music," in *Popular Palestines: Cultures, Communities, and Transnational Circuits*, eds Ted Swedenburg and Rebecca Stein, (Durham, NC: Duke University Press, 2005), pp. 175–201.

7 Cabral, p. 143.

8 Mustafa Abu 'Ali and Hassan Abu Ghanimah, "Nash'at al-Sinama al-Filastiniyyah wa Ittijahatuha" ("The Establishment of Palestinian Cinema and its Orientation," in *Filastin fi al-Sinama*, eds Walid Shamit and Guy Hennebelle (Paris: al-Fajr, 1980), p. 19.

9 Abu 'Ali was recently honored (Fall 2003) at the Isma'iliyyah Film Festival for Short Films in Egypt.

10 Ibid., p. 21.

11 Ibid., pp. 21–2.

12 On such debates see Terry Eagleton, *The Ideology of the Aesthetic* (Oxford: Blackwell, 1990), and Martin Jay, *Marxism and Totality: The Invention of a Concept from Lukács to Habermas* (Berkeley: University of California Press, 1984).

13 Hawal's film includes dramatized scenes of the Palestinian exodus from Haifa.

14 "Hadith ma'Mustafa Abu 'Ali wa Hassan Abu Ghanimah" (interview with Mustafa Abu 'Ali and Hassan Abu Ghanimah), reproduced in *Filastin fi al-Sinama*, p. 26.

15 Elias Khouri, *Bab al-Shams* (Beirut: Dar al-Adab, 1998).

16 Edward Said, "Permission to Narrate," in Edward Said, *The Politics of Dispossession: The Struggle for Palestinian Self-Determination 1969–1994* (New York, Vintage, 1994) pp. 247–68.

17 I borrow the notion of "weapon of culture" from Amilcar Cabral's important notion of the "weapon of theory." See Amilcar Cabral, "The Weapon of Theory," in *Revolution in Guinea: Selected Texts by Amilcar Cabral* (New York: Monthly Review Press, 1972), (pp. 90–111).

18 Gilles Deleuze, "Grandeur du Yasser Arafat," interview with Deleuze conduced by the editor of *Revue d'études Palestiniennes* in September 1983, published in *Revue*, 10, (Winter 1984), and republished in *Revue*, 84, (Summer 2002): 5.

NOTES TO CHAPTER 3

1 Yannis Ritsos (1909–90). [HD]

2 That is, the end of the twentieth century. [HD]

NOTES TO CHAPTER 4

1 For a review of *Route 181* see my 'Journey Towards A Route in Common,' *Middle East Report*, 231 (Summer 2004): 46–47.

2 Benita Parry, 'Liberation Movements: Memories of the Future,' *Interventions*, vol. 1, no. 1 (1998): 45–51. Also, more recently: 'Liberation Theory: Variations on Themes of Marxism and Modernity,' in *Marxism, Modernity and Postcolonialism*, ed. Crystal Bartolovich and Neil Lazarus (Cambridge: Cambridge University Press, 2002).

3 Amilcar Cabral, "National Liberation & Culture," in *Return to the Source: Selected Speeches* (New York: Monthly Review Press, 1973), pp. 39–56 (p. 47).

4 Frantz Fanon, *The Wretched of the Earth* (org. 1965; London: Penguin, 2001), p. 165.

5 I have developed this notion in "Narrating Dispossession, Overcoming Exile: Reading Palestinian Literature." (forthcoming).

6 See the full text of Michel Khleifi's chapter in this volume.

7 Fanon, *Towards the African Revolution* (org. 1967; New York: Grove Press, 1988), p. 103.

8 Estimates go up to 472 villages. See the monumental work of Walid Khalidi, (HD) *All That Remains: The Palestinian Villages Occupied and Depopulated by Israel in 1948.* (Washington: Institute for Palestine Studies, 1992). For information about *Ma'loul*, which I use here, see pp. 346–8.

9 Sabri Jiryis, *The Arabs in Israel* (New York: Monthly Review Press, 1976), p. 85, p. 88. For an extensive discussion of the Absentees Property Law, on which my account is based, see pp. 83–89.

10 See Jiryis, Chapters 4 ("'Redeeming' the Land") and 5 ("'Liberating' the Land"). Jiryis also documents how the collective expulsion of Palestinians continued even after the establishment of Israel, up to as late as 1959. See also Nur Masalha, *A Land Without a People: Israel, Transfer and the Palestinians 1949–96* (London: Faber and Faber, 1997).

11 An excellent recent account of Israel's discrimination against its own Palestinian citizens, and its particularistic and exclusivist national formation, is given by Ahmad H. Sa'di, 'The Peculiarities of Israel's Democracy: Some Theoretical and Practical Implications for Jewish–Arab Relations,' *International Journal of Intercultural Relations*, 12 (2002): 119–133.

12 As Noam Chomsky argued, the main political objectives of the invasion were clear: to destroy the political power of the PLO and crush Palestinian aspirations for full national self-determination. See his meticulous and seminal *Fateful Triangle: The United States, Israel and the Palestinians* (New York: South End Press, 1999). An estimated 10,000–20,000 people were killed in the Israeli invasion of Lebanon.

13 Israel has established a separate educational system for its Palestinian citizens, and controls its curriculum policy, selection of teachers, and budgets. As Sami Khalil Mar'i has argued: "In short, the Arab education system is manipulated by Israel's hegemonic structure in order to serve its ideology, much more than it is intended to address the relevant economic, cultural, and social needs of the Arabs themselves in the present and in the future." ("The Future of Palestinian Arab Education in Israel," *Journal of Palestine Studies*, 14.2 (Winter 1985), 52–73, (p. 59)). See also his *Arab Education in Israel* (Syracuse, NY: Syracuse University Press, 1978).

14 This social custom dates back to the period of military rule under which Palestinians in Israel lived from 1948 to 1966. In that period, the laws curtailing Palestinian freedom of movement were suspended for a day on Independence Day, enabling Palestinians to revisit their destroyed towns and villages.

15 Jean Genet, *Prisoner of Love* (org. 1986; New York: New York Review of Books, 2003), p. 349.

16 Norman Geras, "Language, Truth and Justice,", New Left Review I/209 (January–February 1995): 110–135 (p. 110).

17 Edward Said, *The Question of Palestine* (New York: Vintage, 1992), pp. 56–114. In 'The Burdens of Interpretation and the Question of Palestine,' Said states: 'Everyone who looks into the question of Palestine is engaged in it, but how much better to be engaged openly on the side of justice and truth than to loiter on the margins, vainly seeking impartial solutions and

symmetrical frameworks . . . let me instead enjoin you to call justice justice and truth truth.' (*Journal of Palestine Studies*, vol. 16., no.1 (Autumn 1986): 29–37 (p. 37)

18 The Balfour Declaration was issued on November 2 1917 by British Foreign Minister Arthur James Balfour, promising the Zionist movement a home for the Jews in Palestine.

19 The massacre of Palestinians in Sabra and Shatila refugee camps took place after the expulsion of the PLO from Beirut between 16 and 18 September 1982 and was conducted by Maronite Phalangists under the eyes of their Israeli allies, who had total military command and control of the area. Up to 3,500 defenseless refugees were raped, tortured, and massacred. See Amnon Kapeliouk, *Sabra and Shatila: Inquiry into a Massacre* (Belmont, MA: Association of Arab–American University Graduates, 1984).

20 Edward Said, *After the Last Sky*, p. 149, p. 158.

21 Said, *The Politics of Dispossession*, p. 137.

22 See Joost R. Hiltermann, "Israel's Strategy to Break the Uprising," *Journal of Palestine Studies*, vol.19, no.2 (Winter 1990): pp. 87–98. Hiltermann details gross violations of human rights including collective punishments and assassinations.

23 Norman G. Finkelstein, *The Rise and Fall of Palestine: A Personal Account of the Intifada Years* (Minneapolis: University of Minnesota Press, 1996), p. 13.

24 George Habash, 'Taking Stock: An Interview with George Habash,' *Journal of Palestine Studies*, 28.1 (Autumn 1998): 86–101 (p. 93). Habash is founder and longtime leader of the Popular Front for the Liberation of Palestine.

25 Islah Jad, "From Saloons to the Popular Committees: Palestinian Women, 1919–1989," in *Intifada: Palestine at the Crossroads*, eds Jamal R. Nassar and Roger Heacock (New York: Praeger, 1990), pp. 125–42 (p. 135).

26 Eileen S. Kuttab, "Palestinian Women and the Intifada," *Arab Studies Quarterly* vol.15, no.2 (Spring 1993): 69–85 (p. 81). Also relevant is Rania Khoury, *Palestinian Women and the Intifada* (Bethlehem: International Centre of Bethlehem, 1995); and Joost R. Hiltermann, *Behind the Intifada: Labor and Women's Movements in the Occupied Territories* (Princeton: Princeton University Press, 1991). A good collection of essays on women is: *Palestinian Women of Gaza and the West Bank*, ed. Suha Sabbagh (Bloomington: Indiana University Press, 1998). On the Intifada in general, as well as the Nassar and Heacock collection, see *Intifada: The Palestinian Uprising Against Israeli Occupation*, eds. Zachary Lockman and Joel Beinin, (Washington DC: MERIP, 1989).

27 On the dynamic of the Intifada and the PLO's substitutionism, see the essays on Palestine in Gilbert Achcar, *Eastern Cauldron: Islam, Afghanistan, Palestine and Iraq in a Marxist Mirror* (New York: Monthly Review Press, 2004).

28 The enforcement of the *hijab* by Hamas in Gaza is only one example: see Rema Hammami, "Women, the Hijab, and the Intifada," *Middle East Report*, 164–5 (May–August 1990): 24–8.

29 Said, *After the Last Sky*, p. 38. [On the creative crisis of mimesis in Palestinian cinema see my Introduction. HD].

30 See Dina al-Jundi, "Interview with Michel Khleifi: I Dream of Achieving the Camera-Pen," *Al-Ufuq*, 303 (30 April 1990). (In Arabic.)

31 See *www.sindibad.co.uk*.

32 Peter Wollen, *Signs and Meaning in the Cinema* (Bloomington, IN: Indiana University Press, 1972), p. 48.

33 Khleifi's insistence on the centrality of women's liberation as part of the anti-colonial struggle is a founding preoccupation of his cinema, as *Fertile Memory* and *Wedding in Galilee* testify.

34 Edward Said, "The Morning After," in *Peace and Its Discontents* (New York: Vintage, 1996), pp. 7–20. See also Chomsky, *Fateful Triangle*, pp. 533–65.

NOTES TO CHAPTER 5

1 Lyotard, despite his skepticism about "metanarratives," endorsed the Persian Gulf War in 1990 in a collective manifesto published in *Liberation*, thus endorsing Bush's metanarrative of a "New World Order."

2 I am proposing here the term "post-Third-Worldist" to point to a move beyond the ideology of Third Worldism. Whereas the term "postcolonial" implies going beyond anticolonial nationalist theory and a movement beyond a specific point in history, post-Third-Worldism emphasizes "beyond" a certain ideology – Third World nationalism. See Ella Shohat, "Notes on the Post-Colonial," *Social Text*, vols. 31–32 (Spring 1992).

3 For more on the debate on "location" see, for example, Chandra Talpade Mohanty, "Feminist Encounters: Locating the Politics of Experience," *Copyright*, 1 (Fall 1987): 31; Michele Wallace, "The Politics of Location: Cinema/Theory/Literature/Ethnicity/Sexuality/Me," *Framework*, 36 (1989): 53; Lata Mani, "Multiple Mediations: Feminist Scholarship in the Age of Multi-national Reception," *Inscriptions*, 5 (1989): 4; Inderpal Grewal, "Autobiographic Subjects and Diasporic Locations: *Meatless Days* and *Borderlands*," and Caren Kaplan, "The Politics of Location as Transnational Feminist Practice," both in Inderpal Grewal and Caren Kaplan, *Scattered Hegemonies: Postmodernity and Transnational Feminist Practice* (Minneapolis: University of Minnesota Press, 1994).

4 See J.M. Blaut, *The Colonizer's Model of the World: Geographical Diffusionism and Eurocentric History* (New York and London: Guilford Press, 1993).

5 Chahine portrays Egyptian Jews, positively, as connected to the Socialists fighting for an equal and just Egyptian society, forced to evacuate Egypt fearing the Nazis' arrival, and thus immigrating to Palestine/Israel. Here the film structures point-of-view so that the Egyptian Jew views the clashes between Israelis and Palestinians together with Arabs from the Arab point of view; realizing that the rights of one people are obtained at the expense of another people, he returns to Egypt. The film thus distinguishes between Arab (Sephardi) Jews and European Jews, a distinction reinforced at the end of the film through the protagonist's arrival in the US and his encounter with Ashkenazi Hassidim, implicitly suggesting the distance between his Jewish–Egyptian friends (with whom he shares a similar culture) and European Jews. Such a representation, however, is rather rare in Arab fiction, resulting in the banning of the film by several Arab countries, even though it was approved by Palestinian organizations.

6 The critique of the U.S. must be seen in a context when Sadat was beginning his diplomatic negotiation with Israel, an act that was extremely unpopular in Egypt and the Arab world.

7 See Aijaz Ahmad, "Jameson's Rhetoric of Otherness and the National Allegory," *Social Text*, 17 (Fall 1987), 3–25, and Julianne Burton, "Marginal Cinemas," *Screen*, vol. 26, Numbers 3–4, May–August 1985).

8 See Benedict Anderson, *Imagined Communities: Reflections on the Origins and Spread of Nationalism*

(London: Verso, 1983, and E.J. Hobsbawm and Terence Ranger, eds., *The Invention of Tradition* (Cambridge: Cambridge University Press, 1983).

9 Pontecorvo recently (1991) returned to Algiers to make *Gillo Pontecorvo Returns to Algiers*, a film about the evolution of Algeria during the twenty-five years elapsed since *The Battle of Algiers* was filmed, and focusing on topics such as fundamentalism, the subordinate status of women, the veil, and so forth.

10 Anne McClintock, "No Longer in a Future Heaven: Women and Nationalism in South Africa," *Transition*, 51 (1991): 120.

11 For more on this issue see Ella Shohat, "*Wedding in Galilee*," *Middle East Report*, 154 (September–October 1988).

12 See Fatima Mernissi, *The Forgotten Queens of Islam*, translated by Mary Jo Lakeland (Minneapolis: University of Minnesota Press, 1993).

13 Caren Kaplan, "Deterritorializations: The Rewriting of Home and Exile in Western Feminist Discourse," *Cultural Critique*, 6 (Spring 1987): 198.

14 The friend in question is Ella Habiba Shohat. The letter in the film is based on my essay, "Sephardim in Israel: Zionism from the Standpoint of its Jewish Victims," *Social Text*, 19/29 (Fall 1988), and "Dislocated Identities: Reflections of an Arab Jew," *Movement Research: Performance Journal*, 5 (Fall/Winter 1992).

15 I further elaborate on the subject in "Gender and the Culture of Empire: Toward a Feminist Ethnography of the Cinema," *Quarterly Review of Film and Video*, 131 (Spring 1991), and in *Unthinking Eurocentrism: Multiculturalism and the Media* (with Robert Stam) (London: Routledge, 1994).

16 Or as the letter puts it: "This bloody war takes my daughters to the four corners of the world." The reference to the dispersion of family, as metonym and metaphor for the displacement of a people, is particularly ironic given that Zionist discourse itself has often imaged its own exiles from the four corners of the globe.

17 *Measures of Distance* in this sense goes against the tendency criticized by Hamid Naficy that turns nostalgia into a ritualized denial of history. See "The Poetics and Practice of Iranian Nostalgia in Exile," *Diaspora*, 3 (1992).

NOTES TO CHAPTER 6

1 See Hamid Naficy, *The Making of Exile Cultures: Iranian Television in Los Angeles* (Minneapolis: University of Minnesota Press, 1993).

2 See Hamid Naficy, *An Accented Cinema: Exilic and Diasporic Filmmaking* (Princeton, NJ: Princeton University Press, 2001).

3 See Naficy, *The Making of Exile Cultures*, pp. 17–19.

4 See ibid., pp. 58–60.

5 See Janet Gurkin Altman, *Epistolarity: Approaches to a* Form (Columbus, OH: Ohio State University Press, 1982) p. 4.

6 Among these are Frank Borzage's *A Farewell to Arms* (1933), William Wyler's *The Letter* (1940), Ernst Lubitsch's *The Shop Around the Corner* (1940), Henri-Georges Clouzot's *The Raven* (Le Corbeau, 1943), William Dieterle's *Love Letters* (1945), Max Ophuls's *Letter from an Unknown*

Woman (1948), Jacques Tati's *Jour de Fête* (1948), and Joseph L. Mankiewicz's *A Letter to Three Wives* (1948).

7 See Linda S. Kauffman, *Discourse of Desire: Gender, Genre, and Epistolary Fiction*, (Ithaca, NY: Cornell University Press, 1986) p. 38.

8 See Linda S. Kauffman, *Special Delivery: Epistolary Modes in Modern Fiction*, (Chicago: University of Chicago Press, 1992) p. 19.

9 See Roland Barthes, *S/Z: An Essay*, translated by Richard Miller (org. 1970; New York: Hill & Wang, 1974).

10 See Ella Shohat's own reference to this sequence in Elia Suleiman's film in her chapter in this volume. [HD].

11 See Ella Shohat and Robert Stam, *Unthinking Eurocentrism: Multiculturalism and the Media* (London: Routledge, 1994), p. 319.

12 Compare Naficy's comments about Mona Hatoum's *Measures of Distance* (1988) with those of Ella Shohat in this volume. [HD].

13 See Jacques Derrida, *The Post Card: From Socrates to Freud and Beyond*, translated by Alan Bass (Chicago: University of Chicago Press, 1980).

14 See Hamid Naficy, "History, Memory, and Film: Voices from Inside Lebanon," *Jusur*, vol. 1, no. 3 (1987): 95–102.

15 Kauffman, *Special Delivery*, p. 54.

16 If Masri and Chamoun's *Wild Flowers: Women of South Lebanon* is in the expansive mode, their earlier film, *Under the Rubble* (1983), about the siege of Lebanon, including the harrowing massacre of Palestinians at the Sabra and Shatila refugee camps, is in the claustrophobic mode. While the latter highlights the indigent, violent, and besieged existence of Palestinians, the former, filmed in an equally bad situation of foreign invasion, emphasizes resistance and hope. The filmmakers told me that although there was no dearth of mutilated and dead bodies, they decided not to show them in *Wild Flowers* so as to enhance the mood of hope and expansion. They chose to concentrate on openness of space, mountains, and popular music instead of on closed spaces, death, and silence. As such these two exilic filmmakers have consciously played with both the claustrophobic and the expansive inscription of time–space configuration (chronotopes) in their films.

17 See Hamid Naficy, "Making Films with an Accent: Iranian Emigré Cinema," *Framework*, vol. 43, no. 2 (Fall 2002): 15–41.

NOTES TO CHAPTER 7

1 "Jordan First" was a government-sponsored "public-interest or public-awareness media campaign," which aimed at persuading the Jordanian population that Jordan ought to rank first in the hierarchy of their loyalties. The campaign was launched in the wake of the US preparations for war on Iraq, as Jordan was and remains one of the most important bases for the US army and intelligence services for access to Iraq. The campaign also came in the wake of severe clashes with dissenting Islamist groups, and a crackdown by the Jordanian government. It was aimed mostly at the population of Palestinian origin, which represents the majority in the country (up to 60 per cent) and the massive population of Iraqi exiles that

had flocked to Jordan throughout Saddam's rule, particularly after the outbreak of the first Gulf War. For the Palestinian population, "Jordan First" echoed "Gaza and Jericho First," the slogan launched by the Palestinian delegation negotiating for what later came to be known as the "Oslo Accords 2." The billboards propagating this slogan were pasted in the streets, on buses, and in a number of public spaces, depicting everyday citizens of all ages, from different areas (urban and rural) and of different classes, with blissful expressions on their faces, sometimes in the company of the monarch. In some sense the message to Jordanians of Palestinian descent was simple: Jordan has been good to you, you ought to recognize that. It also appealed to Palestinians living in Jordan who harbored hopes of going back one day to Palestine (i. e., specifically the inhabitants of refugee camps) that their own leadership had signed the Oslo Accords, which promised to betray the right of return. Nizar Hassan is here deriding the Palestinian leadership that seems systematically to betray its poorest populations and has surrendered the rights of return of millions of displaced Palestinians. He is also deriding internecine Arab conflicts, and how fledgling regimes without the legitimacy of real popular support resort to bright and shining advertising campaigns – concocted in Dubai it was rumored – in order to "secure" consent from its population. As soon as the war broke out the campaign was stopped, and all its traces removed. [HD]

NOTES TO CHAPTER 8

1 Gilles Deleuze, *L'image-temps* (Paris: Editions de Minuit, 1985), p. 288.

NOTES TO CHAPTER 9

1 On May 19 2004, the BBC reported that "Israelis fire on crowds in Gaza: dozens of injured were carried to hospital. Israeli troops have opened fire during a protest by Palestinian demonstrators in the town of Rafah in southern Gaza. At least ten people were killed and sixty injured, though some reports put the number of casualties higher." See *http://news.bbc.co.uk/1/ hi/world/middle_east/3728681.stm*. On the very day that this obscene parade was in progress in New York, Israeli Justice Minister Yosef Lapid infuriated his cabinet colleagues by saying the Israeli army offensive in Gaza reminded him of his own family's horrors in World War II. He said that "a TV picture of an elderly Palestinian woman in the rubble reminded him of his grandmother." Prime Minister Ariel Sharon immediately reprimanded Mr. Lapid for the comparison of Rafah to the Holocaust. See BBC, "Gaza political storm hits Israel," in *http:// news.bbc.co.uk/1/hi/world/middle_east/3740649.stm*.

2 Rachel Corrie was a courageous young peace activist from Seattle who was murdered (crushed under a bulldozer) on March 16 2003 by the Israelis while trying to protest the destruction of Palestinian homes in Rafah. In April 2005, Alan Rickman directed a play, *My Name is Rachel Corrie*, at London's Royal Court Theatre, commemorating her life. The subsequent staging of the same play in New York, initially scheduled at the New York Theater Workshop, was abruptly cancelled. No uproar over censorship and freedom of expression was heard anywhere in the world. If anyone dared to utter a word against the terrorizing power of censorship that

Zionists had in commanding the cancellation of a play altogether, they would be immediately branded anti-American, anti-Israeli, anti-Semitic, and of course by definition pro-terrorist. For a critical exposé on the political abuse of branding people anti-Semitic see the extraordinary work of Norman G. Finkelstein, *Beyond Chutzpah: On the Misuse of Anti-Semitism and the Abuse of History* (Berkeley, CA: University of California Press, 2005). The fact that the curse of anti-Semitism is abused by Zionists to silence their critics, however, does not mean that horrid acts of anti-Semitism do not continue to be perpetrated throughout the world, not just in the US and Europe, but also in much of the Arab and the Muslim world. While in the US and Europe, where anti-Semitism was invented, the classical case of anti-Semitism has now shifted its principal focal point away from Jews and directs it towards Muslims, in much of the Arab and Muslim world the legitimate criticism of the atrocities of the apartheid state of Israel often degenerates into the vilest forms of anti-Jewish sentiments. The abuse of the anti-Semitism charge by the US-based Zionists in particular, as Norman Finkelstein has aptly demonstrated, muddies the water, discredits the charge, and thus, while categorically failing to silence the legitimate criticism of the racist state of Israel, lets many actual anti-Semites easily off the hook.

3 "The state," writes Max Weber in his classic essay "Politics as a Vocation," "is considered the sole source of the 'right' to use violence." In another similar formulation, Weber specifies "the state is a relation of men dominating men, a relation supported by means of legitimate (i. e., considered to be legitimate) violence." (Max Weber, "Politics as a Vocation," in *From Max Weber: Essays in Sociology*, eds. Hans Gerth and C. Wright Mills, (Oxford: Oxford University Press, 1946), p. 78.)

4 This crisis of mimesis can lead, and has led, to a variety of creative solutions. Hany Abu Assad's *Ford Transit* (2000) operates through a cross-feeding of documentary and dramatization; Michel Khleifi and Eyal Sivan's *Road 181* (2003) works through a creative collaboration between a Palestinian and an Israeli filmmaker; and Avi Moghrabi's extraordinary *Avenge but One of my Two Eyes* ("Nekam Achat Mishtey Eynay," 2005), via the ingenious act of a noble Israeli filmmaker assuming the double role of both a Jewish witness and a Palestinian victim, whereby bringing the moral authority of the Jewish suffering throughout the ages to become an eyewitness to the contemporary Palestinian predicament (in this respect, Avi Moghrabi becomes the moral equivalent of the extraordinary figure of Naji al-Ali's Hanzalah – a Jewish witness to Palestinian suffering). This crisis of mimesis is usually resolved via a creative act of cross-metaphorizing two sets of cognitively similar but politically estranged metaphors.

5 Conversation with Steve Erickson of indieWIRE. See *http://www.indiewire.com/people/people_030115elia.html*.

6 Conversation with Jason Wood in *Kamera*. See *http://www.kamera.co.uk/interviews/elia_suleiman.html*.

7 For the case that Alan Dershowitz makes for torturing people read Chapter 4 of his *Why Terrorism Works: Understanding the Threat, Responding to the Challenge* (New Haven, CT: Yale University Press, 2003); for an endorsement of the same argument, with added zeal and specific enthusiasm see Michael Ignatieff's *The Lesser Evil: Political Ethics in an Age of Terror* (Princeton, NJ: Princeton University Press, 2004).

8 Xan Brooks, "When we started shooting, so did they," *Guardian*, January 13 2003. See *http://film.guardian.co.uk/interview/interviewpages/0,6737,873837,00.html*.

9 See *http://www.artificial-eye.com/video/ART239/inter.html*.

10 For a harrowing account of the Sabra and Shatila massacre and the role of the Israeli army in it see the Israeli journalist Amnon Kapeliouk's *Sabra and Shatila: Inquiry into a Massacre* (org. 1982). "[T]here is no confusion about who was responsible for the massacre. Israel's very own internal inquiry, the Kahan commission, stated that Ariel Sharon, then defense minister, bore 'personal responsibility' for the atrocities inside the camps." Katharine Viner, "Despair as usual for Palestinians," *Guardian*, February 7 2001. See *http://www.guardian.co.uk/israel/Story/0,2763,434655,00.html.*

11 See Jean Genet, "Four Hours in Shatila," *Journal of Palestine Studies*, vol. 12, no. 3 (Spring 1983): 4–5.

12 The prominent Palestinian poet Mahmud Darwish later immortalized the terror of the second major Israeli invasion of Lebanon, which was launched in 1982, in one of his masterpieces, *Memory for Forgetfulness: August, Beirut, 1982* (Berkeley, CA: University of California Press, 1995).

13 It is imperative to realize that the conspiratorial anti-Semitic assumption that US foreign policy is determined by the Jewish lobby is in fact the reverse of what actually happens. It is not the Jewish lobby (a figment of anti-Semitic imagination) that controls US foreign policy, but US imperial policy that manipulates the legitimate post-Holocaust anxieties of the Jewish community for its own illegitimate purposes. The publication of John Mearsheimer and Stephen Walt's essay, "The Israel Lobby," *London Review of Books* (vol 28, no. 6, March 23 2006), and its extended edition on the Harvard University web page (*http://ksgnotes1.harvard.edu/Research/wpaper.nsf/rwp/RWP06–011*) was of course a landmark event in showing the categorical failure of Zionism in fooling the world with their own self-delusional fantasies. From the very heart of the American power elite and with no connection to any Palestinian, Arab, or Muslim sentiment, Mearsheimer and Walt exposed the half-century-long lie that the pro-Israel lobby had sold American people. Mearsheimer and Walt's open recognition and evident frustration with the Zionist lobby, however, does not mean that they are correct in their categorical blaming of this lobby for the US foreign policy. For an excellent rebuttal to Mearsheimer and Walt's essay, see Joseph Massad's "Blaming the Lobby," in *al-Ahram* (23–29 March 2006); for a similar challenge to Mearsheimer and Walt's position see also Noam Chomsky, "Israel Lobby?" in *Znet* (March 28 2006). The US imperial interest around the globe pre-dates and will outlast the factual evidence of this particular brand of power-mongering, in which Israel possesses a position no more or less glorified than Pakistan, Tajikistan, or Saudi Arabia. The Zionist lobby is exceedingly powerful in the US, but the US global imperialism is not reducible to such specific interests. The Israeli Likudniks and the US neo-cons have now come together and mutated into a third project for global domination that is reducible to neither. This project is neither historically Zionist nor classically conservative. It is a brand new ideology of global domination that recruits freely from the ranks of Jews, Christians, Muslims, and plain old agnostics alike. If Paul Wolfowitz and Bernard Lewis are Jewish, Samuel Huntington and Francis Fukuyama are not – while Fuad Ajami and Azar Nafisi, two lackeys of Paul Wolfowitz and Bernard Lewis, are Shi'i Muslims, one from Lebanon and the other from Iran. Add to them Salman Rushdie, Dinesh D'Souza, and Irshad Manji, and you have a constellation of vulgar neo-cons who are united in nothing but their collective services to US imperial warmongering. The collective victims of this new imperial ideology are not just Palestinians, Iraqis, Afghans, possibly Iranians, and most certainly the increasing number of poor Americans whose dead bodies were floating in the flooded streets of New Orleans in the aftermath of Hurricane

Katrina. Israeli mothers suffering the death of their children are the equal victims of this global warmongering done in part in the name of protecting them from Palestinian violence.

14 From an interview I conducted with Elia Suleiman in New York in October 2002.
15 From an interview I conducted with Elia Suleiman in New York in October 2002.
16 See Ella Shohat's reflections on this scene in her chapter in this book. She is that Jewish friend.
17 From an interview I conducted with Elia Suleiman in New York in October 2002.
18 In the course of a public conversation between Elia Suleiman and me in October 2005 at New York University, he disowned this film and said he had nothing to do with its production.
19 See *http://www.filmfestivalrotterdam.com/en/film/3971.html*.
20 Malcolm X, *Autobiography of Malcolm X: As Told to Alex Haley*. (New York: Ballantine Books, 1964), p. 286. Later Malcolm X regretted this dismissive answer: *Autobiography of Malcolm X*, p. 376.
21 From an interview I conducted with Elia Suleiman in New York in October 2002.
22 From an interview I conducted with Elia Suleiman in New York in October 2002.
23 For a detailed discussion of this relationship see my *Truth and Narrative: The Untimely Thoughts of Ayn al-Qudat al-Hamadhani*. (London: Curzon, 1996).
24 From an interview I conducted with Elia Suleiman in New York in October 2002.
25 Frantz Fanon, *The Wretched of the Earth* (org. 1965, New York: Grove Press, 1963), p. 35.
26 Naji al-Ali (1936–87) was a globally celebrated Palestinian cartoonist, and Hanzalah his principal creation. He was murdered by an assassin in London.

NOTES TO A SELECTED FILMOGRAPHY

1 The film was *Kiss in the Desert* (*Qibla fi al-Sahra*). See Lama's biography in Taysir Khalaf, *Dalil al-Film al-Filastini (1935–2000)* (*A Guide to Palestinian Film, 1935–2000*) (Doha: Arab Screen Independent Film Festival 2001), p. 103.

LIST OF CONTRIBUTORS

Bashir Abu-Manneh is Assistant Professor of English at Barnard College, Columbia University, New York. His most recent essay is "The Illusions of Empire" (*Monthly Review*, June 2004).

Taoufiq bin Amor is a linguist, musician and playwright who teaches Arabic at Columbia University. He received a Ph.D. in linguistics from the University of Tunis in 1991. Among his publications are a play, *al'amira anna'ima*, a textbook, *A Beginners' Course in Tunisian Arabic*, and a composition manual.

Hamid Dabashi is Hagop Kevorkian Professor of Iranian Studies and Comparative Literature at Columbia University and the author of, among other books, *Close-Up: Iranian Cinema, Past, Present, Future* (Verso, 2002). He is the founder of Dreams of a Nation: A Palestinian Film Project.

Nizar Hassan is one of the most distinguished contemporary Palestinian documentary filmmakers. He has written, produced, and directed a number of documentaries, several of which have been featured in international festivals. His most recent film is *Ijtiyah* (*Invasion*, 2003).

Annemarie Jacir is a filmmaker, poet, and activist. She worked in the film industry in Los Angeles before returning to school to obtain her masters degree in film at

Columbia University. Jacir has taught at Columbia, Barnard College, and Birzeit University. Her most recent film, *Like Twenty Impossibles* (2003), premiered in Cannes and has won numerous awards at international festivals. Jacir is named in *Filmmaker* magazine as one of the "25 New Faces of Independent Film." She is a founding member and chief curator of Dreams of a Nation: A Palestinian Film Project.

Michel Khleifi is a pioneering figure in contemporary Palestinian cinema. His feature films and documentaries, including *Fertile Memory* (1980) and *Wedding in Galilee* (1987), brought global attention to Palestinian cinema.

Joseph Massad teaches modern Arab politics and intellectual history at Columbia University. He is author of *Colonial Effects: The Making of National Identity in Jordan* (Columbia University Press, 2001) and *Desiring Arabs* (forthcoming from Harvard University Press).

Hamid Naficy is Nina J. Cullinan Chair in Art and Art History at Rice University and the author of, among other books, *An Accented Cinema: Exilic and Diasporic Filmmaking* (Princeton University Press, 2001).

Omar al-Qattan is a British–Palestinian filmmaker who has directed several documentary films, including *Dreams and Silence* (1991), and produced several other features and documentaries, including Michel Khleifi's *Tale of the Three Jewels* (1995), *Forbidden Marriages in the Holy Land* (1995), and *Route 181* (2003, co-directed with Eyal Sivan). He is the director of the Culture and Science Program at the A.M. Qattan Foundation, a wide-ranging program of grants and prizes in various artistic fields.

Kamran Rastegar is Lecturer in Arabic and Persian at the University of Edinburgh. He is a founding member of the Dreams of a Nation project, and researches modern literary and visual productions of Iran and the Arab world.

Edward W. Said (1935–2003) was University Professor at Columbia University in New York, and the author of numerous books, among them *Orientalism* (Vintage, 1979), and *Culture and Imperialism* (Vintage, 1994).

Ella Shohat is Professor of Cultural Studies at New York University. Her award-winning publications include *Israeli Cinema: East/West and the Politics of Representation, Unthinking Eurocentrism* (co-authored with Robert Stam), *Dangerous Liaisons: Gender, Nation and Postcolonial Perspectives* (co-edited), *Talking Visions: Multicultural Feminism in a Transnational Age, Forbidden Reminiscences*, and *Multiculturalism, Postcoloniality and Transnational Media* (co-edited). *The Culture Wars: A Debate in Translation* (co-authored with Robert Stam) will soon be published by NYU Press. Her writing has been translated into several languages, including French, Spanish, Portuguese, Arabic, Hebrew, German, Polish, and Turkish.

A SELECTED FILMOGRAPHY OF PALESTINIAN CINEMA (1927–2004)

The history of cinema begins with an early reference to Palestine – the Holy Land is an early subject of the cinematic imagination, just as it had provided fodder for traveling photographers and illustrators over the course of the nineteenth century. An early Lumière film shows a gate to the Old City of Jerusalem, a candid window that captures the diverse urban scene of that city around the turn of the century. Yet, the record of filmmaking by Palestinians themselves is only faintly inscribed within the annals of "world cinema." This is despite the fact that the "first Arab narrative film"[1] was directed in 1927 by Ibrahim Lama, a Chilean-born Palestinian who worked in the early Egyptian film industry.

The present filmography is an attempt to bring the rich legacy of engagements with this medium by Palestinian filmmakers to the attention of an English-reading audience. It must be said that to produce a filmography with aspirations of comprehensiveness has been a difficult task, given the contours of the fragmentation of Palestinian society and the erasures and dispossessions that have characterized the experience of post-1948 Palestinians.

It is, thus, worthy of note that at least three significant attempts have been made by cultural historians from the Arab world to collect and register works by Palestinian filmmakers in a comprehensive manner – these efforts have provided a foundation upon which the present filmography has been assembled. They are the filmographies provided in *al-Sinama wa al-Qadiyya al-Filastiniyyah* (*Cinema and the Palestinian Issue*), by Hussein al-'Awdat (Damascus: al-Ahali Li al-Tabi'a wa al-Nashr wa al-Tawzi', 1987) and *al-Sinama al-Filastiniyyah fi al-Qarn al-'Ashrin* (*Palestinian Cinema in the Twentieth Century*), by Bashar Ibrahem (Damascus: The National Organization for Cinema, the Syrian Ministry of Culture, 2001), and *Dalil al-Film al-Filastini* (*1935–2000*) (*A Guide to Palestinian Cinema* (1935–2000)) by Taysir Khalaf (Doha: Arab Screen Independent Film Festival, 2001). Without the careful work of these scholars it would be unlikely that, for example, the pre-1948 films of Ibrahim Hasan Serhan would have been known to me, nor would the wide range of productions carried out by various Palestinian resistance groups in Jordan and Lebanon in the 1960s–80s be as fully mapped out as they have been. However, the latter issue raises one of the more difficult questions for the compiler of this sort of filmography – how to define "Palestinian cinema?"

While the primary measure no doubt would be to limit such a term to works by Palestinians of all backgrounds – those in pre- and post-1948 boundaries of Palestine, those refugees residing in surrounding areas, and those who constitute the global diaspora of Palestinians – the question is more difficult to contend with when looking at the work of the many cultural organizations allied with Palestinian factions. In the lists available of films produced in this context, the national origins of filmmakers have not featured prominently. Committed Arab filmmakers of various national origins were drawn – particularly in the 1970s, and particularly in Lebanon – to join with Palestinian resistance factions (especially nationalist and leftist groups such as the Popular Front for the Liberation of Palestine). In these cases, it has seemed most sensible to me to include these works on the basis of their being produced within the aegis of a Palestinian organization. This exception has applied to, at best, only a handful of filmmakers listed in this filmography, and has only included their works with Palestinian organizations – an example would be the inclusion of the Lebanese filmmaker Jocelyn Saab's *Safina al-Manfa* (*Ship of Exile*, 1982, produced by the Palestinian Da'ira al-Thaqafah wa al-I'lam) but not her many other films which are French and/or Lebanese productions. Such entries are distinguished with an asterisk (*) before the name of the filmmaker.

A second challenge has been to balance the available translations and transliterations of film titles and names against scholarly standards. In many cases, films have appeared in festival listings or press accounts with varying translations of titles. I have in most cases resorted to literal translations of titles, with only some exceptions given to films that have been officially released with different Arabic and English titles. The transliteration of names also reflects a pragmatic approach, accounting for common spellings that have been offered by filmmakers themselves when they have come to my attention.

Despite the shortcomings such compromises may have led to, it is my hope that the following filmography will nonetheless serve the purpose of advancing research into the history of Palestinian cinema, as well as informing the reader of the remarkable expansion of this field even over the past several years.

Abbas, Hiam
Le Pain ("Bread," 2002)
La Danse éternelle ("The Eternal Dance," 2002)

Abdelhadi, Walid
Nour's Dream (2006)

Abdelrahman, Firas
Rachel's War (2003)

Abu 'Ali, Khadija
Atfal, wa Lakin ("Children, But . . ." 1981)

Abu 'Ali, Mustafa
La li al-Hal al-Silmi ("No to Peaceful Solution," 1968)
Bi al-Ruh, Bi al-Dam ("With our Souls, With our Blood," 1971)
'Adwan Sahyuni ("The Zionist Assaults," 1972)
al-Arqub ("The Achilles Heel," 1972)
Mashahid min al-Ihtilal fi Ghazeh ("Scenes from the Occupation of Gaza," 1973)
Laysa Lahum Wujud ("They Do Not Exist," 1974)
'Ala Tariq al-Nasr ("On The Road to Victory," 1975)
Tel al-Za'tar (co-director, 1977)
Filastin fi al-'Ayn ("Palestine in the Eye," 1977)

Abu Assad, Hany
Bayt min al-Waraq ("A House of Cards," 1992)
14e Kippetje ("The 14th Chick," 1998)
Taht al-Mahjar ("Sanctuary," 2000)
Nasseriyya 2000 ("Nazareth 2000," 2001)
Quds fi Youm Akhar ("Jerusalem Another Day: Rana's Wedding," 2002).
Ford Transit ("Ford Transit," 2002)
al-Jinna Alaan ("Paradise Now," 2005)

Abu Dayyeh, Mohammad
Ta'akhar Abi ("My Dad is Late," 2003)

Abu Diqqa, Wael
al-Ghurba ("Exile," 1998)
al-Hawajiz ("Checkpoints," 2000)

Abu Ghoush, Dima
At The Checkpoint (2004)
Sabah al-Khayr Qalqiliya ("Good Morning Qalqiliya," 2004)

Abu Hmud, Saed
Second Halftime (2005)

Aburahme, Dahna
Palestine is Waiting (co-directed with Annemarie Jacir and Suzy Salamy, 2003)
Until When . . . (2004)

Abu Rish, Darwish
Haifawi ("A Man from Haifa," 1999)

Abu Sa'da, Ahmad
Youmiyyat Fida'i ("A Guerrilla's Diary," 1969)
Ma'a al-Tala'i' ("On the Vanguard," 1970)

Abu Salem, François
'Aysh wa Milh ("Bread and Salt," 1976)
al-Quds . . . Abwab al-Madina ("Jerusalem . . . Gates of the City," 1995)

Abu Wael, Tawfiq
Natirin Salah al-Din ("Waiting for Salah al-Din," 2000)
Yaomiyyat Ahir ("Diary of a Male Whore," 2001)
The Fourteenth (2002)
'Atash ("Thirst," 2004)

Adwan, Menem
'An al-'Akhar ("About the Other," 2004)

Ahmed, Imad
Mahalli ("Local,' co-director, 2002)
Buba ("Poppa," 2004)

Aleddin, Ghasoub
Hurub ("Escape," 2004)

* Amiralay, Omar
Ra'iha al-Janna ("The Fragrance of Paradise," 1983)

Andoni, Raed
Irtijal ("Improvisation," 2005)

Andoni, Saed
Jamal, Qissa Shuja'a ("Jamal, A Tale of Courage," 2000)
'Ala Sifr ("A Number Zero," 2002)
al-Hudud al-Akhira ("The Last Frontier," 2002)

Arasoughly, Alia
Hayat Mumazzaqa ("Torn Life," 1993)
Hay Mish Eishi ("This is Not Living," 2001)
Ma Bayn al-Sama' wa al-Ard ("Between Heaven and Earth," 2003)

'Araj, Suha
I am Palestine (2003)

'Arraf, Suha
Fatima (2000)
Qissatuha ("Her Story," 2000)
Sabah al-Khayr ya al-Quds ("Good Morning Jerusalem," 2004)

'Awwad, Gibril
Berlin al-Masida ("Berlin Trap," 1982)
Sabah al-Khayr ya Bayrut ("Good Morning, Beirut," 1983)

'Awwad, Nahed
Mashiyyin? ("Going for a Ride?," 2003)
25 Km (2005)
The Fourth Room (2005)

Ayache, Mohamad
Um Jaber (2000)

Bader, Reem
And Life Goes On (2004)

Badr Khan, Salah al-Din,
Hilm Layla ("Night Dream," 1946)

Badr, Liyana
al-Tariq ila Filastin ("The Path to Palestine," 1984)
Fadwa, Hikayat Sha'ira min Filastin ("Fadwa, a Palestinian Poet," 1999)
Zaytunat ("The Olive Trees," 2000)
Siege (2002)
al-Tir al-Akhdhar ("The Green Bird," 2002)
The Gates are Open Sometimes (2006)

Bakri, Mohammad
1948 (1998)
Jenin, Jenin ("Jenin, Jenin," 2002)
Min Youm Ma Ruhat ("Since You've Been Gone," 2006)

Barakat, Yahya
Masira al-Nidal ("The Path of Struggle," 1981)
Abu Salma 1982)
al-Ayyam al-Mushtaraka ("Days of Cooperation," 1989)
Rimal al-Sawafi (1991)
Fi Bayt Allah ("In God's House," 2003)
Rachel: An American Conscience (2005)

Barrak, Rima
al-Ard al-'48 ("The Land of '48," 2003)

Bishara, Amahl
Across Oceans, Among Colleagues (2002)

Bitar, Hazim
Uncivil Liberties (1998)
Jerusalem's High Cost of Living (2001)

Bitrawi, Walid
Wa Mahuta bi al-Aswar ("And the Walled Enclosure," 1998)

Bokhary, Lina
Fayd ("Deluge," 2002)

al-Buna, Ma'moun
Shuhada 'ala Tariq Filastin ("Martyrs on the Road to Palestine," 1975)

* Chamoun, Jean
Anshuda al-Ahrar ("Anthem of the Free," 1980)
Ma Adhan fi Wajh al-Dammar ("Facing the Destruction," 1999)

Damen, Rawan
Waiting for Light (2000)

Damuni, Nicolas
'Awda Wahida ("Returning Alone," 2002)

* Daoud, Hikmat
Ibda' fi al-Dhakira ("The Beginning of Memory," 1983)

Daoud, Iyad
Dayr Yassin, Zaman al-Waj' ("The Agony . . . Dayr Yassin," 1998)
al-Quds Wa'ad al-Sama ("Jerusalem the Promised of Heavens," 1999)

Darwaza, Sawsan
Ma'i'a Fannanun Yaqulun ("Artists Speak Out," 2000)
al-Murabba' ("The Square," 2003)

Darwish, Ziyad
Intifada Sha'ab ("Intifada of the People," 1991)
Bayt Sahhur Madina al-Samud ("Bayt Sahhur, City of Resistance," 1992)
Murda ("Defiance," 1992)

Daw, Salim
Mafateeh ("Keys," 2003)

al-Deek, Yousef
Case (2005)

Deis, Riyad
al-Kibrita ("The Matchbox," 2004)

Durra, Zeina
The Seventh Dog (2005)

Elias, Hanna
Rahil ("Departure," 1986)
al-Sath ("The Roof," 1987)
al-Subh ("The Morning," 1991)
al-Jabal ("The Mountain," 1991)
Hawajiz al-Tariqat ("Roadblocks," 2002)
Mawsim al-Zaytun ("The Olive Harvest," 2003)

al-Faqih, Rowan
Summer of '85 (2005)

* Fawzi, 'Ali
Shabiba min Filastin ("Palestinian Youth," 1979)

Frej, 'Issa
al-Hurriyya al-Da'i'a ("Lost Freedom," 2000)
Last Supper, Abu Dis, (2005)

Gargour, Maryse
A Palestinian Looks at Palestine (1988)
Watan Blanche ("Blanche's Homeland," 2001)

Habash, Ahmad
Uful al-Qamar ("The Moon Sinking," 2001)
Iyab ("Coming Back," 2003)

Habash, Ismail
Ma Zal Ka'k 'alla al-Rasif ("There is Still Ka'ek on the Sidewalk," 2000)
Apartment (2001)
Mahalli ("Local,' co-director, 2002)
Radi al-Salam ("Say Hi," 2003)

el-Hassan, Azza
al-'Arabiyyat Yatakallimna ("Arab Women Speak," 1996)

Kushan Musa ("A Deed From Moses," 1999)
al-Makan ("The Place," 2000)
Zaman al-Akhbar ("Newstime," 2001)
3 Sant Aqal ("3cm Less," 2003)
Muluk wa Kumbars ("Kings and Extras," 2004)

Hassan, Nizar
Sawa'id al-Ghad ("Hands of Tomorrow," 1991)
al-Nisa fi 'alam al-Rijal ("Women in the World of Men," 1991)
'Ila Ummhu . . . La'ab wa La'aab ("To His Mother . . . Fun and Games," 1991)
Bayt Laham ("Bethlehem," 1992)
Istiqlal ("Independence," 1994)
Yasmin ("1995)
Kalemat ("Words," 1995)
Ustura ("Myth," 1998)
Cut (2000)
Tahaddi ("Challenge', 2001)
Ijtiyah ("Invasion," 2003)
Karem Abou Khalil ("Abou Khalil's Grove' 2005)

* Hawl, Qasim
al-Nahr al-Barid ("al-Nahr al-Barid,'1971)
Limadha Nazra' al-Ward, Limadha Nahmil al-Silah ("Why We Plant Flowers, Why We Carry Arms," 1973)
Ghassan Kanafani, al-Kalima al-Bundughiyya (Ghassan Kanafani, The Word, The Gun," 1973)
Lan Taskut al-Banadiq ("The Guns Will Not Be Silent," 1973)
Buyutina al-Saqirah ("Our Small Homes," 1974)
Hayat Jadidah ("New Life," 1977)
Lubnan . . . Tel al-Za'tar ("Lebanon . . . Tel al-Za'tar," 1978)
'A'id ila Haifa ("Return to Haifa," 1982)
al-Huwiyyah al-Thaqafiyyah ("Cultural Identity," 1984)

al-Helou, Raed
Ba'i' al-Shay fi Ghazza ("Gaza Tea Boy," 1997)
Mahalli ("Local,' co-director, 2002)
La'lo Khayr ("Hopefully for the Best," 2004)

* Hijjar, Rafiq
al-Banadiq Mutahidda ("The United Guns," 1973)
al-Tariq ("The Road," 1973)
Ayar . . . al-Filastiniyyun ("In May . . . the Palestinians," 1974)
al-Intifada ("The Intifada," 1975)
Mawlud fi Filastin ("Born In Palestine," 1975)
Khabar Min Tel al-Za'tar ("News From Tel al-Za'tar," 1976)

Irshaid, Nabila
Travel Agency (2001)

Isma'il, 'Azz al-Din
al-Hilm ("The Dream," 1994)
Gaza, 2006 (1996)
al-'Alam al-Akhar ("Another World," 1999)

Isma'il, Suheir
al-E'eteqal al-Edari ("Administrative Detention," 1998)
Yaomiyyat Arabiyya ("Arab Diary," 2000)

Jacir, Annemarie
A Post-Oslo History, (1998)
Two Hundred Years of American Ideology (2000)
The Satellite Shooters, (2001)
Palestine is Waiting (co-director, 2003)
Ki'annana 'Ashrun Mustahil ("Like Twenty Impossibles," 2003)
Quelques Miettes Pour Les Oiseaux ("A Few Crumbs for the Birds,' co-director, 2005)
An Explanation (and Then Burn the Ahes) (2005)

al-Jafari, Kamal
al-Jahalin ("The Jahalin," 2000)
Visit Iraq (2003)
The Roof (2006)

Jajeh, Jennifer
In My Own Skin (co-director, 2001)
Fruition (2003)

Kayed, Hicham
Ahlamna . . . Emta? ("Our Dreams . . . When?," 2001)
God Forbid! (2001)
Sukkar Yafa ("The Sugar of Yafa," 2002)
Tufula Bayn al-Algham ("Childhood in the Midst of Mines," 2003)
Lemonade (2005)

Khalil, Mahmoud
Taysir ("Facilitation," 1984)

al-Khatib, Basil
Amina . . . Hikaya Filastiniyyah ("Amina . . . a Palestinian Tale," 1982)
La'na ("Curse," 1984)

al-Khatib, Nabil Issa
'Awdat al-Ghazala ("Return of the Deer," 2003)

Khill, Ibrahim
Madinati al-Nassiriyah ("My City Nazareth," 1978)
al-Filastiniyyun wa al-Salam? ("Palestinians and Peace?," 1990)
Bur'am 'ila 'Abad ("Budding to Eternity," 1993)
Bulus al-Najjar ("Paul the Carpenter," 1999)

Khleifi, George
al-Nasik ("The Hermit," 1978)

Bilad al-Bahr wa al-Raml ("Lands of Sea and Sand," 1982)

Khuruj al-Filastiniyyeen min Bayrut ("The Palestinian Evacuation from Beirut," 1982)

Atfal al-Hajjara ("Children of Stones,' co-director, 1988)

Min Qalb 'ila Qalb ("Heart to Heart," 1990)

al-Quds That al-Hisar ("Jerusalem Under Siege," 1991)

Masadir al-Tufula al-Mubakira ("The Source of a Precocious Childhood," 1991)

Shuruq ("Sunrise," 1991)

'Azef al-Nay al-Saghir ("The Player of the Small Flute," 1995)

Anta, Ana, al-Quds ("You, I, Jerusalem," 1997)

Kalb Maryam ("Mariam's Dog,' co-directed with Tayseer Mashareqa, 2004)

Khleifi, Michel

al-Diffa al-Qarbiyya . . . al-'Amal al-Filastiniyyah ("The West Bank . . . Palestinian Hope," 1978)

al-Mustawtinat al-Isra'iliyya fi Sina' ("Israeli Settlements in the Sinai," 1978)

al-'Ashrafiyya ("Ashrafiyya," 1978)

al-Filastiniyyun wa al-Salam ("Palestinians and Peace," 1978)

al-Dhakira al-Khasba ("Fertile Memory," 1980)

Tariq al-Na'im ("The Tranquil Path," 1981)

Ma'lul Tahtafilu bi Damariha ("Ma'lul Celebrates its Destruction," 1985)

'Urs fi al-Jalil ("Wedding in Galilee," 1987)

Nashid al-Hajar ("Canticle of the Stones," 1990)

L'Ordre du Jour (1993)

Hikaya al-Jawahir al-Thalath ("The Tale of Three Jewels," 1994)

al-Zawaj al-Mukhtalit fi al-Aradi al-Muqaddisa ("Mixed Marriages in the Holy Land," 1995)

Route 181: Fragments of a Journey (co-director, 2004)

Khoury, Buthina Canaan

Women in Struggle (2004)

Khoury, Rina

Balala Land (2003)

West . . . East (2005)

Lama, Ibrahim

Qubla fi al-Sahra ("A Kiss in the Desert," 1927)

Fajia'a Fawq al-Haram ("Tragedy of the Pyramids," 1929)

Mu'jiza al-Hub ("Miracle of Love," 1931)

Wakhz al-Damir ("Guilty Conscience," 1932)

al-Dahayat ("The Victims," 1933)

Shabah al-Madi ("Shadow of the Past," 1935)

Ma'ruf al-Badawi ("Maarouf the Bedouin," 1936)

al-Hareb ("The Escaper," 1937)

Nufus Ha'ira ("Souls in Distress," 1938)

'Izz al-Talab ("The Most in Demand," 1938)

Layali al-Qahira ("Cairo Nights," 1939)

al-Kanz al-Mafqud ("The Lost Treasure," 1939)

Qays wa Layla ("Kais and Laila," 1940)

Sarkha fi al-Layl ("A Cry in the Night," 1941)

Rajul Bayn Marratain ("A Man Between Two Women," 1941)

Salaheddine al-'Ayubbi ("Saladin," 1941)

Sarkha fi al-Layl ("A Cry in the Night," 1941)

Khefaya al-Dunia ("The Life's Secrets," 1942)

Cleobatra ("Cleopatra," 1943)

Ibn al-Sahra ("Son of the Desert," 1943)

'Arris al-Hana ("The Ideal Suitor, (1944)

Nida al-Dam ("The Call of Blood," 1944)

Uskutt al-Hub ("Be Silent, Love," 1944)

Wahida ("Alone," 1944)

al-Bey al-Muzayyaf ("The False Bey," 1945)

Bint al-Sharq ("Daughter of the East," 1946)

al-Badawiyya al-Hasana ("The Beautiful Bedouin Girl," 1947)

Kanz al-Sa'ada ("Treasure of Happiness," 1947)

Sikkit al-Salama ("The Safe Road," 1948)

al-Bayt al-Kabir ("The Big House," 1949)

Halaka al-Mafquda ("The Missing Link," 1949)

Kul Bayt illa Rajul ("Each House Has its Man," 1949)

Sitt al-Bayt ("The Lady of the House," 1949)

Assifa ala al-Rabi' ("Storm in Springtime," 1951)
al-Kafela Tassir ("The Caravan Continues," 1951)

Littin, Miguel
Por La Tierra Ajena ("For the Others' Earth," 1965)
El Chacal de Nauhueltoro ("The Jackal of Nauhueltoro," 1969)
La Tierra Prometida, ("Promised Land," 1971)
Compañero Presidente (1971)
Actas de Marusia ("Letters from Marusia," 1976)
Crónica de Tlacotalpan ("Chronicle of Tlacotalpan," 1976)
Recurso del Método ("Recourse to the Method," 1978)
La Viuda de Montiel ("The Widow Montiel," 1979)
Alsino y el Cóndor ("Alsino and the Condor," 1982)
Acta General de Chile ("Clandestine in Chile," 1986)
Sandino (1990)
Los Náufragos (The Shipwrecked," 1994)
Aventureros del Fin Del Mundo ("Adventurers of the End of the World," 1998)
Tierra del Fuego ("Land of Fire," 2000)
Crónicas Palestinas ("Palestinian Chronicles," 2001)
El Abanderado ("The Registered," 2002)
La Última Luna ("The Last Moon," 2004)

* Lutfi, Nabiha
Li'an al-Judhur Lan Tamut ("Because the Roots Will Not Die," 1977)

* Madanat, 'Adnan
Ro'a Filastiniyyah ("Palestinian Visions," 1977)

Mahanna, Seoud
Sa'id ("Said," 2001)

Marcus, Norma
al-'Amal al-Ghamid ("Veiled Hope," 1994)

Masharawi, Rashid

Jiwaz al-Safar ("Passport," 1985)

al-Malja' ("The Shelter," 1989)

Dar wa Dour ("Home and Turn," 1990)

'Ayyam Tawila fi Ghazzeh ("Long Days in Gaza," 1992)

al-Sahar ("Enchanting," 1992)

Hatta 'Esh'ar Akhar (Mana' al-Tajawwul) ("Curfew," 1993)

Entezar ("Waiting," 1994)

Haifa (1995)

Rebab ("Rebab," 1997)

Tawattur ("Tension," 1998)

Khalaf al-Aswar ("Against the Walls," 1999)

Filastin, Ard al-Miy'ad ("Palestine, the Promised Land," 1999)

Ghabash ("Out of Focus," 2000)

Maqluba ("Upside-Down," 2000)

Mawsim Hubb ("Season of Love," 2000)

Bath Mubashir ("Live Broadcast," 2001)

Tadhkira ila al-Quds ("Ticket to Jerusalem," 2002)

Live from Palestine (2003)

Hummus al-Eid ("Hummus for the Festival," 2003)

Arafat, Mon Frère ("Arafat, My Brother," 2005)

Meters Away (2005)

Attente ("Waiting' 2006)

Mashareqa, Tayseer

Kalb Maryam ("Mariam's Dog,' co-directed with George Khleifi, 2004)

al-Masri, Izzidin

Thawb al-Qaws Quzah ("Rainbow Dress," 2004)

al-Masri, Mai

That al-Anqad ("Under the Rubble,' co-director, 1982)

Zahrat al-Kindul ("Wild Flowers: Women of South Lebanon,' co-director, 1986)

War Generation Beirut (co-director, 1988)

Atfal Jebel Nar ("Children of Fire," 1990)
Hanan Ashrawi . . . 'Imra'a fi Zaman al-Tahaddi ("Hanan Ashrawi: A Woman of Her Time," 1995)
Ahlam Mu'alliqa ("Suspended Dreams," 1998)
Atfal Shatila ("Children of Shatila," 1998)
Ahlam Al-Manfa ("Frontiers of Dreams and Fears," 2001)

al-Massad, Mahmoud
Shatir Hassan ("Clever Hassan,' aka 'Shatter Hassan," 2001)

Mer Khamis, Juliano
Arna's Children (2004)

Musallim, Izidore
Layali al-Ghurba ("Foreign Nights," 1989)
Nothing to Lose (1994)
al-Jinna Qabl Mawti ("Heaven Before I Die," 1997)
Adam wa Hawwa ("Adam and Eve," 2003)

Musleh, Hanna
'Urs Sahar ("Marriage of Sahar," 1992)
Jund Allah ("Army of God," 1993)
Ana Malik Saqir ("I'm a Little Angel," 2000)
al-'Aysh bi Karama ("Living with Dignity," 2002)
Fi Shibak al-'Ankabut ("In the Spider's Web," 2004)

Muthaffar, Enas
Ru'ya ("Vision," 1999)
Sabil Sidi Omar ("The Path of Sidi Omar," 2000)
Ah Ya Sitti ("Oh, My Grandmother," 2000)
For Archives Only (2001)
East to West (2005)

Najjar, Najwa

Na'im wa Wadee'a ("Na'im and Wadee'a," 1999)
Walad Ismuhu Muhammad ("A Boy Called Mohammad," 2001)
Jawharat Al-Silwan ("Jewel of Oblivion," 2001)
Yasmine Tughani ("Yasmine's Song," 2006)

Nassar, Ali

Madina 'ala al-Shati' ("The City on the Coast," 1985)
Nabq al-Ata' ("The Source of the Gift," 1992)
al-Marda'a ("The Wet Nurse," 1993)
Darb al-Tabanat ("The Milky Way," 1997)
Fi Shahr al-Tasi' ("In the Ninth Month," 2003)

Nazzal, Omar

The Cage (2004)

* Nimr, Samir

Layla Filastiniyyah ("A Palestinian Night," 1973)
al-Irhab al-Sahyuni ("Zionist Terror," 1973)
Harb al-Ayyam al-Arba'a ("The Four-Day War," 1973)
Riyah al-Tahrir ("The Winds of Freedom," 1974)
Li Man al-Thawra? ("Who is the Revolution For?," 1974)
al-Yemen al-Jadid ("The New Yemen," 1974)
Kafr Shuba ("Kafr Shuba," 1975)
al-Nasr fi 'Uyunihum ("Victory in their Eyes," 1976)
al-Harb fi Lubnan ("The War in Lebanon,' co-director, 1977)
al-Judhur ("Roots," 1984)
Filastin fi al-Lahb ("Palestine on Fire," 1988)

El-Omari, Majdi

So'al Assad ("The Question of Assad," 1988)
'An al-Akhar ("About the Other," 1996)
Athar 'ala Sakhra al-Aqsa ("Traces on the Rock of Elsewhere," 1998)

Othman, Abed
In the Western Boat (2005)
Tahtib (2006)
Madad (2006)

Qadh, Tony
al-Huriyya al-Masluba . . . Filastin al-Muhtalla ("Stolen Freedom . . . Occupied Palestine," 1990)

Qashoo, Osama
My Dear Olive Tree (2004)
Inside Outside (2005)
No Choice Basis (2006)

al-Qattan, Omar
Ahlam fi Firagh ("Dreams and Silence," 1991)
al-'Awda ("Going Home," 1995).
Yaomiyyat Musabiqa Faniyya Taht al-Hisar ("Diary of an Art Competition [Under Curfew]," 2002)

Qazi, Kristan
al-Mawt fi Lubnan ("A Death in Lebanon," 1977)

Rum, Muhammad
Jihad! (co-director, 2004)

* Saab, Jocelyn
Safina al-Manfa ("Ship of Exile," 1982)

Sa'adeh, Mazin
My Friend, My Enemy (2004)
The Guardian of Boredom (2005)

Safadi, Akram
Qissas min al-Quds ("Song on a Narrow Path: Stories From Jerusalem," 2001)

Salama, Marwan
'A'ida ("Returning Home," 1985)
Shajara al-Zaytun ("The Olive Tree," 1986)

Salama, Sherine
Wedding in Ramallah (2002)

Saleh, Liana
Kura wa 'Alba Alwan ("A Ball and a Coloring Box," 2004)

Salloum, Jacqueline
Planet of the Arabs (2003)
Arabs A-Go-Go (2003)
Slingshot Hip Hop: The Palestinian Lyrical Front (2006)

Salti, Ihab
Tilk al-Mara al-Warda ("A Woman Like a Flower," 2001)

Sansour, Larissa
Bethlehem Bandolero (2004)
Tank (2005)

Sansour, Leila
Jeremy Hardy vs. The Israeli Army (2002)
Global Coverage (2002)

al-Sawalmeh, Mahmoud
Intifada (1988)
al-Nar al-Qadima ("The Coming Fire," 1997)
Bawaba li al-Raqam ("The Doorman for the Numeral," 1998)

al-Sawalmeh, Muhammad
Layla al-Junud ("Night of Soldiers," 2002)

Sayegh, Layla
al-Sanduq ("The Trunk," 2004)

Serhan, Ibrahim Hasan
Ziyara al-Malak 'Abd al-'Aziz ("The Visit of King Abd al-Aziz," 1935)
Ahlam Tahaqqaqat ("Dreams Realized," 1939)
Studio Filastin ("Studio Palestine," 1945)
Fi Layla al-'Ayd ("On the Night of the Feast," 1946)
Muqaddimah Sinama'iyyah ("Cinematic Introduction," 1946)
'Ahmad Hilmi Basha ("Ahmad Hilmi Basha," 1946)

Sha'ath, Qalib
al-Miftah ("The Key," 1976)
Yawm al-Ard ("Land Day," 1978)
Qusn al-Zaytun ("Olive Branch," 1978)

Sha'ban, Qasim
al-Nasira '84 ("Nazareth '84," 1984)

* Shahal, Randa
Khatwa, Khatwa ("Step by Step," 1979)

Shamout, Isma'il
Mu'askirat al-Shebab ("Young Soldiers," 1972)
Zikriyyat wa Nar ("Memories and Fire," 1973)
al-Nida' al-Milah ("The Call of Salt," 1973)
'Ala Tariq Filastin ("On The Road to Palestine," 1974)

Shamounki, Nadine
Effaced (2002)

Sharidi, Nazim

Nida' al-Judhur ("Call of the Roots," 1984)

Ghitu al-Dehayshiyya ("The Dehaysha Ghetto," 1988)

Ma Bayn al-Hilm wa al-Dhakira ("Between the Dream and the Memory," 1988)

al-Madina al-Muhasira ("The Surrounded City," 1988)

Bawabat al-Quds ("The Gates of Jerusalem," 1988)

Mawasim al-Khasab ("Fertile Seasons," 1988)

Shehada, Abdel Salam

al-Biy'a ("Innocence," 1994)

Huquq al-Mar'a al-Ensaniyya ("Women's Human Rights," 1995)

al-'Aidai al-Saqira ("Small Hands," 1995)

Bi al-Qarb min al-Mawt ("Close to Death," 1997)

al-Ma', al-Tahadi al-Haqiqi ("Water, the True Challenge," 1998)

al-Zill ("Shadow," 2000)

Hajjar bi Hajjar ("Stone by Stone," 2000)

al-Qasba ("Mirage," 2000)

Radm ("Debris," 2002)

Qaws Quzah ("Rainbow' 2005)

al-Shirqawi, Bakr

al-Harb fi Lubnan ("War in Lebanon,' co-director, 1977)

Sinnokrot, Nida

Palestine Blues (2006)

Srour, Shadi

Sense of Need (2004)

Suleiman, Elia

Muqaddimah li-Nihayat-Jidal ("Introduction to the End of an Argument," co-director, 1990)

Takrim bi al-Qatl ("Homage by Assassination," 1992)

Sijil 'Ikhtifa' ("Chronicle of a Disappearance," 1996)

al-Hilm al-'Arabi ("Arab Dream," 1998)
Cyber-Palestine (2000)
Yadun 'Ilahiyya ("Divine Intervention," 2002)

Tabari, Ula
'Alaqna wa Khalaqna ("Private Investigation," 2002)
Diaspora (2005)

* Tawfiq, Muhammad
Masira al-Esteslam ("The Path of Surrender," 1981)
Umm 'Ali ("Umm 'Ali," 1983)
al-Tifl wa al-La'ba ("The Child and the Game," 1985)
al-Natur ("The Guard," 1988)

Tawil, Helga
Not Going There, Don't Belong Here (2002)
Qalandia (2003)
Isochronism: Twenty-Four Hours in Jabaa (2004)

Terawi, Ghada
Bidna Na'ish ("Staying Alive," 2001)

'Umar, Nasser
al-Huwiyya al-Qatila ("Identity Killed," 1996)
'Awda al-Muwatina ("The Return of the Citizen," 1996)

Yaqubi, Mohanad
Fix (2003)

el-Yasin, Jamal
'Alla Hudud al-Watan ("On the Borders of the Nation," 1993)
Bayan min Maazin al-Quds ("Announcement from the Mosques of Jerusalem," 1993)

el-Yassir, Nada
Sarab ("Mirage," 2000)
Arba'a Aghani Li Filastin ("Four Songs for Palestine," 2001)
Paradise (2001)
All That Remained (2005)

Youssef, Susan
Mamnu' Al-Tajawwul ("Curfew," 2003)

al-Zain, Osama
Transparency (2002)
Palestine Post–9/11 (2005)

Zakharia, Nasri
Tale of Three Mohammeds (2003)

* Zentut, Fu'ad
'Ala Tariq al-Thaura al-Filastiniyyah ("On the Path of the Palestinian Revolution," 1971)
Awraq Sawda' ("Black Pages," 1979)
al-Khiyana ("Treason," 1980)

Zoaabi, Taher
al-Rida ("Satisfaction," 2004)

Zoubi, Sameh
Be Quiet (2004)

al-Zobaidi, Sobhi
Khartati al-Khassa Jiddan ("My Very Private Map," 1998)
Nisa fi al-Shams ("Women in the Sun," 1999)
'Ali wa Ashabhu ("Ali and his Friends," 2000)
Du' fi Akhar al-Nafaq ("Light at the End of the Tunnel," 2000)
Shawwal ("Looking Awry," 2001)

'Ubur Kalandia ("Crossing Kalandia," 2002)
Uqniyya Ta'ir Sijjin ("A Caged Bird's Song," 2003)
Film Arabi Tawil ("A Long Arab Film," 2006)

* al-Zubaidi, Kais
Sawt min al-Quds ("A Voice from Jerusalem," 1977)
Watan al-Aslak al-Sha'ika ("The Nation of Barbed Wire," 1980)
Filastin, Sijl Sha'b ("Palestine: a People's Record," 1984)
Muwajihha ("Opposition," 1984)
Milf al-Mujazirra ("Dossier of a Massacre," 1984)

A SELECTED BIBLIOGRAPHY ON PALESTINIAN CINEMA

Abdel Malek, K., *The Rhetoric of Violence: Arab-Jewish Encounters in Contemporary Palestinian Literature and Film*. New York: Palgrave Macmillan, 2005.

Abu Ghanimah, Hassan, *Filasteen wa al-'Ayn al-Sinama'iyyah* ("Palestine in the Cinematic Eye"). Damascus: Union of Arab Writers, 1981.

Abu-Lughod, Lila, et.al. "Dreams of a Nation: Reviews from a Palestinian Film Festival," *American Anthropologist*, March 2004, vol. 106, no. 1, pp. 150–60.

Alexander, L., "On the Right to Dream, Love and Be Free: an Interview with Michel Khleifi," *Middle East Report*, 1996, vol. 26, no. 4, pp. 31–3.

Asfour, N., "The Politics of Arab Cinema: Middle Eastern Filmmakers Face Up to Their Reality." *Cineaste*, 2000. 26(1): p. 46–8.

Auty, C., "Palestine," *Monthly Film Bulletin*, 1982, vol. XLIX, no. 585, p. 240.

al-'Awdat, Hussein, *al-Sinama wa al-Qadiyya al-Filastiniyyah* ("Cinema and the Palestinian Issue") Damascus: al-Ahali Li al-Tabi'a wa al-Nashr wa al-Tawzi', 1987.

Baecque, A.d., "Noce en Galilée," *Cahiers du Cinéma*, 1987, no. 401, pp. 45–7.

Benedict, S., "Intervention Divine," *Cahiers du Cinéma*, 2002, no. 572, pp. 18–19.

Bosséno, C. and J. Roy, "Entretien avec Mustafa Abu Ali, Chef de l'Unité Cinéma de l'O.L.P.," *Image et Son*, 1980, no. 350, pp. 89, 91–2.

Bourlond, A., "A Cinema of Nowhere: an Interview with Elia Suleiman," *Journal of Palestine Studies*, 2000, vol. 29, no. 2, pp. 95–101.

Brooks, X. 'We have no film industry because we have no country.' *Guardian*, London (UK), 12 April 2006, p. 22.

Brumm, A. M., "Migration, Marginality, and Cultural Conflict in Recent Israeli and Palestinian Cinema," *Canadian Review of Comparative Literature*, 1996, vol. 23, no. 2, p. 561–77.

Brumm, A. M., "Palestinian Film Week." *New Outlook*, 1992, vol. 35, no. 5, p. 33.

Bruyn, O.D., F. Garbarz, and Y. Tobin, "Elia Suleiman," *Positif*, 2002, no. 500, pp. 202–9.

Carter, M., "The Palestinian," *Majority Report*, 1978, vol. 8, no. 14, p. 5.

Causo, M., "Haifa," *Cineforum*, 1996, vol. XXXVI, no. 355, p. 27.

Chauvin, J.-S., "Etat du Cinema Palestinien," *Cahiers du Cinéma*, 2002, no. 572, p. 16–17.

Dodd, P., "Homelands," *Sight & Sound*, 1992, vol. 1, no. 10, p. 18–21.

Downing, T., *Palestine on Film*, London: Council for the Advancement of Arab-British Understanding, 1979.

El-Hassan, A., "When the Exiled Films Home," *Framework*, 2002, vol. XLIII, no. 2, p. 64–70.

Fareed, Samir, *al-Sinama al-Filastiniyah fi al-Ard al-Muhtallah* ("Palestinian Cinema in the Occupied Territory"). Cairo: The Higher General Committee to Culture, Horizons of Cinema Series, no. 3, 1997, pp. 81 ff.

Fusco, C., "Allegories of Palestine: an Interview with Michel Khleifi," *Afterimage*, 1988, no. 16, p. 14–16.

Gertz, N., "Space and Gender in the New Israeli and Palestinian Cinema," *Prooftexts*, 2002, vol. 22, nos. 1 & 2, pp. 553–79.

Gertz, N. and George Khleifi, *Landscape in Mist: Space and Memory in Palestinian Cinema*. Tel Aviv: Am Oved and the Open University 2005.

Goodfellow, M., "Festival Report: A Palestinian Festival Collects Work by Directors Scattered Worldwide," *Sight & Sound*, May 2004, vol. 14, no. 5, pp. 4–6

Heijnen, W., "Palestina," *Skrien*, 1978, nos. 76–7, p. 52–53.

Hennebelle, Guy "Arab Cinema" *MERIP Reports*, November 1976, no. 52, pp. 4–12.

Hennebelle, Guy, "The National Question in Palestinian Cinema," *Cinéaste*, 1979, vol. 10, no. 1, p. 32.

Ibrahim, Bashar, *al-Sinama al-Filastiniyyah fi al-Qarn al-'Ishriyn* ("Palestinian Cinema in the Twentieth Century"). Damascus: the National Organization for Cinema, the Syrian Ministry of Culture, 2001.

Indiana, G., "Elia Suleiman," *Film Comment*, 2003, vol. 39, no. 1, pp. 28–32.

Joyard, O., "Dans l'Oeil d'Elia Suleiman le Nomade," *Cahiers du Cinéma*, 2002, vol. 572, pp. 12–16.

Joyard, O., "Chimères Humanitaires," *Cahiers du Cinéma*, 2001, no. 558, pp. 16–17.

Katunun, A., *Srazajuscijsja kinematograf* ("Notes on Palestinian documentary films"). *Iskusstvo Kino*, 1979, no. 11, pp. 151–61.

Kelly, R. and S.F. Said, "Zero Gravity," *Sight & Sound*, 2003, vol. XIII, no. 1, pp. 16–18, 42–3.

Khalaf, T., *Dalil al-Film al-Filastini* (1935–2000). ("Facts on Palestinian Film, 1935–2000") Doha: Arab Screen Independent Film Festival, 2001.

Layoun, M.N., "A Guest at the Wedding: Honor, Memory, and (National) Desire in Michel Khleifi's *Wedding in Galilee*," in Between Woman and Nation: Nationalisms, *Transnational Feminisms*, and the State, C. Kaplan, N. Alarcan, and M. Moallem, eds., 1999, Durham, NC: Duke University Press, pp. 92–107.

Morice, J., "Intervention Divine," *Beaux Arts Magazine*, 2002, no. 221, p. 22.

Naficy, H., "Palestinian Film Letters," *Critique*, 1995, no. 7, pp. 53–61.

Nesselson, L., "Curfew," *Variety*, 1994, vol. CCCLV, no. 3, p. 41.

Ostria, V., "Sur Tous les Fronts," *Cahiers du Cinéma*, 1996, no. 501, p. 10.

Passevant, C., "Le Mariage de Rana," *Jeune Cinéma*, 2002, no. 279, pp. 63–5.

Porton, Richard, "Notes from the Palestinian Diaspora: An Interview with Elia Suleiman," *Cinéaste*, Summer 2003, vol. 28, no. 3, pp. 24-7

Rich, Ruby, "Divine Comedy: Elia Suleiman's Surreal Slapstick Fights Brutality with Imagination," *San Francisco Bay Guardian*, March 26, 2003.

Rosen, M., "Wedding In Galilee," *Cinéaste*, 1988, vol. 16, no. 4, p. 51.

Rubenstein, L., "We Are the Palestinian People," *Cinéaste*, 1974, vol. 6, no. 3, p. 35.

Sabouraud, F., "Noce en Galilee," *Cahiers du Cinéma*, 1987, no. 397, p. 50.

Sabouraud, F. and S. Toubiana, "La Force du Faible," *Cahiers du Cinéma*, 1987(401): p. iii.

Said, S.F., "Zero Gravity," *Sight & Sound*, 2003, vol. 13, no. 1, pp. 16–20.

Shamit, Walid and Guy Hennebelle, *Filastin fi al-Sinama*. Paris: al-Fajr, 1980.

Shlegel, S.J., "Film't kato or'zhie i sredstvo za samoutv' rzhdavane" (Report on the 3rd International Palestinian film festival, held in Baghdad 18–25 March 1978). *Kinoizkustvo*, 1978, vol. XXXIII, no. 7, pp. 68–70.

Shmeit, Walid and Guy Hennebelle's, *Filasteen fi al-Sinama* ("Palestine and Cinema").

Beirut and Paris: al-Fajr, 1980.

Shohat, E., "Anomalies of the National: Representing Israel/Palestine," *Wide Angle*, 1989, vol. XI, no. 3, p. 33–41.

Shohat, E., "The Palestinian Wave In Recent Israeli Cinema," *Cinéaste*, 1987, vol. 15, no. 3, p. 10.

Shohat, Ella, et. al. "Review Essays on 'Wedding in Galilee,'" Middle East Report, September-October 1988, no. 154, pp. 44-6.

Strauss, F., "Cinéma Palestinien: le Processus de Création," *Cahiers du Cinéma*, 1997, no. 514, pp. 54–8.

Suleiman, E. and H. Frappat, "Illusions Nécessaires," *Cahiers du Cinéma*, 2001, no. 560, pp. 54–6.

Suleiman, E. "A Cinema of Nowhere," *Journal of Palestine Studies*, Winter 2000, vol. 29, no. 2, pp. 95–101.

White, A., "Wedding in Galilee," *Film Comment*, 1988, no. 24, pp. 57–8.

ACKNOWLEDGMENTS

Dreams of a Nation: A Palestinian Film Festival, the Palestinian Film Project that it initiated, and now this volume are all the results of a collaborative work by a small band of academic and community activists. Annemarie Jacir has been chiefly responsible for curating the festival and the project that occasioned the appearance of this book. I am grateful for her untiring effort in making this dream come true. She is the soul of this project and in the generosity of her grace beats the heart of our collective commitment to Palestinian cinema. Equally instrumental in making the Dreams of a Nation project come true were Fatima Ali, Kareem Fahim, Ahmed Issawi, Ghada Jiha, Nicole Marcote, and Kamran Rastegar. They all devoted much of their invaluable time, their labor of love, and the entirety of their care and confidence in what we were set to do. I am honored to be one of them.

When we took the festival to Palestine itself, the Yabous cultural organization was chiefly responsible for facilitating our event. Rania Elias-Khoury and Joan Abu Jebara Assali in particular were gracious hosts and tireless organizers in making our mutual event possible. Equally instrumental in the success of our festival in Palestine were the other staff members of Yabous – Randa Antar, Majed Musafer, Rawan Sharaf, and Juliet Tuma; as were the Yabous board members: Khaled Al-Assali, Nazmi Al-Ju'beh, Mazen Bazbaz, Givara Budeiri, Hidaya Dajani, Dalia Habash, Mark Khano, and Suhail Khoury. I thank them all. Without their institutional support and dedicated commitment to our project we could not have taken our festival to Palestine.

I would also like to thank Ihab Salti for hosting our festival in the wonderful Cinematheque that he runs in Nazareth. My equal gratitude goes to Sara Qatamesh at the Popular Arts Center and Reem Fadda at the Sakakini Cultural Center in Ramallah, as well as to Hanan Lozon at the Cultural Center Cinema/PRCS in Gaza. The Dreams of a Nation film festival would not have reached Palestinians inside their homeland without their support.

To give a critical dimension to our festival in Palestine, we had organized a panel discussion in Jerusalem to which we invited such leading Palestinian filmmakers as Mustafa Abu Ali, Daoud Barakat, Nizar Hassan, George Khleifi, Najwa Najjar, and Ula Tabari. We are grateful for their support. Alia Arasoughly, Rania Elias-Khoury, Rashid and Mona Khalidi, and George Khleifi were invaluable help in the selection process. Peter Lagerquist was a joy to have as an all-round help during the festival.

Hany Abu Assad and his cast and crew, getting ready to shoot his critically acclaimed *Paradise Now* in Nablus at the time, facilitated my visit to that ancient and devastated city; and George Khleifi and his exceptionally kind and gracious family were the exemplary models of generosity and hospitality, under exceedingly difficult circumstances, while I was in Palestine. I thank them all.

We all owe a special note of gratitude to the distinguished Chilean–Palestinian filmmaker Miguel Littin, who graciously accepted our invitation and joined us in Palestine. His trip from Chile to Palestine was a gift of grace far beyond our hope and expectation. It is impossible to explain the grace with which he restored hope and underlined the dignity of Palestinians while he traveled with us from one city to another. Gracefully helping us carry his luggage through one military checkpoint after another, he was the defiant soul of a Palestinian fighter in the aging body of a Latin American revolutionary, as he held his proud head high, while the magnificent posture of his moral rectitude, and the stare of his contemptuous gaze, made the barefaced occupiers of his ancestral homeland look away in defeat. The night in the late February 2004, when Miguel Littin gave a lecture on cinema at the al-Qattan Foundation, precisely at the moment that the Israeli army was robbing a bank in downtown Ramallah and the audience could hear the sounds of bullets over his voice, will forever remain in my mind as the very definition of the indomitable spirit of Palestinians, wherever they are, claiming and achieving their inalienable right to their homeland.

I would like to thank Riham Barghouti for graciously hosting my visit to Birzeit

University, where I was able to meet my colleagues Professors Ina'am E-Obeidi and Suleiman Rabadi to plan our future projects in Palestine. I am equally grateful to Professors May Jayyusi and Samir Awad for having made time to see me while I was at Birzeit.

I cannot thank these dear friends and esteemed colleagues enough for making my trip to Palestine, and through it this book, possible. I will forever cherish the memory of being so graciously hosted in Palestine by its rightful inhabitants, while they were under a disgraceful military occupation. To be the exemplary model of graceful hospitality under such dire circumstances is simply beyond belief.

I thank all my distinguished colleagues at Columbia University who defied the atmosphere of fear and intimidation generated against us and joined our initial conference that we had organized in conjunction with the festival. Lila Abu-Lughod, Coco Fusco, Stathis Gourgouris, Joseph Massad, Rosalind Morris, Richard Peña, James Schamus, and Gayatri Spivak were exemplary models of courage in lending our festival the authority of their good names and being instrumental in making our event possible. We will never forget their noble stand for the indomitable cause of justice under very hostile circumstances. Under the terrorizing condition of post-9/11 New York – where street thugs, neo-con charlatans and hazardous millionaires have had a rendezvous with power – we were all put to test, and precious few of us passed the historic trial. I am particularly grateful to my dear friend and distinguished colleague Jonathan Cole, then our courageous Provost, for having withstood extraordinary pressure to safeguard our academic freedom. His untimely departure from that crucial post was tragic, and he is sorely missed at Columbia's helm. I do not believe that in my lifetime Columbia will again see the likes of Jonathan Cole or benefit from the visionary leadership with which he steered us through very troubled times.

As in many other instances, the late Edward W. Said (1935–2003) was the principal inspiration behind the idea of this film festival and the project it commenced. From the very inception of this idea, I consulted with Edward Said on a regular basis and solicited his help and advice on many occasions. I also thank Zainab Astarabadi, for many years Edward Said's assistant, for her help in the initial, preparatory, stages of our festival, as well as Sandra Fahy, her successor, who was equally helpful and supportive. Although the presence of Edward Said is missed amongst us as this volume goes to print, his soaring soul sustains our hopes. We were blessed by his presence among us to deliver the keynote speech of the festival, and this volume is graced by his name and privileged by his words. I am grateful to Mariam Said for giving us permission to publish Edward Said's opening remarks as the preface to this book.

I thank all the subsequent friends and colleagues who accepted my invitation to join this volume: Bashir Abu-Manneh, Taoufiq bin Amor, Nizar Hassan, Hamid Naficy, Kamran Rastegar, and Ella Shohat. Their collective wisdom and caring knowledge are definitive to what I hoped to achieve with this project. I am also grateful to Joseph Massad for his comments on an earlier draft of my own chapter in this book.

Above all my gratitude goes to the Palestinian filmmakers themselves – the chroniclers of their own national appearance on the global screen. It has been a rare and precious privilege for me to get to know them as friends, and feel welcomed in their midst as a pious pilgrim to the joyous occasion of their art, and a committed comrade in their noble cause. They trusted our project and lent the dignity of their name and the honor of their reputation to the legitimacy of our project. On behalf of our collective, I thank them all. I hope and trust that this volume, which is the modest measure of my love and admiration for the beauty and brilliance of their national cinema, is not too much of a disappointment.

During the semester that he spent with us at Columbia, Michel Khleifi in particular was grace incarnate and a source of joy and hope to have around in otherwise desperate times. I thank him for the confidence he sustained in all of us as we were paying homage to a cinema with his graceful signature all over its map. My prolonged conversations with Michel Khleifi, Elia Suleiman, Hany Abu Assad, Nizar Hassan, Omar al-Qattan, George Khleifi, Annemarie Jacir, and Mai Masri have been the principal source of my knowledge, love, and admiration for Palestinian cinema. I am grateful to and honored by their having graciously accepted me in their midst – a mere *Ajam* who still cannot even tell a *qaf* from a *ghayn*, and yet a Palestinian at heart.

The administrative staff of the Department of Middle East and Asian Languages and Cultures at Columbia University, which I chaired at the time we organized our festival, came under severe pressure and unconscionable harassment by people who did not like our Palestinian film project. Jessica Rechtschaffer and Michael Fishman, in particular, I would like to thank for the grace and patience with which they endured those difficult days.

Anything I have ever done on cinema and any word I have ever written about a film are undeservedly graced by my friendship with Amir Naderi, whom I thank for the precious presence of his noble soul – and his unsurpassed knowledge of world cinema – in our midst in New York.

The publication of this volume is made possible by generous grants from CAME and University Seminars publication funds at Columbia University. I am grateful to my distinguished colleagues, Professors William Theodore de Bary and Robert Belknap, and their respective committees, for their support of our subvention request.

Finally, I need to thank Amy Scholder, my extraordinary editor at Verso, who as usual put together a text of meaningful and purposeful ideas from a scattered pot-pourri of possibilities I put at her disposal. Without her generous patience and keen and caring eyes this volume would not have been possible.

Hamid Dabashi
New York
April 2006

Printed in the United States
by Baker & Taylor Publisher Services